The British Women's Suffrage Movement in 100 Objects

The British Women's Suffrage Movement in 100 Objects

A Material History

Elizabeth Crawford

BLOOMSBURY ACADEMIC

LONDON · NEW YORK · OXFORD · NEW DELHI · SYDNEY

BLOOMSBURY ACADEMIC
Bloomsbury Publishing Plc, 50 Bedford Square, London, WC1B 3DP, UK
Bloomsbury Publishing Inc, 1359 Broadway, New York, NY 10018, USA
Bloomsbury Publishing Ireland, 29 Earlsfort Terrace, Dublin 2, D02 AY28, Ireland

BLOOMSBURY, BLOOMSBURY ACADEMIC and the Diana logo are trademarks
of Bloomsbury Publishing Plc

First published in Great Britain 2026

Cover design by Aneeka Makwana
Cover image: China figurine, Suffragette trampling a policeman © Lesley Mees

A catalogue record for this book is available from the British Library.

A catalog record for this book is available from the Library of Congress.

ISBN: HB: 978-1-350-52077-6
          PB: 978-1-350-52078-3
          ePDF: 978-1-350-52079-0
          eBook: 978-1-350-52080-6

Typeset by Integra Software Services Pvt. Ltd.
Printed and bound in Great Britain

For product safety related questions contact productsafety@bloomsbury.com.

To find out more about our authors and books visit www.bloomsbury.com
and sign up for our newsletters.

For Grant. For Everything.

CONTENTS

ACKNOWLEDGEMENTS

This work would not have been possible without the generosity of all those who have allowed me to show you these 100 objects. Institutions and private collectors alike could not have been more helpful. I drew particularly on the Women's Library collection at the London School of Economics and Political Science and am most grateful to LSE for not only allowing free use of their images but also for arranging for some objects to be specially photographed. Over the years I have enjoyed many conversations with Dr Gillian Murphy, the curator of the Women's Library collection, who was as efficient and kind as ever in helping with this project, looking out items in which I was interested and arranging a most enjoyable photographic session. At other institutions I am grateful for help from Jenny Blackhurst at Girton Library; Beverley Cook at the London Museum; Lisa Coombes at The Box, Plymouth; Krystyna Campbell-Pretty and the National Gallery of Victoria; Sue John at the Glasgow Women's Library; and Emma McBeath and Hannah Priest, successively, at the Pankhurst Museum. For many decades I have enjoyed contact, indeed friendship, with leading collectors in the suffrage field and would like particularly to thank Ken Florey and Emmy van Beugen, Martin Last, and Chris and Lesley Mees for taking such trouble to ensure that I had images of any of their objects I requested. In Dublin Professor Diana Spencer made a special journey to St Stephen's Green to photograph the Haslam Memorial Seat for me and, on a flying visit to London, Agnes Crawford photographed Millicent Fawcett's statue. I would also like to thank Mary Branson, AntikBar Vintage Posters, Cambridge University Library, Forum Auctions, Lucy Gibbon at Orkney Archives and the National Library of Ireland for dealing efficiently with my reproduction requests. In addition, Catherne Clay, June Hannam, Mari Takayanagi, Zoe Thomas, Jacqui Turner and Melanie Unwin have taken an interest and solved various riddles for me. My family has, as ever, been my delight.

1

Introduction

The women's suffrage movement was a political campaign that began in 1866 and in 1928 finally achieved its goal of 'the vote as it was or may be granted to men'.

In the mid-nineteenth century, most of the British population thought the idea of a woman voting was ridiculous. Voters were men, just as vicars, lawyers, soldiers and sailors were men. However, by no means all men were voters and in 1866 middle-class men, unwilling to be excluded any longer from having a say in the way the country was governed, were pressing for a new Reform Bill.[1] Taking advantage of the ensuing political discussion, a small group of women determined to do what they could to lobby for women to be included in the Bill. If a woman fulfilled the property qualification that allowed a man a vote, why should she not also be a voter? To this end they very swiftly drafted a petition, found 1,521 women willing to sign and arranged for the political philosopher and Liberal MP, John Stuart Mill, to present it to Parliament. At the time this was seen as the correct way in which to exert pressure; methods were to change over the years.

Women had no right to participate formally in the parliamentary political system. Parliament had evolved to run a patriarchal society in which women were subjected to inequality and injustice in all areas of life, their concerns subsumed in those of men. Campaigners did not believe they could rely on men to understand and protect their interests, or that progressive social, economic and political reforms, benefitting all, would be enacted unless women took part in the political process. The parliamentary vote would be the ticket to full citizenship, allowing women to be citizens rather than subjects.

Based on primary printed sources, the historiography of the suffrage movement is extensive. But, as well as producing documents, to achieve their political end the suffrage campaigners created, caused to be created or used all manner of objects, while wider society was stimulated to produce others in reaction to their ideas and activities. Although the campaigners may no longer be with us, thousands of objects associated with their campaign, for and against, survive. From these I have selected one hundred, arranged in a chronological chain, with which to 'read' the suffrage narrative. Printed material, such as *The Women's Suffrage Journal* (Object 9) or *The Suffrage Annual* (Object 77), is not excluded, but is just one type of object, interrogated as any other to discover the reason for and method of its creation. For, while a study of a suffrage object, such as Object 36, the Women's Freedom League Proclamation Banner or Object 41, the suffrage medals, highlights an important stage of the campaign, it can also bring more shadowy areas into sharp focus. Thus Object 13, the poster advertising Helen Taylor's

1885 parliamentary candidature, draws attention to a suffrage byway that was until recently unremarked, and Object 24 highlights the Women's Freedom League's first Minute Book, an item whose existence was unknown before bought at an internet auction and lent to the Women's Library collection. Moreover, by studying Objects 67, the 'comic' forcible feeding postcard, and 68, the ceramic figurine of a suffragette, we can comprehend more viscerally than by reading disparaging comments in newspapers something of the misogyny prevalent in the society of the day.

In her adept survey of the state of the field of material culture within the discipline of history, Dr Serena Dyer notes that, while there 'is no unified material culture methodology', Professor Jules Prown's system of 'description, deduction and speculation continues to be influential'.[2] Constituting a close reading of each object in its time, this is the approach that informs the study of my chosen 100 objects. To my mind it is necessary to describe an object before attempting to deduce how it fits into the narrative. Once that is established, it is then possible to speculate as to its meaning, purpose and effectiveness. Moreover, although a political movement, the suffrage campaign was enmeshed in all areas of life, with each of the objects fitting into at least one of the six categories by which Prown classifies material culture: Art, Diversions, Adornment, Architecture, Applied Arts and Devices.[3] In the last several decades work has been published relevant to most of these categories as applied to the suffrage movement.

Although in her influential study, *The Spectacle of Women*, Lisa Tickner mourned the lack of interest then shown by both political and art historians in the material produced by the early-twentieth-century suffrage campaign, it was her work in describing and analysing so attractively the methods and imagery employed and effects created by the movement's artists that encouraged historians to step away from purely political analysis.[4] Her work was swiftly given a reality by the inclusion of her selection of suffrage artefacts in the 'Edwardian Era' Exhibition, held at the Barbican Art Gallery 1987/8.[5] A few years later another exhibition, 'Suffragettes in the Purple, White and Green', curated by Diane Atkinson at the Museum of London (1992/3), gave the public an opportunity of viewing the panoply of WSPU creativity,[6] while The Women's Library, first in its purpose-built premises in Whitechapel and then at LSE, has mounted exhibitions demonstrating the power of suffragist propaganda.[7]

Publications, some of them listed in this book's Select Bibliography, provide evidence of the suffrage campaign's relationship to material culture in the fields of, for example, fine art, fiction, theatre, dress, vegetarianism, architecture, jewellery, photography, interior design, periodicals, coinage, textiles and shopping. However, it may be that my observations on Objects 31–34 and 97 are the first in relation to the suffrage movement that Prown would categorize as 'Devices'.

There is yet no survey devoted to the memorabilia of the British women's suffrage campaign such as Kenneth Florey has produced for that of the United States.[8] Even so, that book does include a considerable number of British items and, with knowledge drawn from his formidable collection, Florey has contributed a chapter on British suffrage badges to *Suffrage and the Arts* (eds Miranda Garrett and Zoe Thomas, 2018). This work and another, *Women's Suffrage in Word, Image, Music, Stage and Screen: The Making of a Movement* (eds Christopher Wiley and Lucy Ella Rose, 2021), comprising essays that consider the role played in the suffrage movement by fine and applied artists and their created objects, are manifestations of the women's suffrage movement's 'material turn'. Indeed, the most recent survey of suffrage history writing, *The Routledge Companion to British Women's Suffrage* (ed. Krista Cowman, 2025), devotes one of its four sections to chapters on material culture. These include a contribution by Beverley Cook, curator of social history at the London Museum, on 'curating, collecting and displaying suffrage', which illustrates very effectively the difficulties faced in creating a nuanced display out of so many competing objects. Each has their own story to tell but those that involve sacrifice or violence are more obviously 'sensational'. With the London Museum collection holding material evidence of physical force perpetrated by both the suffragettes and the State, there is a danger that is the story that gets told, it being what visitors and sponsors expect. Similarly, Women's Social and Political Union (WSPU) marketing continues to be so effective that the centenary of partial enfranchisement in 2018 was dominated by purple, white and green, whether or not the colours were appropriate to the occasion. Those celebrations not only produced a laudable programme of exhibitions but also teased out collections of suffrage objects that had lain dormant within families. Some came onto the market, but others were given to museums; it is to be hoped this pattern may be repeated in 2028 when we celebrate the centenary of full enfranchisement. Such is the power of marketing that, to the despair of the historian, purple, white and green may again be the colour motif, despite the WSPU playing no part in the final stage of the campaign.

Having established my approach to the objects, I surveyed the span of the campaign, perceiving it as falling into five unequal sections, the first four of which cover the years of campaigning and the fifth the aftermath. The number of objects within each section was chosen to reflect the relative intensity of the campaign in that period. Thus Objects 1–18 cover 1866 to 1903; Objects 19–78, 1903 to 1914; Objects 79–83, 1914 to 1918; Objects 84–93, 1918 to 1928; and Objects 94–100, 1929 to 2025. Although, for the sake of succinctness, the title of this book refers to the 'British' women's suffrage campaign, Ireland was, of course, an integral part of the wider UK movement until partition in 1922 and is represented here by Objects 8 and 79.

The objects are drawn from institutional and private collections, some with known provenance, others not. Some have been donated to institutional archives, others bought from dealers, antique fairs, book fairs, or at auction, terrestrial or internet. One consideration in making the selection was to demonstrate the diversity of suffrage-related objects, each photograph, painting, engraving, figurine, textile, piece of china, furniture, poster, recording, film, statue, medal, diary, board game, silver, library or typewriter having its own biography. To assess its significance and the part it played in the suffrage narrative we need to discover what it is, who made it, when, where and why. To verify its authenticity, we need to know its provenance, that is, who made it or owned it. That is possible if the object is held in an archive composed by the original activists, such as those in the Women's Library at the London School of Economics or the London Museum, or if bought with a credible provenance from a reputable dealer or auction house. But quantities of suffrage objects survive at random, quite detached from their original owner and knowledge and judgement must be employed in deciding on the authenticity of such items. It is regrettable that the suffrage movement has attracted the attention of rogue dealers who are not above manufacturing spurious 'suffrage' objects. Miss Turquand's silver basket (Object 70), engraved with its history of being sold for 'King's Taxes', is indisputably 'right', a silver cigarette case on which a figure of a 'suffragette' has been crudely scratched is probably not. But even when not engraved with a history, all the objects have a story to tell, whether sturdy, as Helen Blackburn's bookcase (Object 17), or ephemeral, as the lily carried at Emily Wilding Davison's funeral (Object 73).

When making the selection the other consideration was to choose objects to represent as many developments in the suffrage movement as possible. For, over the years the campaign was anything but cohesive, societies rose and fell, each having its own time-specific reason, powered by its own leaders, guided by its own principles but which, as situations or personnel changed, sank out of view, or split, or merged, or devoured other societies. At its most basic the campaign can be viewed as consisting of two wings, the constitutional, led from the end of the nineteenth century by Mrs Fawcett, and the militant, led from 1903 by Mrs Pankhurst. The former are known as 'suffragists' and the latter as 'suffragettes', a name, meant to be derogatory, first applied to the emergent WSPU by the *Daily Mail* on 10 January 1906. Christabel Pankhurst, Mrs Pankhurst's eldest daughter, parsed the distinction between the two names as 'Just "['jist']" want the vote" was the notion conveyed by the older appellation and, as a famous anecdote had it, "the Suffragettes [hardening the 'g'] they mean to get it."'[9] Although this is a neat summary, the reality was more complex. As methods of campaigning changed, individuals moved not only between suffrage societies, but from one wing to another, from militant to constitutional and vice versa. Suffrage materials can bear witness to these changes of allegiance. For instance, in the early twentieth century the numerous badges owned by Mrs Lilian Hicks and her daughter, Amy, testify to the wide range of societies to which they successively or concurrently belonged. These, together with Amy's hunger-strike medal, were, long after their deaths, mounted and framed, not only creating an impressive display but making manifest the complexities of the suffrage campaign as experienced by two individuals.[10]

Each of the hundred objects has been identified and, if known, the reason for its creation, its maker and present whereabouts noted. This information forms the basis for a short discussion, placing each object in the historical narrative to explain how it helped develop the suffrage campaign. Discussions are at times confined to the specific, such as the 1866 petition (Object 1), or Mrs Pankhurst's shoe (Object 78), but many, such as the 'Votes for Women' train (Object 31) or suffrage plays (Object 53), while placing the chosen object in context, do briefly mention others of the same genre. For, from the quantities of suffrage objects surviving, the possible permutations of any one hundred are endless. Although informed by many years of researching suffrage material, this selection is personal. Other historians will emphasize different aspects of the suffrage story by making a different selection.

But whatever the choice, there is no doubting the power of suffrage objects, felt not only by the original campaigners but also by subsequent curators. For a short period immediately before the Second World War each wing of the suffrage campaign housed its archive of printed material and artefacts in Westminster buildings. Those interested in women's history could consult the suffragists' Women's Service House library (Object 95), as Virginia Woolf did when seeking verification of the facts that fuelled the anger expressed in *Three Guineas*, while the Suffragette Fellowship intended the younger generation to be moved by the power of the prison relics, banners and battle trophies they had arranged on display close by at Women's Record House (Object 96). Nearly a century later, while events have brought the original Women's Service House library, now the Women's Library, to the LSE and the original Suffragette Fellowship collection to the London Museum, the distinction is less clear, with each accruing donated or purchased items from across the suffrage spectrum. While in the late 1930s the Suffragette Fellowship piled donated objects into a single glass case, in the second decade of the twenty-first century museums not only employ more sophisticated methods of display, but have made progress in digitizing their holdings and making them available online.[11] The London Museum, the Women's Library at LSE, the Glasgow Women's Library, the National Museum of Wales, the National Museum of Scotland and the People's History Museum, Manchester, all provide online access to digitized suffrage objects in their collections. All these institutions and many local museums also have suffrage material either on display or in store and available for research. Even when nothing appears in an online catalogue, it is always worth asking if a museum holds any suffrage objects. Increasingly, museums offer handling sessions, the Victoria and Albert, for instance, has several suffrage items available through its 'Order an Object' service at its V. & A. East Storehouse.

Although many objects are held in private collections, those in institutions accessible to the public provide ample scope for further research. A study of any suffrage object or group of objects would be revealing of life during the campaigning period. For instance, there is much still to be discovered about the production and consumption of commercial suffrage objects, such as china figurines (Object 68). Who bought them? Was the availability of such items ever advertised? What type of shop stocked them? Would they have been given as a present to a known anti-suffragist or as 'a bit of a laugh' to a supporter? Where in the home were items like this placed? Was it on the mantlepiece over the range in a kitchen, or on a shelf in a 'front room', or in a display case in a drawing-room? Under Object 68, I mention that the design of the figurine was registered in 1909. Do others of this genre appear in the National Archive's Design Register? If so, who were their creators? In fact, in the hunt for all kinds of suffrage-related objects the Design Register is ripe for investigation.

As I explain under Object 50, postcards were a phenomenon of the suffrage campaign. Both postcards sympathetic to suffrage, designed by suffrage artists, and those antipathetic, published by commercial firms lampooning the movement, have attracted some attention. My belief is that the misogynist image of 'the suffragette' depicted on the commercial cards was but one stage in the history of portraying transgressive women and not specifically anti-suffrage. In researching a subject such as this, in effect cartooning, it is necessary to take the long view, back into the nineteenth century and forward through the twentieth. The fact that the heyday of the comic picture postcard coincided with the 'suffragette' years has perhaps concentrated undue attention on that medium. What would be useful to know is how well those cards sold compared with those of other comic genres? Were they produced so prolifically because they were profitable, or because the publisher had a discernible antipathy to the women's movement? Is any publisher or artist known to have supported a pro- or anti-suffrage society? Being the least expensive suffrage objects on the market, it would still be possible to make and research a small collection of these comic cards, focusing perhaps on an individual publishing firm or artist.

Of cards produced by the suffrage societies, little focus has yet been concentrated on photographic cards of suffrage personalities, that is, portrait cards that carry a caption that associate them with one of the societies. While the leaders appear on any number of cards, those of lower rank may only feature on one. Is it possible to ascertain why an individual was given this accolade? Can the postcard be correlated with any activity, such as appointment as an organizer or the serving of a prison sentence? Is there any pattern in the way the sitters chose to be presented? It is a misfortune that few, if any, postcard albums remain intact as originally constructed, cards having been extracted to be sold separately. But if one were to be encountered that would be an excellent subject for investigation.

Photographs, whether or not produced as postcards, may prove more helpful than print when attempting to research one particular aspect of the suffrage campaign. For, although printed sources reveal little evidence of racial diversity, the British women's suffrage movement differed markedly from that in the United States in that there was no overt discrimination. An African-American woman, Sarah Remond, was one of the signatories to the 1866 petition (see Object 1) and other Black and minority ethnic men and women may have been among the campaign's supporters. However, they are now 'hidden from history'; census records only documented a person's place of birth, which is no guide to ethnic origin as so many white British men and women were born in countries of the Empire. While we have yet to discover supporters whose ethnicity linked them to Africa or the West Indies, the involvement of elite Indian women is evidenced by the well-known photograph of Princess Sophia Duleep Singh, daughter of the last maharaja of the Sikh empire and god-daughter to Queen Victoria, as she sells copies of *The Suffragette* outside Hampton Court Palace, and of that of Indian women, in saris, representing their country in the 1911 suffragette Coronation Procession. That spectacular had at its heart an adulation of Empire, to which the majority of both suffragists and suffragettes were sympathetic. This was a time when Indian suffrage activists believed that by joining the campaign in the Imperial metropolis they would gain favour that would eventually prove useful to their own cause.[12] A few such women have already been identified, but it was a photograph (see Object 76) that added two hitherto unremarked sisters to their number. It is worthwhile carefully scanning photographs, photographic postcards and, indeed, film, in an attempt to uncover any further evidence of racial diversity.

Although suffrage fiction has been studied for its content, little attention has been paid to how such works came to be published. How receptive were publishers, invariably male, to commissioning or accepting for publication manuscripts on the subject? Under Object 54 I mention briefly the involvement of one small publisher but there is ample scope for more ambitious enquiries. Related to this, publishers of suffrage novels and non-fiction were not only reliant on the individual consumer but needed to capture the attention of all types of libraries. In the entry 'Libraries' in *The Women's Suffrage Movement: A Reference Guide*, I made a necessarily brief survey of the books made available to readers in a selection of public libraries between the late-nineteenth century and 1914, but a more detailed analytical study of library catalogues could give a very useful insight into the reading habits of the men and women of the day. The suffrage connections to a more self-selecting readership, that of members of the London Library, have been teased out in a short article.[13] In this subscription library, one of whose founders was John Stuart Mill, objects of print culture, that is, books, dating from the early days of the suffrage movement, are still held on the open shelves, many with inscriptions noting they were presented to the Library by suffrage activists. Are there any other libraries whose catalogues and shelves can be interrogated in this way?

Some types of suffrage objects, particularly those such as hunger-strike medals that embody heightened emotion, have a very high financial value, driven both by the sacrifice they symbolize and by their comparative scarcity. But they, too, would benefit from further investigation. Under Object 41 I set out my research into the development of the form of the medal, but the significance of the different clasps has not yet been definitively established, although various theories have been mooted. As well as studying the medals held in institutional collections, details of many others that have passed through the sale rooms can be viewed on auction house websites. The latter can be very informative on all types of suffrage objects and are just one of the less obvious sources that can be utilized when researching.

Curiosity is to be recommended, both as an approach to discovering objects and to their interpretation. For, studying suffrage objects offers a means of entering the mindset not only of the campaigners but also of the politicians with whom they were engaging and their fellow countrymen and women, witnesses to the campaign.

Note on the text

To focus on the objects and to keep the text within a manageable word length, I have not included here details of the lives of the many suffrage activists mentioned, other than to include their life dates against their entry in the index. Thanks to the explosion of interest in the suffrage movement in the last couple of decades, readers will find biographical information readily available on the internet, on sites such as Wikipedia and Spartacus Educational, and, through library membership, in the *Oxford Dictionary of National Biography* or as links to published biographies. This book will be successful if it stimulates readers to discover more about the suffrage campaign and its campaigners.

Object 1

The printed pamphlet form of the 1866 women's suffrage petition

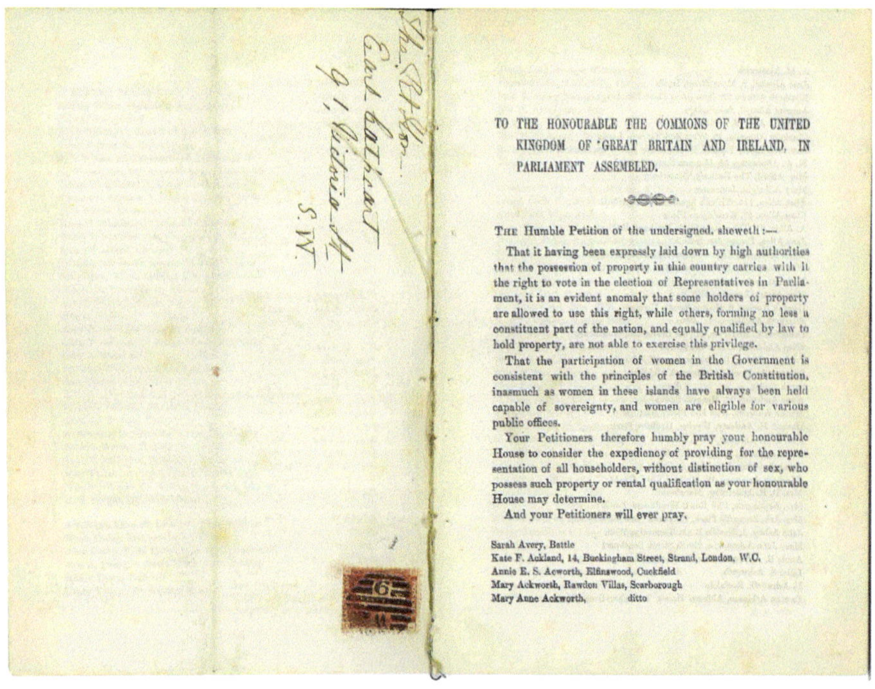

TO THE HONOURABLE THE COMMONS OF THE UNITED KINGDOM OF 'GREAT BRITAIN AND IRELAND, IN PARLIAMENT ASSEMBLED.

THE Humble Petition of the undersigned, sheweth :—

That it having been expressly laid down by high authorities that the possession of property in this country carries with it the right to vote in the election of Representatives in Parliament, it is an evident anomaly that some holders of property are allowed to use this right, while others, forming no less a constituent part of the nation, and equally qualified by law to hold property, are not able to exercise this privilege.

That the participation of women in the Government is consistent with the principles of the British Constitution, inasmuch as women in these islands have always been held capable of sovereignty, and women are eligible for various public offices.

Your Petitioners therefore humbly pray your honourable House to consider the expediency of providing for the representation of all householders, without distinction of sex, who possess such property or rental qualification as your honourable House may determine.

And your Petitioners will ever pray.

Sarah Avery, Battle
Kate F. Ackland, 14, Buckingham Street, Strand, London, W.C.
Annie E. S. Acworth, Elfinswood, Cuckfield
Mary Ackworth, Rawdon Villas, Scarborough
Mary Anne Ackworth,   ditto

Object 1 is the pamphlet form of the women's suffrage petition presented to Parliament in 1866. 40 pages, no printer noted. Back cover and first page shown. (SC/20, The Women's Library collection, London School of Economics and Political Science.)

Object 1 is a rare, printed example of the first of the 16,433 mass petitions delivered to Parliament during the long 'votes for women' campaign.[1] Revealing the names of the signatories, it is important not only as a created object, evidence of the work undertaken to launch the suffrage campaign, but also as a document, a primary source of information on the earliest campaigners.[2]

In May 1866, with parliamentary reform under discussion and middle-class men vociferously protesting their lack of a vote, members of the Kensington Society, a woman-only discussion group, seized the opportunity to lobby for the inclusion of women in any new Bill. In July 1865 they had campaigned for the election to Parliament of the political philosopher John Stuart Mill who, in his manifesto, suggested that women should be given the parliamentary vote on the same terms as men. It was Mill's stepdaughter, Helen Taylor, who now drafted the petition, to be signed only by women, calling for 'the representation of all householders, without the distinction of sex, who possess such property or rental qualification as your honourable House may determine'. At the time, petitioning was the most effective method of exerting pressure on the legislature.

A small committee ordered the printing of petition forms and posted them with explanatory letters to friends and relations, requesting signatures. They, in turn, utilizing their own networks, distributed the forms further around Britain's cities, towns and villages, some even being prepared to canvass door-to-door.[3] In less than three weeks 1,521 signatures were returned to the organizers, who pasted them together into a long roll. On 7 June this unwieldy petition was taken to Westminster Hall by Emily Davies and Elizabeth Garrett, and handed to Mill, who presented it in the House of Commons, describing it as from '1500 ladies, praying that the franchise might be granted to females who were independent householders. The petitioners were of the higher and middle classes of society, many of them very well known'.[4]

It is thanks to Davies' expertise in creating the material culture of persuasion, developed while campaigning for greater educational opportunities for girls and women, that we can interrogate Mill's description of the social rankings of the signatories. For, although the original petition was destroyed, as were all presented between 1834 and 1946, Davies decided that the name and address of each signatory should be listed in a printed pamphlet and sent to members of both Houses of Parliament and to the weekly papers so that, 'in case they take any notice, they may know what they are commenting on'.[5]

Object 1 was sent to Earl Cathcart, a member of the House of Lords. Addressed by hand, with a perforated Penny Red postage stamp affixed, it was delivered to his London address.[6] With no office, working in domestic surroundings, the women had acquired addresses of hundreds of UK newspapers, together with names and addresses of all MPs and peers, and then laboriously addressed and dispatched over 1,000 pamphlets, of which mailing only this copy survived, to be discovered on a stall in the Portobello Road market in the 1990s.

Object 1 is a landmark in women's history, marking the beginning of the long suffrage campaign and providing a lens through which to view the women who in 1866 had 'not hesitated to affix their names to a public document, and to pronounce a decided opinion, open to the controversy and criticism of all the world'.[7] At a macro-level, the printed petition allows us to investigate the family, geographical, economic, religious and social networks that connected women not only to each other across the UK, but to the idea of political emancipation and to the parallel campaigns they were waging to improve their opportunities and status. At a micro-level, analysis reveals details of individual women, who were by no means confined, as Mill intimated, to 'the higher and middle classes of society'. Although many were the wives or widows of professional men or lived off inherited funds, many were women working to support themselves as governesses, shopkeepers or dressmakers, or were wives or widows of tradesmen. No distinction was made as to class or colour; those signing included a widowed Leeds charwoman, Mrs Emma Tingle, and the African-American abolitionist campaigner, Sarah Parker Remond.[8] By publicizing the 1,521 names, the creators of Object 1 were not only employing an unusual tactic but launching a campaign that was to become legendary for its increasingly inventive methods and for the range of objects produced in the attainment of its goal.

Although, on 7 June 1866, neither Davies nor Garrett waited in the Ladies' Gallery of the House of Commons to see Mill present their petition, a year later, on 20 May 1867, Garrett's younger sister, Mrs Millicent Garrett Fawcett, watched as he moved an amendment to the Representation of the People Bill that, if it had been successful, by substituting the word 'person' for 'man', would have allowed some women to qualify under any new voting arrangements. The vote, however, was not to be so easily won.

Object 2

Lydia Becker's dress, 1889

Object 2 is a dress made for Lydia Becker by a court dressmaker, Madame Brownjohn, 1889. (TWL.2003.665, The Women's Library collection, London School of Economics and Political Science.)

Lydia Becker played a major role in the nineteenth-century suffrage movement, while always regretting that her signature had not appeared on the 1866 suffrage petition.[1] For, having only recently moved into Manchester, she only heard mention of the suffrage movement in October 1866 when Barbara Bodichon's paper on 'Reasons for the Enfranchisement of Women' was delivered at the annual meeting of the National Association for the Promotion of Social Science, held that year in the city. She immediately contacted Emily Davies in London, offered to organize a Manchester petition and published an article on 'Female Suffrage' that elicited much favourable comment in newspapers throughout the country.[2] Thus began an involvement in the suffrage campaign that was to dominate the rest of Becker's life.

In February 1867 she made her first appearance at a meeting held by those who had collected the Manchester signatures to the 1866 petition. Although a newcomer to the group, she clearly impressed and was immediately elected honorary secretary of the Manchester women's suffrage committee, continuing the campaign after the defeat of Mill's women's suffrage amendment to the 1867 Reform Act. Unmarried, she had been responsible for the upbringing of her fourteen younger siblings after their mother's early death, and the skills acquired in managing a large middle-class household translated well into the organizing of a political campaign. Moreover, her botanical studies, which had been her particular interest, had inculcated the systematic and scientific approach she was to apply to matters of business.

Becker's appearance reflected her capabilities; she was the epitome of what was considered a 'strong-minded' woman. Tall, her buxom figure firmly corseted, her hair pulled back from a high forehead and plaited into a neat crown, she was invariably depicted wearing metal-rimmed spectacles. The image of a strong-minded spinster was not, however, that which those in London who saw themselves as the leaders of the movement wished to promote. But, even if she was neither married, young nor pretty, Becker's style of dress could not be faulted in its adherence to what was considered suitable for a woman of her class and position.

In the 1880s, Becker firmly, with humour, espoused the cause of corsets, citing the benefits of the support given, although many of her fellow suffrage campaigners, members of the Rational Dress Society, spoke out against them.[3] There is no doubt the outfits she wore would have reassured any audience or, indeed, any lobbied MP, that Miss Becker of the Manchester Women's Suffrage Society was a respectable middle-class woman who, whatever her opinion on women's enfranchisement, was unlikely to foment revolution.

As Becker clearly took care over her appearance, it might have pleased her to know that Object 2, one of the last costumes she had made, survives. Worn in 1889 at the wedding of her youngest brother, its appearance was recorded in detail in a newspaper report as 'a redingote of rich faille, in the new shade of bronze green, trimmed down each side with handsome passementerie, Medici collar and cuffs to match, worn over vest, and underskirt of duchesse satin, bonnet of rich red roses, with green foliage'.[4] Both the bronze green shade of the silk and the Medici collar, a style raised at the back and open at the front, indicated an awareness of what was new in fashion.[5] For this outfit Becker had commissioned Madame Brownjohn, who was not only a London 'court dressmaker' but was also highly recommended by the Rational Dress Society.[6] However, Becker's graceful costume was entirely conventional, most certainly necessitating the wearing not only of corsets but also of a small bustle pad to create a fashionable slight fullness at the rear. Object 2 was memorialized not only in words, but also in a photograph and in a painted portrait, worn by Becker in the photograph that Helen Blackburn included on page 180 of her *Record of Women's Suffrage* (1902), and on which Elizabeth Guinness based the portrait with which she decorated Blackburn's bookcase (see Object 17).

Becker died in 1890 but her dress, which can have been little worn, survived, in its afterlife continuing to promote feminist concerns. In 1932 it was lent for a fund-raising dress pageant organized by the Manchester branch of the Women's Citizen Association and was eventually given to the Fawcett Society.[7] In 2016 Becker's importance to the early suffrage campaign was represented by this dress, hanging at the back of a display case that also contained Object 1, in the LSE Library's exhibition 'Endless Endeavours: from the 1866 Women's Suffrage Petition to the Fawcett Society'. However, to be photographed as Object 2, the outfit received the attention of a costume mounter who has brought it to life, recreating for us the presence of Lydia Becker.

Object 3

Cartoon of Lydia Becker and Jacob Bright, *c.*1868

Object 3 is a cartoon depicting Lydia Becker and Jacob Bright MP. Artist and place of publication unknown, possibly 1868. (From the Collection of Dr Kenneth Florey. Photograph by Emilia van Beugen.)

With the abolition of stamp duty in 1855 and of paper duty in 1861 the number of newspapers rose and, as literacy increased, stimulated by the 1870 Education Act, so did the market for printed news. With the passing of the 1867 Reform Act the (male) electorate doubled, creating a new readership for political news, the names of political figures, both local and national, becoming increasingly familiar. Thus, after her appointment in early 1867 as honorary secretary of the Manchester suffrage committee and her appearance a year later audaciously speaking from the platform in the Free Trade Hall at the first public meeting of the Manchester National Society for Women's Suffrage (MNSWS), Lydia Becker's name soon achieved national recognition, and, to her dismay, her caricatured figure began to appear in political cartoons.[1]

There is little evidence to suggest that the cartoons featuring Becker were published in newspapers or magazines but, rather, were issued as small posters at election time, covering the windows of bookshops and newsagents, pasted up in coffee shops and inns. Offering the public a range of visual images to augment newsprint descriptions, the political cartoon was a diverting means of commenting on current issues. In these Becker is invariably linked with Jacob Bright, Radical Liberal MP for Manchester, who succeeded as parliamentary spokesman for the suffrage campaign after Mill lost his seat in the 1868 general election. Bright entered Parliament at a Manchester by-election in November 1867, held the seat in 1868, lost in 1874, but reclaimed it in 1876, thereby giving cartoonists numerous opportunities to chart his fortunes. In one form or another, Lydia Becker is well represented in the surviving cartoons.[2] However, nothing is known of these cartoonists; artwork is unsigned, and little evidence survives of the only two named printers.[3]

Probably commenting on the Manchester 1868 general election, Object 3's cartoonist is seeking to stir the viewer's emotions by depicting Bright as dominated by Becker and her fellow suffrage campaigners. For, pushing a pram labelled 'Only Women's Rights', he is unmanned, while Becker, despite her ruffles and bustle, is careless of revealing her ankles and is defined by her spectacles and broom as a 'woman's righter'. It did not take long for another cartoonist to transform Becker's broom into an umbrella, which became, as depicted on twentieth-century comic postcards (see Object 50), the suffragette's standard accessory. In an 1876 cartoon, carrying an umbrella labelled 'Women's Rights', Becker is the very antithesis of the image she and her fellow campaigners wished to project.[4] The visual rhetoric of Object 3 is augmented by a caption that plays on the word 'Becker', rendering it 'Becca' (ie 'Rebecca'), which, together with 'Jacob', would create a (somewhat nonsensical?) biblical association in the minds of church/chapel-going readers, and 'Pecker' by way of alluding to a common phrase of general exhortation.

It is noticeable that Becker attracted more attention from cartoonists than any other suffrage leader. For instance, in the twentieth century, although 'the suffragette' was a common target, the Pankhursts, mother and daughters, were rarely lampooned. It may be that Becker proved irresistible because she was seen to work so closely with Bright, or merely that, despite the care she took with her appearance (see Object 2), her manner exemplified the very characteristics cartoonists expected to find in a 'woman's righter'. Mrs Millicent Fawcett, although she too was very close to an MP and spoke from public platforms around the country, did not receive this treatment, but the MP was her husband, and she was young, pretty, wealthier and of higher status than Becker.

Object 3 is important in making early acknowledgement of the existence of the MNSWS, whose members are offering encouragement to their MP and their honorary secretary. For, although the London National Society for Women's Suffrage (LNSWS), dominated by Mill and Helen Taylor, may have considered itself the 'mother committee', by 1868 Manchester was determined to direct its own campaign. While the LNSWS wished only to continue petitioning, Manchester took a bolder step, deciding to test the state of the law, encouraging around 6,000 women to register as voters. The argument, promoted by a lawyer, Thomas Chisholm Anstey, with support from Dr Richard Pankhurst, was that women's ancient right to the franchise had only been removed by the 1832 Reform Act. Although one Manchester woman, Mrs Lilly Maxwell, did vote in the November 1867 by-election, her name having inadvertently been accepted on the register, the tactic of registering women who fulfilled the property qualification ultimately failed when tested in the courts in November 1868.[5] However, twenty-four women who had been allowed to register in the Manchester area did vote in the November/December 1868 general election, a slight consolation to Becker as she embarked on the next stage of the campaign.

Object 4

An advertisement in the *Orkney Herald*, 4 October 1871

WOMEN'S SUFFRAGE.
PUBLIC MEETING.
MISS TAYLOUR, of Belmont, Stranraer. Honorary
Secretary of the Galloway Society for Women's Suf-
frage, will deliver a LECTURE on the above subject
IN THE
VOLUNTEER HALL, KIRKWALL,
On Monday Evening, 9th October,
AND IN THE
TOWN HALL, STROMNESS,
On Tuesday Evening, 10th October,
At a Quarter-past 8 o'clock.
After the Lecture, a Petition to Parliament will be
submitted to the Meeting, in support of Mr Jacob
Bright's Bill for conferring the Franchise on Women
Householders who pay Rates.
COLLECTION AT THE DOOR TO DEFRAY EXPENSES.

Object 4 is an advertisement in the 4 October 1871 issue of the *Orkney Herald*. (Courtesy of Orkney Library and Archive.)

In 1869 Jacob Bright succeeded in pushing his 'women's rights' pram (see Object 3) some way into the House of Commons, successfully promoting an amendment to a Municipal Franchise Bill that allowed spinster and widowed ratepayers in England the right to vote in local elections.[1]

Taking heart from this achievement, in 1870 Bright introduced a Bill for the Removal of the Electoral Disabilities of Women, which passed its Second Reading before being defeated. In 1871 it was again defeated but, undeterred, the suffrage campaigners planned for Bright to reintroduce it in 1872. In the meantime, women campaigners continued to petition. But, rather than simply contacting friends and relations, as in 1866 (see Object 1), they now sought signatures to petitions from the strangers flocking to 'Women's Suffrage' meetings. For, not only was the subject novel, but so was the prospect of being addressed by a 'woman's rights' woman.

Although Lydia Becker was the most well-known of the new breed of suffrage speakers, other women had also begun touring the country, lecturing on women's right to the parliamentary vote, inviting the formation of local suffrage committees and requesting signatures to petitions in support of the latest suffrage bill. One of the first was 'Miss Taylour, of Belmont, Stranraer' who in July 1869 had attended a women's suffrage meeting held by the London National Society for Women's Suffrage (LNSWS), and in February 1870 began a well-advertised lecture tour in the north of England, at the request of the LNSWS. Less than two years after Becker, by taking to the platform in Manchester, had shattered the shibboleth that denied women the freedom to address the public on political matters, it was already acceptable for the name of a middle-class woman to be advertised in a newspaper in association with the women's cause. Moreover, barely three months later an advertisement for one of Taylour's lectures mentioned there would be a 'Collection at the door to defray expenses'.[2] So, not only were suffrage speakers advertised in newspapers, but it was no longer necessary to disassociate them from any mention of money.

Jane Taylour was the daughter of a former soldier who had farming and business interests in the south-west of Scotland. One of eleven children, Taylour was the only unmarried daughter and, after her father's death in 1867, was free to follow her own interests, one of which was to campaign for enfranchisement. No papers survive to explain the arrangements for these early suffrage tours, though one press report indicated that, in advance of Taylour's arrival in Paisley, a local committee had been formed to make arrangements such as booking the hall and creating an audience.[3] With Taylour's standing as 'a lady' emphasized, it is likely she was offered 'hospitality', that is, invited to stay with one of the organizers, rather than in a hotel.

In 1871, now honorary secretary of the Galloway branch of the National Society, Taylour gave over fifty lectures. In October, acting on behalf of the Edinburgh National Society for Women's Suffrage (ENSWS), accompanied by Agnes McLaren, stepdaughter of Mrs Priscilla McLaren, the latter being sister to Jacob Bright and the ENSWS president, Taylour carried the suffrage message to the most northerly point yet, Object 4 heralding their arrival in Orkney. The wording is identical to advertisements for Taylour's lectures in other Scottish local papers, with only details of venue changed.

Although the editor of the *Orkney Herald*, William Peace, was a Liberal, he felt obliged to state that the paper, which circulated in Orkney and Shetland and backed Liberal interests, was not 'committing ourselves to support of the movement'.[4] But Taylour's Kirkwall lecture, delivered on 9 October in a wooden hall in the town centre, was reported quickly, favourably and at great length, the writer commenting that 'while eloquent, Miss Taylour is also logical'.[5] That attribute tells us something about the audience's expectation of a woman lecturer. Meetings had been very crowded and Taylour and McLaren well-received, publicity continuing in the letter column after their departure, their *'womanly'* appearance prayed in aid against criticism from a clerical element.

Travelling to Orkney had not been easy, involving journeys by train, steamship and coach. In her address McLaren noted, 'In many respects the mission on which we have come was a trying one, and only undertaken from the strong conviction that it was our duty to do so.' With the knowledge that a Kirkwall suffrage committee had been formed, that petitions were to follow and that the meeting's chairman who, in advance, had expressed himself in opposition to the views held by the speaker had at the end declared, 'I confess for myself, that, after listening to her address, my former opinions have been considerably shaken', Taylour and McLaren may have been assured that the 'trying' mission had been worthwhile.[6] Those signing the Orkney petitions were among the 330,000 who in 1871 petitioned Parliament in support of women's suffrage.

Object 5

An engraving of a suffrage meeting, 1872

Object 5 is an engraving of the platform speakers at a London suffrage meeting, *The Graphic,* **25 May 1872. From the left: Mrs Millicent Fawcett, Mrs Mark Pattison, Mrs Ernestine Rose, Miss Lydia Becker, Lyon Playfair MP (chairman) and (standing) Miss Rhoda Garrett.** (TWL.1998.58, The Women's Library collection, London School of Economics and Political Science.)

As Taylour and McLaren toured the north of Scotland, in England the balance of power between the London and the Manchester suffrage societies was shifting, with London rather losing momentum after Mill failed to hold his Westminster seat in 1868. For, although revered as the philosopher of the women's cause, as president of the London National Society for Women's Suffrage (LNSWS) Mill exercised a somewhat repressive influence, reluctant for the society to be involved in active campaigning. This was not the view of the Manchester society, led by

Jacob Bright, now spokesman for the suffrage cause in Parliament. To exercise pressure on MPs, he decided that an umbrella committee, based in London, representing all suffrage societies, was required. Despite some acrimony, the result was the formation in late 1871 of the Central Committee of the National Society for Women's Suffrage. Thus, there were now two London-based suffrage societies, for the Central Committee was not synonymous with the LNSWS and, indeed, some members of the latter took objection to the Central Committee, many members of which, including Bright and Lydia Becker, were also working with Mrs Josephine Butler for the repeal of the Contagious Diseases Acts. Mill was adamant that the CDA campaign should not be associated with that for suffrage.

On 1 May 1872, the Bill to Remove the Electoral Disabilities of Women, introduced in Parliament by Bright, suffered yet another defeat on its Second Reading and, in response, on the evening of 10 May, the suffrage campaigners held a public meeting in central London. Although most speakers were connected to the Central Committee, Millicent Fawcett of the LNSWS, despite her personal attachment to Mill, joined them on the platform.

The suffrage campaign was to be long and, in its later stages, highly visible, but the scene in the Hanover Square Rooms is the first of its events to be illustrated in the press, in an engraving that appeared in a relatively new weekly paper, *The Graphic*.[1] The paper's main selling point was the number and quality of its engravings, its founder, wood-engraver William Luson Thomas, believing pictures could exert a powerful influence on public opinion. Published on a Saturday, priced at 6d, *The Graphic* had a circulation of *c*.100,000, its artists considered 'among the best to be found'.[2] Recognizing that a depiction of platform speakers at a women's suffrage meeting would create an arresting picture, the editor devoted an entire page to the scene, printing the image sideways to take full advantage of the generous paper size.

It is worth considering why the anonymous artist chose to depict the moment when, of all the speakers, Rhoda Garrett was holding the floor.[3] Indeed, to appeal to *The Graphic*'s principally middle-class readership, Millicent Fawcett, the youthful wife of a well-known MP, conventionally attractive and immutably respectable, might have seemed a more obvious choice. However, barely a year since she had given her first suffrage speech, Garrett's fame as a touring speaker for the Central Committee had grown. Moreover, she projected an image distinctly different from that of the others on the platform, but which, most crucially, was also attractive. At a time when it was conventional for women to wear their hair 'up', hers falls loosely over her shoulders, and instead of a close-fitting dress and shawl, she wears a resolutely un-corseted two-piece, a tailored skirt and a double-breasted jacket with velvet revers. Although no report commented on Garrett's appearance, it is evident she caught the artist's eye, presumably as the speaker best embodying the spirit of the evening.

Having made his sketch, the artist did not have to rely on memory to produce the finished work, for *The Graphic* revealed that 'the portraits of the speakers at the Women's Suffrage Meetings are assisted by photographs taken by Messrs Elliot and Fry, of Baker Street'.[4] Although that firm's archive was later destroyed, an Elliot and Fry photograph of Fawcett from this period survives, showing her head inclined at the same angle, her hairstyle and dress identical to that in the engraving.[5]

At this time at least one publisher thought there might be a market for photographic portraits of suffrage speakers for, under the heading 'Woman Suffrage', Messrs Dando, Hulson and Co. advertised 'Excellent Photographic Portraits of Miss Lilias Ashworth, Mrs Fawcett, Miss Rhoda Garrett, Mrs Rose and other ladies interested in the movement'.[6] This niche market was not enough, however, to save Dando, a serially unsuccessful opportunist, from bankruptcy.[7] Perhaps surprisingly, in view of the great demand for photographs of suffrage campaigners in the early twentieth century, no similar enthusiasm was evident in the nineteenth.

Object 6

Statue of John Stuart Mill, erected 1878

Object 6 is the statue of John Stuart Mill by Thomas Woolner, 1878. Bronze statue on Portland stone pedestal. Here photographed in 1927 for a postcard published by the National Union of Societies for Equal Citizenship. (TWL.2009.02.186, The Women's Library collection, London School of Economics and Political Science.)

In the 1870s, while cartoonists were caricaturing Lydia Becker and Jacob Bright (see Object 3) and photographs of Millicent Fawcett and Rhoda Garrett were offered for sale (see Object 5), the features of John Stuart Mill were also receiving artistic attention. For, after his sudden death in May 1873, a committee was formed to raise money to erect a statue in Westminster to commemorate Mill's life and work.[1]

Although the committee was dominated by men, it did include women such as Elizabeth Garrett Anderson and Millicent Fawcett with whom Mill had worked to present the 1866 petition and move the amendment to the 1867 Reform Bill. In addition, he had sponsored the Married Women's Property Bill and in 1869 published *The Subjection of Women*, an important essay, heavily influenced by discussions with his late wife, Harriet Taylor, and his stepdaughter, Helen Taylor.

A site was reserved in the Embankment's recently created Temple Gardens, the commission given to sculptor Thomas Woolner and the statue finally unveiled on 24 January 1878, with Millicent Fawcett among those present to hear her husband, Professor Henry Fawcett, MP for Hackney, give the eulogy. It was reported that the statue 'of heroic size is represented as sitting upon a garden seat, the right hand holding a book. At the feet of the figure is a newspaper, apparently carelessly dropped. The face is looking towards the Houses of Parliament'.[2]

During the following thirty years, although Mill's politics and philosophy were much discussed in the press, his statue attracted little attention. However, on 20 May 1908, which, besides being Mill's birthday, was also the day in 1867 on which he moved the Reform Bill amendment, the spotlight was once more directed on his statue when Charlotte Despard and Teresa Billington-Greig, leaders of the recently founded Women's Freedom League (WFL, see Object 24), attempted to present him with a garland into which flowers were woven spelling out 'Votes for Women'. However, the garden authority objected to this 'advertisement', forbidding the ceremony until the florist had removed the inflammatory phrase, this hiatus garnering for the WFL even more publicity. At least two press photographers recorded the event.[3] It is likely the idea of harnessing Mill to their campaign had originated with the WFL's organizing secretary, Billington-Greig, a strategic thinker, who recognized that such an association lent political and philosophical legitimacy to a campaign that was by now increasingly overshadowed by the active militancy of Mrs Pankhurst's Women's Social and Political Union (see Object 21). Rather than merely quoting his words, the WFL considered it expedient to be associated physically with Mill's image.

In 1909 the WFL produced a postcard portrait of Mill and on 21 May 1910 returned to the statue bearing wreaths, the ceremony organized by an artistic organization, the Suffrage Atelier. An even larger demonstration was held at the statue in 1911 when the WFL was joined by many other societies.[4] In 1912 and 1914 Mill Memorial Meetings were held by the WFL, but in Caxton Hall rather than at the statue, possibly because 'Votes for Women' demonstrations were no longer permitted in Temple Gardens. In 1913 models of the statue were offered for sale to suffrage sympathizers by the sculptor's daughter.[5]

On 21 May 1917 the WFL held a Caxton Hall meeting to commemorate the fiftieth anniversary of Mill's parliamentary intervention, and on 24 May 1918, three months after the passing of the Representation of the People Act, the WFL and other organizations returned to his statue to lay celebratory wreaths. Such a ceremony was not repeated until 20 May 1927, a month after the prime minister had declared his intention of introducing legislation to give women the vote on the same terms as men (see Object 91). Therefore, with the final goal in sight, a photographer was hired to capture the image shown on Object 6, that of Millicent Fawcett, on behalf of the National Union of Societies for Equal Citizenship (NUSEC), and Emmeline Pethick-Lawrence, now president of the WFL, together with many members of the new inter-war women's organizations, laying wreaths to honour their champion.

A year later, on 19 May 1928, shortly before the passing of the Equal Franchise Act, Fawcett again led a wreath-laying ceremony, returning for the last time on 20 May 1929. Having witnessed the unveiling fifty-one years previously, she now made a final obeisance to Mill's statue on the day that serendipitously coincided with Nomination Day for candidates in the first general election at which all women could vote on the same terms as men. Fifty-eight years later, on 20 May 1987, Mary Stott, a revered feminist journalist, laid a wreath at his statue on behalf of the Fawcett Society. Thus, on the 120th anniversary of the day Mill had stood up for women in the House of Commons, his statue served to mediate the link between the London National Society for Women's Suffrage, of which he had been president, and its direct descendant, the Fawcett Society, still championing gender equality and women's rights.

Object 7

Annual reports of nineteenth-century suffrage societies

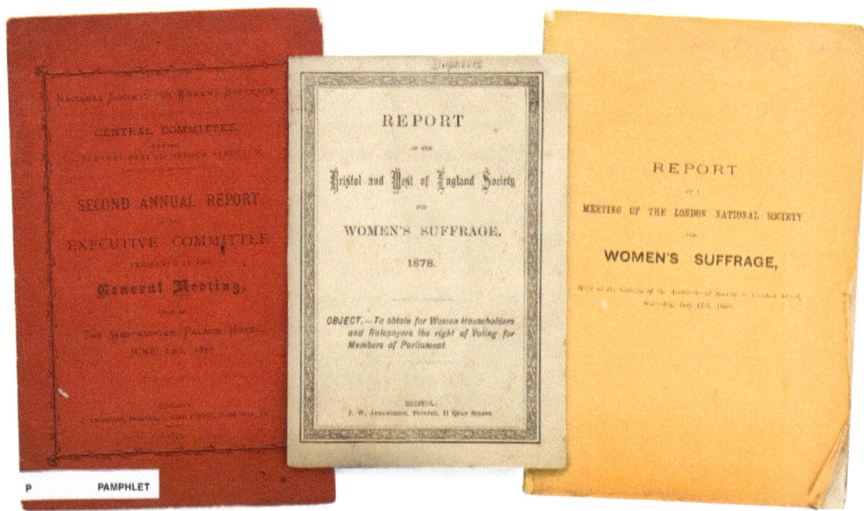

Object 7 comprises three of the early annual reports issued by suffrage societies. (Left) Central Committee Second Annual Report, 1873. (Centre) Bristol and West of England Society for Women's Suffrage Annual Report, 1878. (Right) Report of a meeting of the London National Society for Women's Suffrage, 17 July 1869. (2LSW/A/1/2/02, PC/06/396-11/27, PC/06/396-11/28, The Women's Library collection, London School of Economics and Political Science.)

It is through their published annual reports that we can trace the development of the women's suffrage societies. In the aftermath of the 1866 suffrage petition, its organizers haltingly formed themselves into a group that by the summer of 1867 was known as the London National Society for Women's Suffrage (LNSWS). On 17 July 1869 the LNSWS held its first public meeting, in central London, later publishing a verbatim report of the proceedings, shown on the right in Object 7. On this occasion the audience, who included Miss Taylour (see Object 4), heard women for the first time speak from a London platform in the furtherance of their cause. Although most of the speakers were men, the chair was taken by Mrs Clementia Taylor, with Millicent Fawcett proposing a resolution 'that this society pledges itself to use every lawful means to extend the franchise to women'.

As we have seen under Object 2, the Manchester suffrage committee was already in existence when Lydia Becker was elected its honorary secretary in early 1867 and, under Object 3, that she was determined the society should follow its own course, rather than being directed by London. She did, however, concede that the committee should be known as the Manchester National Society for Women's Suffrage, tacitly agreeing to a federated scheme that was enlarged in November 1867 with the formation of the Edinburgh National Society for Women's Suffrage, under the leadership of Mrs Priscilla McLaren. These three were the main societies, to which committees in Bristol and Birmingham affiliated in 1868 and those in Dublin and Belfast in 1871.

However, as we have seen under Object 5, with the formation of the Central Committee of the National Society in late 1871 there was a shift in the balance of power, giving pre-eminence to those sympathetic to the aims and methods of the Manchester society, and, as a corollary, a decline in the influence of the LNSWS, exacerbated by the death of Mill in 1873. While the LNSWS always worked in domestic surroundings, the Central Committee had a London office, 9 Berners Street, from which emerged business-like annual reports that, while giving a survey of each year's work, also set out the names of its officers and subscribers/donors, lists of members, details of all the local committees, with names and addresses of their officers, together with details of the society's publications and accounts. From the latter we can discover, for instance, that in 1872/3 £37 10s was spent on rent (for the three-quarters of that year for which they were in occupation); £43 16s 4d on postage, carriage, telegrams and omnibus fares; £4 16s 4d for coals, candles and attendance; £102 7s 6d for Secretary's salary and payment for copying and £164 14s 5d expended on agents in London, Portsmouth Rugby, Boston, Ipswich, Peterborough, Bury St Edmunds, Berkhampstead, Chelmsford, Norwich, Northampton and Woolwich. Every one of these components of an annual report provides us with an entry point into the life of a society and is a springboard for further research.

As noted under Object 17, as early as 1903 Lilias Ashworth Hallett commented on the value to future researchers of the material contained in annual reports. Although not all have survived, some reports may now be found in local archives, while many, held by the Women's Library collection at LSE, have been digitized, with access freely available.[1] Covering societies, constitutional and militant, throughout the country in both the nineteenth and the twentieth centuries, these reports are an essential research tool not only as a primary source of information on the suffrage campaign but, as printed objects, revealing, for instance, connections between the societies and their printers and changes over time in design and typography.

Object 8

The Haslam memorial seat, St Stephen's Green, Dublin

Object 8 is a seat of Kilkenny limestone sculpted by Albert Power. Dedicated to Anna Maria and Thomas Haslam 'in honour of their long years of public service chiefly devoted to the enfranchisement of women', it was erected on St Stephen's Green in the centre of Dublin, November 1925. (Courtesy of Professor Diana Spencer.)

Anna Maria Haslam was one of the few Irishwomen to sign the 1866 suffrage petition (see Object 1).[1] Both she and her husband had been born into Quaker families and in 1867, after the defeat of his amendment to include women in the Reform Bill, John Stuart Mill consulted the Quaker network about the possibility of pursuing the women's suffrage campaign in Dublin. The answer was pessimistic but Lydia Becker of the Manchester Suffrage Society was more successful in finding support, encouraging Anne Robertson, a novelist living at Blackrock on the outskirts of Dublin, to set up an Irish committee affiliated to the National Society for

Women's Suffrage. Petitions soon streamed over from Ireland and suffrage speakers made the reverse voyage from England.[2] In Dublin in 1870 Millicent Fawcett held a successful meeting, attended by Mrs Haslam, and in the next couple of years Becker toured Ireland, as did her ally, Isabella Tod, who in 1871 had formed the North of Ireland Women's Suffrage Society in Belfast. However, there was a hiatus when the first Dublin committee failed until it was replaced in 1876 by the Dublin Women's Suffrage Association (DWSA), of which Anna Maria Haslam was for the next thirty-seven years secretary.[3]

In the final two decades of the nineteenth century, one of the principal shapers of the British women's suffrage movement was its participants' attitude to the Irish Question. Suffrage leaders in both the north and south of Ireland were not sympathetic to the 1886 Home Rule Bill, believing that all social and economic progress made by women in the previous twenty years would be threatened if Irishmen were elected to an Irish parliament. In 1888, after the split in the main London suffrage society (see Object 14), the Dublin and Belfast committees affiliated to the Central Committee led by Mrs Fawcett, who in the ensuing years made many speeches condemning home rule. At this point a number of home rulers withdrew their support from the DWSA.

The Dublin and Belfast societies were physically distant from Westminster and felt doubly at a disadvantage, lobbying for entry into a political system that not only prevented access to women but was also considered by many in Ireland to be that of a colonial power. Perhaps as a result, and because Ireland had been excluded from the acts (1869 and 1882 respectively) that enfranchised single and widowed women ratepayers in England and Scotland, in the 1880s and 1890s the Irish societies concentrated their efforts on local emancipation, campaigning to gain women the municipal franchise. In 1896 the Dublin Women's Suffrage and Poor Law Guardian Association (as the DWSA was now called) campaigned successfully for the Poor Law Guardians (Women) Act for Ireland and that October Mrs Haslam travelled to Birmingham for the national conference at which the idea of forming the National Union of Women's Suffrage Societies (NUWSS) was first mooted and to which in the following year both the Dublin and Belfast societies affiliated. In 1901 the DWSA changed its name to the Irish Women's Suffrage and Local Government Association (IWSLGA) in recognition of the spread of the movement to other towns apart from Dublin and Belfast.

As the suffrage campaign began to change character in the twentieth century, the Haslams were still active participants. In October 1903 Mrs Haslam attended the National Convention in London (see Object 18) and in June 1908 both took part in the NUWSS Hyde Park demonstration. When, a few months later, Hanna Sheehy-Skeffington and Margaret Cousins, previously members of the IWSLGA, formed the Irish Women's Franchise League (IWFL), they immediately went to see 'Mrs Anna Haslam, to inform her that we younger women were ready to start a new women's suffrage society on militant lines'.[4] The split reflected not only differences of tactics, but also of politics, the younger women being strongly nationalist, Mrs Haslam a unionist. There remained, however, a degree of mutual respect; in 1913 Mrs Haslam visited Sheehy-Skeffington, imprisoned in Mountjoy Jail as a result of her IWFL activities. (For the IWFL's attitude to the outbreak of war in 1914, see Object 79.)

In 1918, as she voted at the general election, Anna Maria Haslam was fêted as Ireland's oldest suffragist by members of all political parties, among whom were several women who, after her death in 1922, formed the Haslam Memorial Committee to commission the St Stephen's Green seat. They included Sheehy-Skeffington and Sarah Harrison, Dublin councillor and painter of the 1908 portrait of the Haslams.[5] The work of Albert Power, a leading Irish nationalist sculptor, the elegantly substantial seat stands only a few paces from a bust of Constance Markievicz, the only woman to win a parliamentary seat at the 1918 general election (see Object 84).

Object 9

The Women's Suffrage Journal

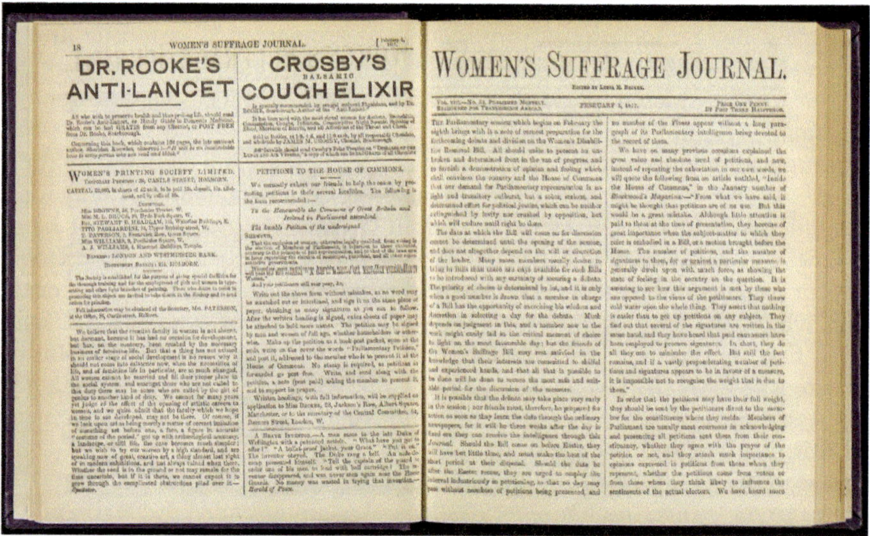

Object 9 is an 1877 volume of *The Women's Suffrage Journal*. (https://digital.library.lse.ac.uk/documents/detail/184293, The Women's Library collection, London School of Economics and Political Science.)

In 1870 women on both sides of the Atlantic launched a trio of women-centred political journals, the better to broadcast information and opinion on matters affecting their lives. In the United States the *Woman's Journal*, edited by Lucy Stone, first appeared on 8 January, followed in the UK on 1 March by the *Journal of the Manchester National Women's Suffrage Society*, edited by Lydia Becker and then, on 8 March, by *The Shield*, edited by Josephine Butler. Becker's publication was soon renamed *The Women's Suffrage Journal* (*WSJ*), although it did not confine itself to suffrage but covered other campaigns, such as that of the rights of married women to both their property and their children. However, it did eschew the anti-Contagious Diseases Acts campaign for, like J.S. Mill, Becker, while supporting Butler's work, recognized that any public association would only harm the suffrage cause. Thus, from 1870 until it ceased publication on

Becker's death in 1890, each development in the suffrage campaign can be followed in detail in the *WSJ* which Helen Blackburn eulogized as 'a record which served to keep the workers in touch, which gave the cue to their common policy, and was a ready reference for Members of Parliament and others engaged in political questions'.[1]

Becker had no need to look far for a printer for, among the early subscribers to the Manchester National Society for Women's Suffrage (MNSWS) was Alexander Ireland, co-proprietor of the *Manchester Examiner and Times*, whose firm printed the MNSWS annual reports.[2] Moreover, Becker's Manchester office in Jackson's Row was close to the printer at 7 Pall Mall Court. From its first issue the *WSJ* presented a professional appearance, its typography and layout clear. Becker was to remain the *WSJ*'s editor and main contributor for the rest of her life, in addition to her work as honorary secretary of the MNSWS, member of the Manchester School Board (MSB), paid secretary of the executive committee of the Central Committee, 1881–4 and parliamentary agent for the Central Committee, 1884–8.[3]

From October 1870 she was relieved of some *WSJ* work when Trubner & Co., a London firm associated with radical causes, took over as publisher, dealing with distribution and, eventually, advertising.

The *WSJ* was remarkably good value. Copies were sent free to MNSWS subscribers, but individual copies could be bought for 1d, an annual post-free subscription and the bound yearly volumes both being 1s 6d. One annual subscriber was Mrs Sophia Goulden, whose daughter, Emmeline (later Pankhurst), remembered the *WSJ* being delivered to their Manchester home.[4] An issue consisted of at least eight pages, often sixteen, and when times were exciting could extend to as many as thirty-six.[5] Besides its news, the journal included an abundance of names, allowing readers the satisfaction of knowing they were part of a growing band of sympathizers who were writing letters, attending meetings, signing petitions, and subscribing to suffrage societies across the four nations of the UK. In the twenty-first century those names allow readers the possibility of encountering women who have left no other trace in nineteenth-century suffrage history and are a springboard for local research.

The *WSJ* also served as a promotional tool, sent to all members of Parliament and left in libraries and waiting rooms to attract new recruits. Copies were exchanged with other women-centred journals, sent overseas and to national and provincial newspapers, many of which mentioned the *WSJ* in their summaries of monthly magazines. It is, however, difficult to assess the journal's circulation. The 1888 rupture in the National Society is likely to have affected sales; the *WSJ* remained associated with the Central Committee, the interests of the new Central National Society for Women's Suffrage now represented by another journal, the *Women's Penny Paper*. Only after February 1877 did the journal gain some income from classified and display advertisements. Many of the former advertised suffrage speeches and pamphlets, whereas the latter were taken by manufacturers of products aimed at woman in her domestic sphere, such as Reckitts blue (for the laundress), cough elixir (for the nurse) and cornflour (for the cook). But the reader only had to turn the page to encounter the world of practical politics, to receive explicit directions on the preparation of petitions, details of the previous month's tally of those presented, verbatim reports of parliamentary suffrage debates and of the votes cast by individual MPs on suffrage-related matter.

For twenty years the *WSJ* dropped through letterboxes and was passed around the family and between neighbours, yet, of the thousands of copies printed, very few have survived. A bound volume is now rarely found outside an institutional library, single issues are virtually non-existent, but a digitized version of the complete *WSJ* can be found in the Women's Library Journals Collection in the LSE Digital Library.[6]

Object 10

Invitation card to 'A National Demonstration of Women', 6 May 1880

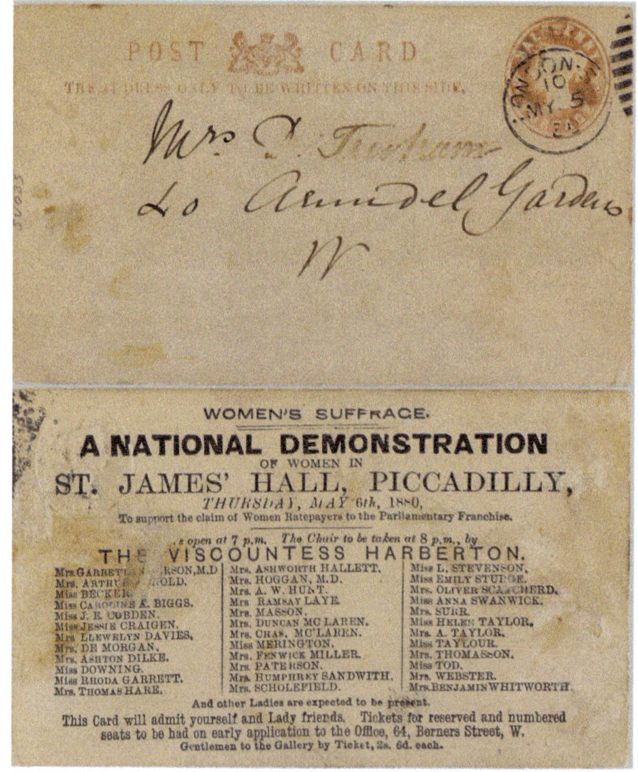

Object 10 is a printed card, an invitation to 'A National Demonstration of Women'. 6 May 1880. The card was posted, without an envelope, on 5 May 1880. Both sides shown. (Martin Last collection, Zurich.)

Noting the success of Gladstone's new style of populist campaigning and the enthusiasm with which Manchester women ratepayers had crowded municipal election meetings, in late 1879 Lydia Becker suggested the time had come to organize mass suffrage meetings at which women, and only women, would speak and officiate.[1] Women would be admitted free, but men would be required to pay. A first meeting, held in Manchester's Free Trade Hall on 8 February 1880, was so successful that a 'Demonstration Fund' was launched to pay for future meetings, the next planned for London, to be organized by Helen Blackburn of the Central Committee for Women's Suffrage.

The March general election brought in a Liberal government, sending a surge of optimism through the suffrage movement. By April the Demonstration's ambitious organizers had booked St James' Hall, close to Piccadilly Circus, where, thanks to its excellent acoustics, an audience of over 2,000, sitting under a red and gold barrel-vaulted ceiling, enveloped in a Moorish-style decor, would catch every word uttered by the speakers. The wording and typography of an advertisement for 'A National Demonstration of Women' in the May *Women's Suffrage Journal* are identical to that of Object 10, suggesting the cards were printed by the journal's printer.[2] In 1880 these cards could only be sent 'stamped to order', that is, bought in sheets of forty-two, already embossed with a pink halfpenny stamp, and then printed with the desired text and posted to members of suffrage societies and other sympathizers. Although, before the end of April, there was little mention of the London Demonstration in the press, names of likely attendees were gathered at meetings in middle-class drawing rooms and in halls in poorer districts, such as Bermondsey and Tower Hamlets. As Blackburn commented, the National Demonstrations filled 'the largest hall of the city, packed from floor to ceiling with women of all ranks and occupations, working women in very large proportions'.[3]

However, the recipient of Object 10, Mrs Dermina Tristram, was most definitely middle-class. Born in Smyrna (Izmir) into an English family who had lived there since the late eighteenth century, she was barely fifteen years old when in 1852 she married Uvedale Barrington Tristram. The family eventually moved to England, where, in 1879 in Kensington, their youngest child was born. They stayed only briefly at 40 Arundel Gardens, a tall, stuccoed house, soon moving to nearby Oxford Gardens, which remained their London address until their deaths. No family papers relating to Mrs Tristram survive except this card, nor is her name mentioned in any suffrage-related documents. It is not inconceivable the card was sent to her after a drawing-room meeting held on 4 May by Miss Caroline Williams of 4 Vicarage Gate, Kensington, for it was posted the next day, bearing a South Kensington postmark.[4] If Mrs Tristram did accept the invitation, she left at home, besides her husband and servants, ten children, the eldest twenty-one and the youngest a few months.[5]

Widely reported, the Demonstration was noted for the fact that 'women, and none but women, occupied the floor and the platform. Women organized and conducted the meeting from the beginning to its close'.[6] *The Christian World* reporter described 'the rustle of silks, the sweep of velvets, the shrill buzz of a thousand feminine voices, the triumphant pealing of the organ overhead' and noted the speech by 'a clever, but somewhat saucy young lady, Miss Rhoda Garrett'.[7] Once again, it was Garrett who attracted the eye of *The Graphic* artist (see Object 5). Aesthetically attired, she is the central figure in a half-page illustration, standing on the platform, caught mid-flow, addressing the packed hall.[8] Other suffrage leaders, such as Becker and Mrs Priscilla McLaren, sit each side of her, as two women lay in front a large sheet of paper on which is emblazoned her name. This method of identifying speakers was an innovation *The Christian World* thought organizers of other meetings should emulate.

Such was the demand that an overflow meeting was held in another room, where Garrett's cousin, Millicent Fawcett, whose name is absent from the invitation card, explained she had initially refused to participate 'declaring it was certain to be a failure, that there was not enthusiasm enough amongst the women of London to fill St James's Hall' but she was 'proved to have been wrong and she gladly confessed her error'.[9]

Estimated to have cost £500, the Demonstration was considered a triumph, garnering extensive, sympathetic press coverage and was followed by seven others, in Bristol, Birmingham, Bradford, Nottingham, Sheffield (see Object 12), Glasgow and Edinburgh.

Object 11

Oil painting by Richard Staunton Cahill, 1888, 'Mary Smith Lecturing on Woman's Rights'

Object 11 is an 1888 oil painting by Richard Staunton Cahill, 'Mary Smith Lecturing on Woman's Rights, Cockermouth'. 38 x 28.2 cm. (National Gallery Victoria, Melbourne, Gift of Krystyna Campbell-Pretty AM and Family through the Australian Government's Cultural Gifts Program, 2020.)

In a scene very different from a 'National Demonstration' a woman in plain attire stands on a platform addressing an unseen audience.[1] Behind her a poster reads, 'A Lecture on Woman's Rights Will Be Delivered in the Lecture Hall of the Young Men's Christian Association Cockermouth on Wednesday Mrs Smith'. This, the earliest known painting of a woman actively promoting 'woman's rights', is dated 1888, but the event it records probably took place some years previously.

The artist, Richard Staunton Cahill, born in Co. Clare, Ireland, trained from 1850 at the Royal Hibernian Academy, Dublin, moving first to London and then to Nottingham, where he taught at the Government School of Art, before being appointed in 1877 master of a new School of Art in Keswick, Cumberland. There he lived with his sister and, when a lack of pupils caused the closure of the art school in 1883, he continued teaching on his own account. In February 1884 Oscar Wilde, in the area to lecture, visited his studio and admired his paintings of the Irish coast.[2]

Although it has proved impossible to find evidence for the scene that Cahill portrays, the lecture is not, for instance, mentioned in *The Women's Suffrage Journal* (see Object 9), yet the information he has painted on the poster rings true. There was indeed a Young Men's Christian Association (YMCA) Lecture Room in Cockermouth, although the association became defunct and its premises were taken over in 1882 by a new society, the Wordsworth Institute, for whom Cahill held art classes. The name of the building having likewise changed, the use of 'YMCA' on the poster suggests that the lecture pre-dated 1882. In addition, although 'Mrs Smith' might be thought merely a generic name to place on the poster, in the early years of the suffrage campaign the leading activist in Cumberland was Miss Mary Smith of Carlisle, whom Lydia Becker, in a letter of 20 May 1868, addressed as 'Mrs' Smith, that honorific still sometimes used for older women. Smith was a non-conformist schoolmistress and poet who had supported Chartism in the 1840s, was involved with the campaigns to repeal the Contagious Diseases Acts and for the property rights for married women. For many years she ran a girls' school from her home in Finkle Street and was renowned for her Penny Readings. It was with Smith's encouragement that in 1869 Becker gave a 'woman's rights' lecture in Carlisle, which led to the founding of the Carlisle branch of the National Society for Women's Suffrage, with Smith as its honorary secretary. In her posthumously published autobiography, Smith mentions speaking and lecturing in public and writing letters to the press on 'Woman's Suffrage'.[3] Smith comments in her autobiography, as might the figure on the platform, 'Nor was I ashamed of being plainly dressed.'[4] As Smith suffered declining health for about seven years before her death in 1889, it is even more likely the lecture had taken place no later than the early 1880s.

This painting is the only evidence of an event, just one of an unknown number held over the decades in small public rooms in towns and villages throughout the country. With no journalist there to record it and without the imprimatur of a suffrage society, Smith is giving her lecture to an audience who did not commit their experience to posterity. Cahill is our only witness, the details he included giving veracity to the scene, while also raising questions. He records not only the poster and the speaker, but the umbrella and shawl, accessories necessary for the journey from Carlisle. But how had Smith travelled to Cockermouth? Had she gone by train to Penrith and then taken the new Cockermouth, Keswick, Penrith line? Had she booked and paid for the room herself? It is unlikely she had been invited by the YMCA as that organization relied only on male lecturers. Had she arranged for a chairman to be present, another figure sitting, out of sight, at that rather rickety table? Certainly, someone had supplied her with the speaker's standard equipment, a water jug and glass. Finally, could the small roll of paper resting on the table be a petition, ready for signing?

As an object, the painting is silent as to its history. When he painted it, Cahill may have already left Keswick, where the growing success of the new Keswick School of Industrial Art may have proved fatal to his attempts to earn a living. He was in London by 1890 and returned to Ireland some years later, dying at Lahinch, Co. Clare, in 1905. In 1888, noting the growing interest in women's suffrage, did he work up a sketch he had taken years earlier in that lecture room in Cockermouth? Surfacing at a Dublin auction in 2014, Object 11 may have accompanied Cahill on his return home. In this, the only known example of his figure work that does not depict an Irish genre scene, Cahill has produced for us the only visual evidence of early suffrage grassroots campaigning.

Object 12

Carte de visite photograph, Sheffield 1882, annotated

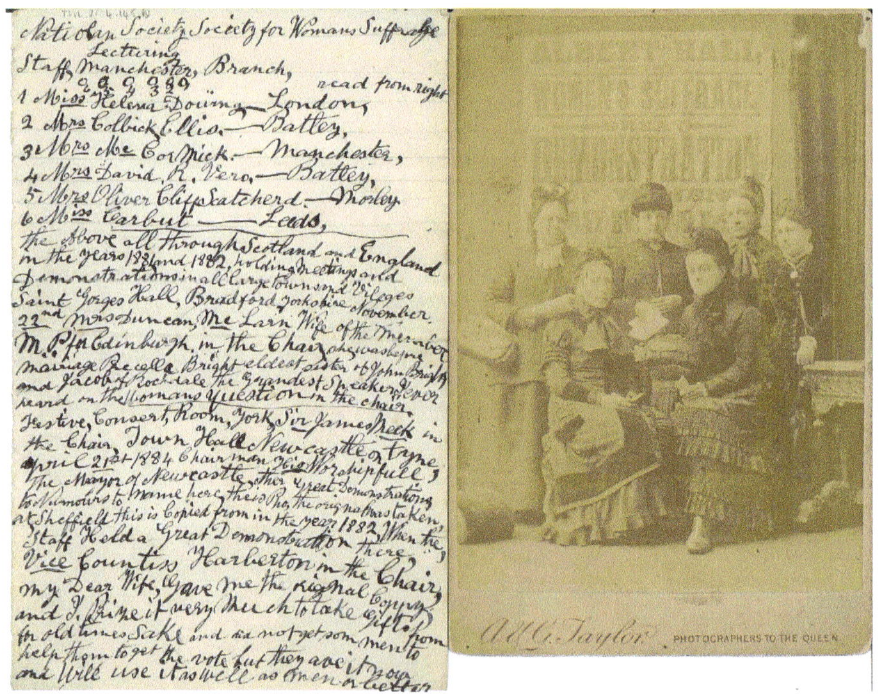

Object 12 is a *carte de visite* photograph by A. & G. Taylor, Sheffield, 1882, accompanied by an explanatory text written post-1918. (TWL.2004.145a and b, The Women's Library collection, London School of Economics and Political Science.)

In 1882, perhaps around the time 'Mrs Smith' was lecturing in Cockermouth (see Object 11), six suffrage campaigners posed for Object 12 to commemorate the seventh 'Great Demonstration', held on 27 February in Sheffield's opulent Albert Hall. Taken a short distance away, in the studio of A. & G. Taylor at Furnival Chambers, 101 Norfolk Street, this is the earliest known photograph to record post-1866 activists. Coincidentally, thirty years earlier, Anne Knight, one of the leaders of the Sheffield Female Political Association, was probably the first suffragist captured on camera, photographed holding a large sheet of paper on which was written her call to 'Be Free'. Similarly, in 1882, to convey their message, the campaigners brought to the studio a large 'Demonstration' poster, such as had been pasted up around the city.

That Object 12, a photograph mounted on thick card, the reverse giving details of the photographic firm, not only survives but is accompanied by an explanatory text, is due to the efforts of a man who placed great value on it, writing, 'My dear wife gave me the original coppy [*sic*]. I prize it very much to take gifts from for old time's sake.' He was David Vero, a millwright, whose wife Maria stands on the far left in the photograph.[1] The couple lived in Batley, a Yorkshire mill town, as did Mrs Ann Ellis, standing second from right. A millworker for over twenty years, she had represented the Yorkshire Heavy Woollen association at the 1880 Trades Union Congress. Both these working-class Yorkshire women worked with middle-class Mrs Alice Cliff Scatcherd, the honorary secretary of the Yorkshire Society for Women's Suffrage, not only for suffrage but also to improve conditions for women workers in the woollen industry.[2] In 1878 Scatcherd, who chaired an overflow meeting at Sheffield, had held suffrage meetings in the homes of Vero and Ellis, reading to the company excerpts from the current issue of *The Women's Suffrage Journal*.

Standing second from the left is Mrs Ann McCormick, who lived in Salford and from *c.* 1877–85 was the paid organizer for the Manchester National Society for Women's Suffrage (MNSWS).[3] An experienced businesswoman, she undertook administrative work in the MNSWS office, addressed public meetings in and around Manchester and helped to organize the Demonstrations in London, 1880, Birmingham, 1881 and Glasgow, 1882. At the Sheffield Demonstration the three working-class women sat on the platform alongside more middle-class campaigners. Their dedication to the cause lasted the rest of their lives; after her engagement with the MNSWS ended in 1885, McCormick was by 1890 an organizer for the Women's Franchise League, in 1902 Ellis gathered signatures in Batley for a petition from Yorkshire textile workers and was a member of the deputation presenting it to Parliament, while Vero's affectionate widower ensured her gravestone recorded for posterity that 'she was a member of the National Society for Women's Suffrage (Manchester Branch)'.[4]

Whether by chance, the seated women in the photograph are two middle-class members of what David Vero describes as the 'National Society for Women's Suffrage Lecturing Staff, Manchester Branch'. On the left is Louisa Carbutt, who signed the 1866 petition, was an early member of the Leeds Suffrage Society and elected a poor law guardian, 1883. Beside her is Scatcherd and standing on the far right is Mrs Helena Shearer, whom Vero remembered as 'Miss Downing', but who had married in Bradford in 1881, after speaking at that city's Demonstration. In the 1881 census Downing described herself as a 'political organizing clerk'.

It seems likely that the photograph was taken for promotional purposes, rather than merely for sentiment. Close inspection shows that the women are holding a variety of paper objects, surely brought to convey a message. What is the significance of the papers McCormick, Carbutt and Scatcherd hold and of the satchel the latter so prominently displays? Is Mrs Vero perhaps holding the petition signed at the meeting? There were to be many more such petitions presented before the vote was won. However, the Demonstrations, the last held in Edinburgh in March 1884, failed to influence the passage of the 1884 Reform Bill; the new Act, while enfranchising many more men, firmly rejected the women's cause.

Object 12 speaks of the cross-class nature of this stage of the suffrage campaign and of the media awareness of its organizers. Its survival is due to the affectionate support of one old man who thought to record events of forty years previously, believing that now women had the vote 'they will use it as well as men or better'.

Object 13

Election handbill for Helen Taylor's candidature at the North Camberwell parliamentary election, 1885

Object 13 is an election handbill promoting Helen Taylor's candidature at the North Camberwell Parliamentary Election, 1885. (Mill-Taylor/Box 7, The Women's Library collection, London School of Economics and Political Science.)

Issued a year after the 1884 Reform Act failed to enfranchise women, Object 13 is material evidence of an episode in suffrage history that those recording the nineteenth-century campaign chose to ignore, but which demonstrates another method by which a woman attempted to engage with the machinery of government. For, as, in 1868, Richard Pankhurst and Lydia Becker had tried to prove that women had a right to register to vote (see Object 3), so, in November 1885, Helen Taylor, John Stuart Mill's stepdaughter, accepted an invitation from the Camberwell Radical Club to stand in the general election as the Independent Radical Democrat candidate for the south London constituency of North Camberwell. As with the 1868 registration campaign, this move represented a challenge to the 1832 Reform Act, the contention being that under its terms women were not expressly excluded from standing for Parliament. However, so unpopular in suffrage circles was Taylor's association with the Radicals, that neither Becker, in *The Women's Suffrage Journal*, nor Helen Blackburn, in her *Record of Women's Suffrage* (1902), mentioned her candidature, even though by selecting a woman, Mrs Ethel Leach, as her election agent, Taylor had taken another step in advancing the cause.[1] Perhaps because Taylor failed to achieve her goal, this by-way of suffrage history was overlooked in later suffrage narratives, only recently receiving detailed attention.[2]

Although Taylor, as a member of the executive committee of the London National Society for Women's Suffrage, continued after Mill's death to insist that the society should abstain from campaigning, elsewhere she was playing an active part in politics. In 1876, as a Liberal, she was elected to the Southwark seat on the London School Board (LSB), and then, as a Radical, topped the poll when re-elected in 1879 and 1882, only standing down to launch her parliamentary campaign. She was also supporting home rule for Ireland, campaigning with Anna Parnell for land nationalization, organizing an English branch of the Irish Ladies' Land League and in 1881 was involved in founding the Democratic Federation, the precursor of Britain's first socialist political party. None of these campaigns found favour with the leaders of the mainstream suffrage societies.

In advance of the election a long, black-and-white handbill was published, setting out the ten pledges of Taylor's manifesto: fair pay, no wars, free justice, free education, home rule, restoration of the land to the people, direct taxation, annual parliaments, pay for MPs and universal suffrage. As was conventional, it carried the printer's name and the addresses of the election committee rooms, as did other handbills published by her official campaign. However, Object 13 carries none of this official information and, instead, may be linked to a four-page leaflet, addressed to 'Working Men and Women', issued by working-class Jessie Craigen, who from the 1870s had been a roving suffrage speaker and in the 1880s had taken part in eight of the 'Grand Demonstrations'. Devoted to Taylor, she had campaigned with her for the Irish Land League in England and Ireland before causing some offence that had led to her ostracism.[3] Despite this, in 1885 Craigen campaigned ardently for Taylor in Camberwell. Her four-page leaflet explains that a few working men and women, not connected with the official committee and 'not in communication with Miss Taylor herself in any way', were calling themselves 'Miss Taylor Election Independent Aid Committee ' – the red-printed handbill being the only remaining vestige of this endeavour.[4] The message on Craigen's handbill is simple, vote for the 'Tried Friend of the People and their Children', an allusion to Taylor's LSB support for the education of working-class children, which she believed should be free and secular, without physical punishment and with girls accessing the same curriculum as boys. However, although Craigen appeared regularly in newspaper reports through the first ten months of 1885, there is no mention of her, nor of the 'Independent Aid Committee', in November and December, during the election and its aftermath. Was Craigen silent, or, if not, why were her meetings not reported?

She was living nearby, in Peckham, was renowned for the power of her oratory and was a well-known 'character', having often been before the courts the previous year for breaking by-laws that prevented her speaking at meetings in public parks.

Taylor's campaign ran smoothly, if noisily, receiving wide press coverage, but when she and Leach presented her nomination papers to the Returning Officer on the first day of the election, 24 November, they were, despite Taylor's protests, rejected. The seat was won by the Liberal candidate. It was to be another thirty-three years before a woman again published her own parliamentary election handbill.

Object 14

An engraving of a meeting of the Women's Franchise League, 1891

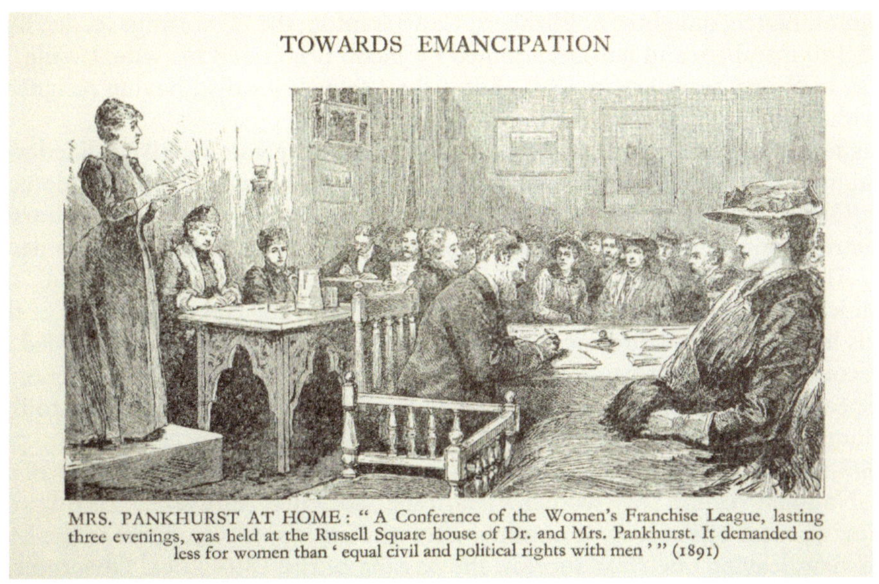

MRS. PANKHURST AT HOME: " A Conference of the Women's Franchise League, lasting three evenings, was held at the Russell Square house of Dr. and Mrs. Pankhurst. It demanded no less for women than ' equal civil and political rights with men ' " (1891)

Object 14 is a **1932 reproduction of an engraving, originally published in The Graphic, 1891, depicting a meeting of the Women's Franchise League.** (Author's collection.)

After the success of the Grand Demonstrations of the early 1880s, the failure to pass a women's suffrage amendment to the 1884 Reform Bill led to a period of disappointment, compounded by the intrusion of national politics into the life of the Central Committee, which, in 1888, split over the issue of home rule for Ireland.[1] Its leaders, Lydia Becker and Millicent Fawcett, sided with the Liberal Unionists, retaining the name Central Committee of the National Society for Women's Suffrage, with Fawcett as honorary secretary, while a smaller, more radical, pro-home rule element broke away to become the Central National Society for Women's Suffrage.

The disruption brought to the surface long dormant differences, put aside as the campaigners worked together in the hope of passing a suffrage bill. On one side were those who thought all women with the requisite property qualification, married or single, should be eligible for the vote and, on the other, those who, for pragmatic political reasons, considered married women must be excluded. Although not without opposition, this latter stance had been the Central Committee's policy since 1874. After the 1888 split, the Central National Society then lost its radical wing to a group even more extreme, the Women's Franchise League, whose founders were adamant that married women must be included in any future suffrage bill.[2]

Those who took this action had previously been responsible for the campaign that resulted in the passing of the Married Women's Property Acts of 1870 and 1882. As the principle of coverture, by which a married woman's legal existence was subsumed in that of her husband, was now undermined, campaigners such as Mrs Elizabeth Wolstenholme Elmy and Mrs Alice Scatcherd were no longer prepared to back the usual 'spinsters' suffrage bill but, instead, proposed a Women's Electoral Disabilities Removal Bill, drafted by Elmy, giving the vote to all women with the necessary qualification. Other leading members of the League included Dr Richard Pankhurst, who had worked with Elmy in Manchester since the 1860s; his wife, Emmeline; Mr and Mrs P.A. Taylor, in whose house the first suffrage petition had been assembled; and Mrs Harriot Stanton Blatch, daughter of Elizabeth Cady Stanton, the US suffrage leader. By 1890 the League had 140 members and had been joined by Jacob Bright and his wife, Ursula. The latter took over as honorary secretary in 1891, Elmy, the League's idealist, having resigned in 1890, unhappy with what she perceived as mistreatment.

The League's aims were far reaching, not only to achieve the vote for all qualified women, but also 'to establish for all women equal civil and political rights with men'. The London conference depicted in Object 14 was held over three days in December 1891 in the Pankhurst home in Russell Square, Bloomsbury, the engraving allowing us a rare glimpse of a room decorated by Emmeline.[3] The first evening was devoted to 'The Economic Position of Women', the second to 'The Political Rights and Duties of Women' and the third to 'The Programme of the League and the Bills it has promoted and supported'. It is likely *The Graphic* artist recorded a moment from the second evening, that being the only session at which a woman, Ursula Bright, was in the chair. Speakers that evening included Blatch, who bears a close resemblance to the woman on the podium, as captured by the artist.

In 1896/7 the League, funded in the main by Scatcherd, became a member of the newly organized National Union of Women's Suffrage Societies. However, relying on strong personalities, who, for one reason or another, were no longer able to support it, the League then faded from view, leaving one clear success, the passing of the 1894 Local Government Act, by which married women with the appropriate qualification were enabled to vote at local elections.

The 1891 conference might have been forgotten had it not been for *The Graphic* illustration, to which the original caption was 'Conference of the Women's Franchise League in Russell Square'.[4] But, forty years later, by which time the Pankhurst name was famous, perhaps notorious, it was as 'Mrs Pankhurst at Home' that it was reproduced in *Our Mothers*, a useful research source for images explaining the world of the late-Victorian woman.[5] The assimilation of the ghostly traces of the Women's Franchise League into the Pankhurst legend was furthered by Sylvia Pankhurst's evaluation in *The Suffragette Movement*, in which, not unnaturally, she highlighted the involvement of her parents.[6] Although by no means a Pankhurst fiefdom, the Women's Franchise League did mark an important development in the suffrage campaign, its members espousing causes that were to mature in the twentieth century, but, with evidence of its existence confined to small archival collections, *The Graphic* engraving is its most conspicuous legacy.

Object 15

Photograph of Elizabeth Wolstenholme Elmy

Mrs. Wolstenholme Elmy.

Mrs. Wolstenholme Elmy has been a keen Suffragist since 1866. It was largely due to her efforts that the Married Women's Property Act and the Guardianship of Children (1886) Act were passed. Mrs. Elmy helped to found the original Manchester Women's Suffrage Society. We deeply regret to say that whilst this number of THE COMMON CAUSE was being printed a telegram reached us announcing the death of MRS. WOLSTENHOLME ELMY, on March 12th.

Object 15 is an undated photograph of Elizabeth Wolstenholme Elmy, reproduced in *The Common Cause*, 15 March 1918. (The Women's Library collection, London School of Economics and Political Science.)

It was with Object 15, showing Elizabeth Wolstenholme Elmy at work as a writer, that the National Union of Women's Suffrage Societies (NUWSS) chose to accompany her death notice in their paper. Details of the photographer have been all but obliterated from the only known original of the photograph, held in Congleton Museum, but, from that, research would suggest the photographer was F.W. Schmidt, in business in Manchester's Victoria Street from 1902.[1] It is likely the photograph was taken *c*.1907, although whether at home or at Schmidt's studio is unknown. However, we can see the photographer had learned enough of his client to capture her in her most typical pose. For, although little remains of her prodigious correspondence, what survives indicates the breadth and depth of her life-long campaigning for political and social equality for women, conducted, in the main, by means of her pen.[2] Although regarded as an elder stateswoman by the early leaders of the Women's Social and Political Union (WSPU), Elmy and her work were neglected until comparatively recently, not fitting easily into the narrative of nineteenth-century suffrage history.

Wolstenholme Elmy, then 'Miss Wolstenholme', a school mistress, had been the instigator of a small committee gathering names in Manchester for the 1866 petition. Over the previous five years she had worked to improve girls' education and, as a member of the Kensington Society, was in touch with Emily Davies. The committee became the Manchester National Society for Women's Suffrage, Wolstenholme Elmy, who had moved from Manchester to Congleton, resigning in favour of Lydia Becker (see Object 2). Subsequently she became secretary of the Married Women's Property Committee (MWPC), from 1872 based in London, although her position became difficult after it was known she, as a believer in free love, had conceived a child out of wedlock. She was forced to bow to the demands of her co-workers, Millicent Fawcett being particularly vociferous, and in 1874, before the birth, married the child's father, Ben Elmy. In 1881 Wolstenholme Elmy and her son spent three months in London on behalf of the MWPC, lobbying MPs before the passing of the 1882 Married Women's Property Act. Her next campaign,1883–6, during which she distributed nearly half a million leaflets and over 40,000 pamphlets, resulted in the passing of the Guardianship of Infants Act.

Wolstenholme Elmy joined the Central National Society (CNS) after the 1888 split in the Central Committee but when it became clear that the CNS was prepared to accept the clause explicitly excluding married women from any new suffrage bill, she broke away to found the Women's Franchise League (see Object 14), before resigning from that in 1890 and in 1891 setting up the Women's Emancipation Union (WEU), 'An Association of Workers to Secure the Political, Social and Economic Independence of Women'. Wolstenholme Elmy, a secular humanist with republican tendencies, was emphatic the WEU should be non-party, open to all classes and to men as well as women, although, in the event, the small membership was mainly middle class. While the title of the Women's Franchise League still associated it with the campaign for the vote, that of the WEU reflected its aim for a more extensive emancipation. Rather than being a 'mere suffrage society', it claimed for women 'equality of right and duty with men in all matters affecting the service of the community and the State. Equality of opportunity for self-development by the education of the schools and of life. Equality in industry by equal freedom of choice of career. Equality in marriage and equality of parental rights'.[3]

In 1892 the WEU became notorious when, at its first conference, Mary Cozens suggested, 'If they had a regiment of women who could shoot, they would have the franchise in a week.'[4] Cozens was soon eased out of the WEU, too radical for even that most radical of nineteenth-century societies, but, later, like Wolstenholme Elmy, joined the Women's Social and Political Union. In 1897 the WEU backed the Parliamentary Franchise (Extension to Women) Bill which would have given the vote to qualified women, regardless of marital status. For this and for a Special Appeal, signed by 257,796 women, the WEU worked alongside the NUWSS, while choosing to stay outside this new umbrella organization, whose purely suffrage aims Wolstenholme Elmy now considered too narrow. However, by 1899 the WEU was no longer able to attract sufficient funding and dissolved, after holding a final conference and printing a report of its achievements. Wolstenholme Elmy was conscious of the necessity of preserving her work and, as she had done with the numerous pamphlets published during the Guardianship of Infants campaign, ensured that WEU publications were sent to the British Museum, to be held in its library (now the British Library). There one can still study them and, thanks to Object 15, picture their creator and the circumstances of their creation.

Object 16

Portrait of Mary Wollstonecraft

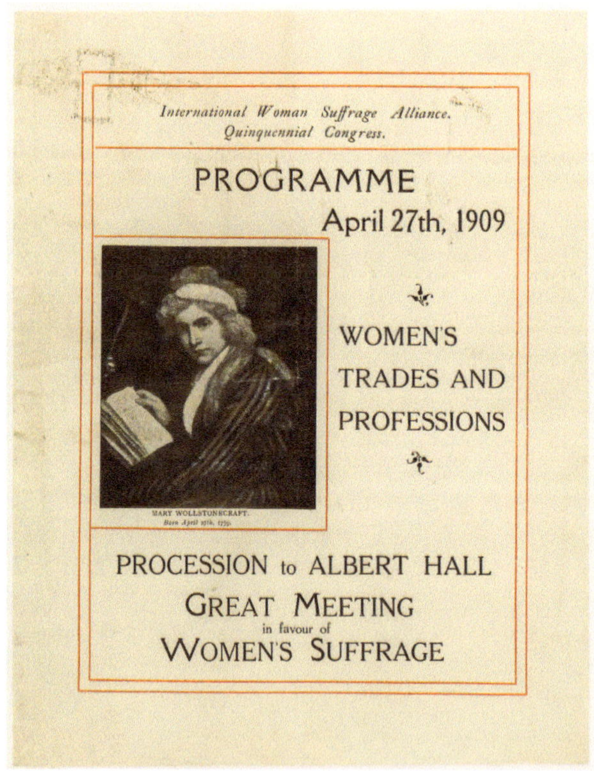

Object 16 is a portrait of Mary Wollstonecraft as featured on a programme for a 1909 event organized by the National Union of Women's Suffrage Societies (NUWSS). (2ASL/11/49, The Women's Library collection, London School of Economics and Political Science.)

Although it may seem anachronistic to place Object 16, created in 1909, at this stage of the suffrage narrative, it was the work of late-nineteenth-century campaigners that had made the portrait of Mary Wollstonecraft, author of *A Vindication of the Rights of Woman* (1792), a natural choice with which to decorate this programme for an event held in London on the 150th anniversary of the day of her birth. Such was the calumny heaped on her around the time of her death in 1797 that it was only within the previous twenty years it had become possible for Wollstonecraft to be mentioned in polite society, far less placed at the centre of a public celebration. But, in October 1890, at a time when Elizabeth Wolstenholme Elmy was cultivating the idea of the Women's Emancipation Union (see Object 15), Fisher Unwin had published a new edition of Wollstonecraft's *Vindication*, for which he commissioned Millicent Fawcett to write the Introduction.[1] Long tainted by its author's personal history, which involved attempted suicide and bearing a child while unmarried, this was *Vindication*'s first reissue since 1844, with Fawcett, a well-connected paragon of rectitude, a necessarily benign link between Wollstonecraft and the modern reader. While expressing disapproval of the 'errors of Mary Wollstonecraft's own life' and her 'irregular relations', an attitude with which Wolstenholme Elmy would have been only too familiar, Fawcett revealed a close knowledge of the author's thinking, presenting her as a pioneer feminist. Thus, on the cusp of the centennial year of her most famous text, this edition launched the rehabilitation of Wollstonecraft, who swiftly became a heroine of the suffrage movement.

Vindication was not referenced by John Stuart Mill in *The Subjection of Women* (1869) and it was only in 1886 that Fawcett had begun to refer publicly to Wollstonecraft, remarking, for instance, in a lecture in Newcastle that when 'tracing the growth of the movement she thought the initiative must be conceded to Mary Wollstonecraft'.[2] It may or may not be coincidental, but the previous year a new biography of Wollstonecraft, the first since 1800, was published in London.[3] In it the author, Elizabeth Robins Pennell, a UK-based American, demonstrated empathy for Wollstonecraft, finding every practical excuse for her behaviour, subtly characterizing her so as to appeal to late-Victorian sentiment and, offering an analysis of *Vindication*, commenting that it was little read. It would be inconceivable that Fawcett had not read this work of redemption which, in turn, allowed her, in the Unwin Introduction, to present Wollstonecraft as a pioneer of the suffrage movement. Two years later Pennell was to provide a preface to another, cheaper, reissue of *Vindication*. Wollstonecraft was now available to all, with the editions held on public library shelves and articles about her appearing in the women's press.[4] In addition to the relaunching of her work, in 1884 the portrait later chosen to decorate Object 16 became the first representation of Wollstonecraft to enter a national collection, bought by the National Gallery.[5] One of her two portraits by John Opie, this was painted around the time of the publication of *Vindication* (1790–1) and, presenting her as a scholar, fitted very well with the image of the intellectual foremother that suffrage campaigners wished to construct.

In 1907 Fawcett contributed a very lightly updated version of her 1890 Introduction as 'A Pioneer of the Movement', a chapter on Wollstonecraft in another Fisher Unwin publication, *The Case for Women's Suffrage*, edited by Brougham Villiers. This book, which looked to the future of the movement while recognizing its past, also included contributions from Emmeline and Christabel Pankhurst, Charlotte Despard and Keir Hardie MP. An article on Wollstonecraft by 'An Admirer' in the suffrage paper, *Women's Franchise*, and the creation of a 'Mary Wollstonecraft' banner for the June 1908 NUWSS procession both invoked her as a 'Pioneer', while a cheap (threepenny) pamphlet, 'Mary Wollstonecraft and the Women's Movement of Today', cited passages from *Vindication* to indicate its relevance to women in the early twentieth century.[6] All survive, their creation a testament to the work of the nineteenth-century campaigners who, by slowly effecting a change in the laws of property and marriage and in attitudes to female education, allowed a re-evaluation in the twentieth century of Wollstonecraft and her ideas.[7]

Object 17

Helen Blackburn's bookcase, 1897

Object 17 is Helen Blackburn's bookcase, made in 1897, now in Girton College, Cambridge. (The Mistress and Fellows, Girton College, Cambridge.)

One of Mary Wollstonecraft's scarcest works, *Thoughts on the Education of Daughters* (1788), was among the extensive collection of books and pamphlets relating to women's suffrage, education, employment, temperance and social and domestic duties collected by Helen Blackburn during a lifetime devoted to the women's cause. In 1897, to hold this library, she designed for it Object 17, a glazed mahogany bookcase which, on her death, she left, with its contents, to Girton College, Cambridge.

Blackburn had acquired much of the collection while holding the paid positions of, from 1874–7, secretary to the first incarnation of the Central Committee of Women's Suffrage, from 1888–97 secretary to that society, as reorganized, and, in tandem, secretary from 1880 to 1895 to the Bristol and West of England Women's Suffrage Society. In addition, she was editor (1880–90) and joint editor (1890–5) of the *Englishwoman's Review* and author of numerous pamphlets and handbooks promoting the campaigns for both suffrage and improvements in women's working conditions. As Lady Frances Balfour commented, Blackburn was 'a born chronicler and antiquarian, particularly in one line of research, what she used to call "the spindle side"'.[1] Blackburn had demonstrated an early appreciation of a library when, in 1865, she had applied to join the London Library, a subscription lending library of which John Stuart Mill had, in 1841, been a founder. Being both young and a woman, Blackburn's membership rendered her at that time a decided anomaly in the Library's demographic.

Blackburn probably began her suffrage collection around 1874 and then continued to build it while living, from 1880, in Bristol. When she returned to London in 1889 as secretary to the Central Committee, re-organized after the 1888 split (see Object 14), her suffrage library moved with her. Lady Frances Balfour describes Blackburn's 'small panelled room stacked with endless files of Suffrage papers. There was a sofa couch, which was her bed, and I used to see a frugal meal unnoticed on the hob'.[2] From this room Blackburn conducted a worldwide correspondence and consequently her library has a strong international perspective, containing books and pamphlets in English, Dutch, French, German and Italian.

Blackburn acquired a number of antiquarian volumes, such as *The Lawes Resolutions of Womens Rights: or, the Lawes Provision for Women* (1632), and Mary Astell's *Serious Proposal to Ladies*, which, with 'full access to all the materials which could be furnished by the Women's Suffrage offices', enabled her to research and write her survey of the campaign, *Women's Suffrage: A Record of the Women's Suffrage Movement in the British Isles* (1902).[3] As Blackburn explains, her intention was to write a factual history, showing how 'the effort to bring political liberty to the daily lives of women' formed part of 'the continuity of history'.[4] A particular strength of the work is its long 'Bibliography of the Women's Suffrage Movement', listing books and articles published between 1792 and 1901, many once owned by Blackburn.

It was presumably in 1897, on her retirement as secretary to the Central Committee, that Blackburn designed the bookcase to house the material she would take with her from her office. To decorate it, she commissioned from Elizabeth Guinness, an artist and suffrage sympathizer, portraits of Lydia Becker (see Object 2) and Caroline Ashurst Biggs, her predecessors in the secretaryship.[5] Blackburn recognized the appeal of the visual for, as a parallel to her book collection, she had compiled, as a consciousness-raising object for an 1885 Exhibition of Women's Industries, a collection of portraits of women who had opened new fields of endeavour to women. Displayed at the Chicago World Fair, 1893, on its return given by Blackburn to Bristol University to decorate its women's reading room and, although, as devised, subsequently lost, forty-two images have survived and are now held with Blackburn's Papers in Girton College.

It is likely that the upper glazed section of Object 17 originally held books and that Blackburn's extensive collection of loose pamphlets and ephemera was housed in the drawers and lower cupboards. The pamphlets were soon bound into volumes, the work paid for by Lilias Ashworth Hallett, a long-time colleague who saw the value of preserving the movement's history. As she remarked to the College Bursar of the Annual Reports, 'they have lists of all the early workers and early subscriptions and I believe that these will be of lasting interest. There will always be a few women who will look back through the years with interest and gratitude to the struggles of the early workers'.[6]

The bookcase may still be seen in Girton Library, a material testament to the devotion of a collector and colleague, while its contents are held by the College as a discrete entity, allowing the modern historian to understand what resources were available to early researchers.

Object 18

Scenes at the National Convention for the Civic Rights of Women, magazine illustration, 1903

Object 18 illustrates scenes from the National Convention for the Civic Rights of Women, drawn by Robert B. Paxton for *Black and White*, 24 October 1903. (Reproduced by kind permission of the Syndics of Cambridge University Library.)

At the end of the nineteenth century, the demise of the Women's Franchise League and the Women's Emancipation Union, the erstwhile 'ginger groups' of the suffrage movement (see Objects 14 and 15), left the now rather torpid suffrage campaign in the hands of the National Union of Women's Suffrage Societies (NUWSS). This umbrella organization was formed in 1897, uniting all local suffrage societies, regardless of party allegiance, to present a common front and ensure that the enfranchisement bills presented to Parliament received maximum support. Millicent Fawcett, who had gravitated to the forefront of the suffrage campaign after the death of Lydia Becker in 1890, presided over the 1896 meeting that set the process in motion, but was not formally appointed president until 1907.

The early years of the NUWSS coincided with a real reversal of the local government rights that had been won by women over the previous decades. For instance, through changes in organization, on local councils married women ratepayers were losing their votes, and all women their seats. The most drastic change came in 1902 when the Education Act abolished school boards, to which women had since their inception in 1870 had a right of election; it was feared that women's position as poor law guardians might similarly be threatened. Long-time campaigners, such as Elizabeth Wolstenholme Elmy, could see their life's work being dismantled and it was as a result of her persistence that a National Convention for the Civic Rights of Women was held in London, in Holborn Town Hall on 16 and 17 October 1903.[1] The Convention was backed by the newspaper publisher W.T. Stead, sponsored by the NUWSS and attracted 200 delegates. It was addressed by a wide range of women speakers who were actively engaged in public work.

The first day of the Convention was open to the public, with details of the speeches widely reported in the press, but only the magazine *Black and White* sent an artist, Robert B.M. Paxton, to record a visual impression.[2] Reading the spread from left to right, Paxton places Wolstenholme Elmy, her ringlets distinctive, in the first place, speaking on 'Women's Highest Mission', before moving to the Rev. Steinthal, a stalwart of the Manchester Suffrage Society, who chaired the afternoon session, which was devoted to 'The Parliamentary Franchise and its bearing on the legal and industrial position of women'. This was the particular interest of Eva Gore-Booth, who is shown as a speaker, with Wolstenholme Elmy and Esther Roper (wearing spectacles) in attendance (see also Object 20). Paxton also notes the presence of Mrs Green, president of the Women's Co-operative Guild, who 'said she was the representative of 16,000 working women, who felt that they were among the greatest sufferers from the want of a franchise'.[3] His sketch of the audience is not unduly unsympathetic; such scenes were always an easy target for mockery by the male-dominated publishing world.

At the following day's session, open only to NUWSS members, Wolstenholme Elmy pressed for the raising of a fund of £2,000 a year for three years to finance a mass suffrage campaign in the run-up to the next general election; £570 was raised that day. As a result of the Convention the NUWSS was instructed to ask all Cabinet members and leaders of the Opposition to receive deputations on women's suffrage and for pressure to be brought on political party associations to select only candidates in favour of women's suffrage.

The Convention is often overlooked in the history of the suffrage movement, but by openly discussing the retrogressive effect of new legislation, bringing together women from across Britain and Ireland to take cognizance of their changing position and at least giving some consideration to a scheme to rouse the country, it may be considered as a 'hinge', linking the nineteenth-century campaign to that of the twentieth. Although unaware of it, those viewing Paxton's scenes were witnessing an early sowing of seeds of change which, taken with the contemporaneous events discussed under Object 19, were to revolutionize the suffrage campaign.

Object 19

The Pankhurst home, 62 Nelson Street, Chorlton-on-Medlock, Manchester

Object 19 is 62 Nelson Street, Chorlton-on-Medlock, Manchester, home of the Pankhurst family and the site of the creation of the Women's Social and Political Union WSPU. (The Pankhurst Centre.)

Emmeline Pankhurst did not attend the National Convention for the Civic Rights for Women, 16–17 October 1903 (see Object 18) but, instead, on Saturday 10 October, invited a few women from the Manchester Independent Labour party (ILP) to her home, 62 Nelson Street. It was as members of the newly formed WSPU that they left. With the goal of achieving the parliamentary vote for women on the same terms as men, the WSPU was to be women-only and free of party affiliation. Moreover, as Pankhurst declared, it was 'to be satisfied with nothing but action on our question. Deeds, not words, was to be our permanent motto'.[1]

Forced to economize after Richard Pankhurst's sudden death, Emmeline, her four children and two servants had moved in 1898 to 62 Nelson Street, Chorlton, a district less salubrious than their former surroundings in Victoria Park. When previously advertised, number 62 was described as offering 'three entertaining rooms, five bedrooms, dressing room, bath, w.c. and well-appointed domestic offices'.[2] It was in these domestic surroundings that what was to be the most militant of the suffrage societies was founded, the latest in a succession of organizations with which Pankhurst had been involved. For, after the family returned to Manchester from London in 1893, she had been a member of the executive committee of the Manchester National Society for Women's Suffrage, while remaining a leader of the Women's Franchise League (see Object 14). She had, in 1891, declared, 'I am a radical, devoted to the politics of the people', left her local Women's Liberal Association in 1894 and was an energetic ILP-elected poor law guardian until, widowed, she resigned to take up very necessary paid work as registrar of births and deaths in Chorlton.[3]

The timing of the launch of the WSPU was a fortuitous mix of the personal and political. Although Pankhurst's daughters, Christabel, Sylvia and Adela, were living at home, none is noted as present at the 10 October meeting. According to Sylvia, her mother, who had hoped the ILP would back the call for women's enfranchisement, was dismayed to discover women were not allowed to join the North Salford branch of the ILP because its Pankhurst Hall, built three years earlier in memory of Richard Pankhurst, was barred to women.[4] However, this much-cited cause of ill-feeling is confusingly contradicted by contemporary newspaper reports showing that women were certainly not excluded from the hall.[5] Perhaps, more likely, Emmeline not only did not believe the NUWSS could campaign effectively but, by creating a new society, would keep her eldest daughter, Christabel, within her sphere of influence.[6] The latter had been working closely with Esther Roper and Eva Gore-Booth in the North of England Society for Women's Suffrage (NESWS) and was about to begin a law degree at the University of Manchester.[7]

Over the next two years, using the Nelson Street address, Christabel published several letters on women's suffrage in the press, although none mentioned the WSPU. It was only in 1905 that the society began to make its mark, first, in Westminster on 12 May, when Emmeline led members, including Elizabeth Wolstenholme Elmy, to protest the 'talking out' of a private member's suffrage bill. Then, in the autumn, with a general election expected, she became disenchanted with lack of support from the ILP and directed attention instead towards the prospective Liberal government. Thus, on 13 October, Christabel walked from 62 Nelson Street to Manchester's Free Trade Hall, where she and Annie Kenney put to a leading Liberal, Sir Edward Grey, the question, 'Will the Liberal Government give women the vote?' Such heckling was not unusual, but, conducted by young women, brought swift reprisals. Christabel and Annie were found guilty of obstruction and assaulting a policeman, refused to pay a fine, went to prison (for seven and three days respectively), thereby achieving national press coverage for the WSPU. On their release, each returned, first to 62 Nelson Street and, on 20 October, to the Free Trade Hall, this time as guests of honour at a reception organized by the WSPU and the Manchester Central ILP.[8] In mid-1906, after graduating with first-class honours, Christabel left Manchester for London, where Sylvia was studying at the Royal College of Art and to where Kenney had brought the WSPU campaign. Emmeline then gave up 62 Nelson Street, moving into a cheaper apartment at 60 Upper Brook Street, and by autumn 1907, resigning her position as registrar of births and deaths, had made London her base and the WSPU her sole occupation.

Seventy years passed before the house again featured in the press, in 1977 saved from demolition and listed Grade 2*, entirely on account of its association with the Pankhurst family.[9]

Interest had been growing since 1974 when the BBC had screened 'Shoulder to Shoulder', a powerful and very popular series dramatizing the militant campaign through the lives of the Pankhursts. Once restored, on 10 October 1984 number 62, together with 60, was re-opened as The Pankhurst Centre, combining a small museum dedicated to the Pankhurst and suffragette legacy (see Object 97) with the headquarters of Manchester Women's Aid, a charity supporting women and children in need.[10]

Object 20

Photographic postcard of the 'Lancashire and Cheshire Delegates on the Women's Franchise Deputation to the Prime Minister', May 1906

Lancashire and Cheshire Delegates on the Women's Franchise Deputation to the Prime Minister. [Copyright. F. R. CLARK.

Object 20 is a photographic postcard of the 'Lancashire and Cheshire Delegates on the Women's Franchise Deputation to the Prime Minister', May 1906. The photographer is F.R. Clark, the exact site in London is unknown. (TWL.2002.378, The Women's Library collection, London School of Economics and Political Science.)

During the spring of 1906, Mrs Pankhurst left 62 Nelson Street for London on several occasions, one being the weekend of Friday 18 May. Also in London was the group of women from Lancashire and Cheshire shown in Object 20, who had travelled there for the same reason as Pankhurst, to persuade the Prime Minister, Campbell-Bannerman, to grant the franchise to women. On Saturday 20th, with members of other suffrage organizations, they carried their banners in a procession from the Embankment to Downing Street, where leaders of the movement interviewed Campbell-Bannerman. After lunch they rallied in Trafalgar Square and on Sunday joined another mass meeting in Hyde Park.

Most of the women were employed in cotton mills and were losing a day's pay as they posed for F.R. Clark.[1] There is no clue as to where or when the photograph was taken, other than that it was after their arrival in London, for one of their leaders, Mrs Selina Cooper, had travelled south some days earlier.[2] Some thought had been given to the positioning of the women, for three of the leaders are in the centre, seated in the second row. Sarah Reddish is hatless, with Eva Gore-Booth to her left and Selina Cooper next-but-one on the right, holding a sheaf of leaflets. Sarah Dickenson could be the woman between Reddish and Cooper and Esther Roper the woman on the right of that row. Some faces transcend the years; others have either not been recorded or lack definition. The result is both a souvenir of the group's determination to speak to power and evidence that someone had an eye for a new form of publicity, for it was barely four years since the Post Office permitted photographs to be used on postcards.

Not only is the postcard, as an object, evidence of involvement in the Deputation, but the objects within the photograph allow us to identify the women's political affiliations. Although it is impossible to read the message on their badges, the wording on their banners is clear. On the right is that of the Lancashire and Cheshire Textile and Other Workers Representation Committee (LCWTOWRC), formed in the summer of 1903 by Reddish, Cooper, Dickenson, Roper and Gore-Booth, which brought suffragists together with women organizers from the trade union and cooperative movement to sponsor a Labour parliamentary candidate pledged to support enfranchisement for working women. They had been the 'radical suffragist' element within the North of England Society for Women's Suffrage (NESWS), of which, until 1905, Roper was secretary.[3] Disillusioned with the performance of David Shackleton, the Labour MP for whom they had campaigned in the 1902 Clitheroe by-election, the radical suffragists fielded their own Labour candidate at Wigan in the 1906 general election. Although defeated, he did beat the Liberal candidate into third place.

At the back right of the photograph is the banner of the Union of Patent Cap Winders, Hank and Bobbin Winders, Cassers, Doublers and Reelers and on the left that of Manchester and Salford District Women's Trade and Labour Council (MSWTUC), both of which were mentioned in press reports, the latter revealed as 'bright yellow'.[4] Led by Dickenson and Gore-Booth, the MSWTUC was the most recently formed of the organizations, having split from another body, the Women's Trade Union Council (WTUC), which was backing the call for adult suffrage. As the suffrage campaign had, in the nineteenth century, been bedevilled by differences around the position of 'married women' versus 'spinsters and widows', so in the twentieth there was a division between the 'equal suffrage' and the 'adult suffrage' factions.

The weekend's events were well covered in the press, 'the visitors from the north' described as 'an orderly, neatly-dressed little band of about 50 women of all ages', contrasting favourably with the 'women of the Bromley and Poplar section [who carried] their babies at their breasts'.[5] For the occasion Annie Kenney of the WSPU resumed her former attire of clogs and shawl, representing herself as the stereotypical 'mill girl', giving the press an attractive subject on which to focus both words and pictures.[6]

After this demonstration there was little further cooperation between the radical suffragists and the WSPU, the groups differing not only in methods but in aims. Radical suffragists preferred to campaign along constitutional lines and, supporting Labour, could not back the WSPU's election policy. This, devised by Christabel, was to favour no political party but to campaign for any that would keep the Liberal, that is, the government candidate, out. Cooper became a full-time NUWSS organizer, Reddish worked with the NUWSS Bolton Suffrage Society, while Roper and Gore-Booth had launched a new organization, the National Industrial and Professional Women's Suffrage Society, embodying their ideal of cross-class cooperation. The parliamentary vote, seen as a panacea for so many societal ills, was a goal approached along increasingly diverse and diverging paths.

Object 21

A German photographic postcard, 23 October 1906

Object 21 is a photographic postcard of the Women's Social and Political Union (WSPU) demonstration at the House of Commons on 23 October 1906, published by Hermann Hillger Publishers, Berlin. (Martin Last collection, Zurich.)

At the beginning of 1906, Annie Kenney, who appeared in her mill-girl attire before the Prime Minister in May (see Object 20), had been sent from Manchester 'to rouse London'.[1] Initially she renewed contact with East End Independent Labour party supporters, such as Mrs Minnie Baldock, with whom in December 1905 she had heckled Liberal rallies by way of introducing WSPU tactics to London. Then, as a first step in bringing the campaign assertively to the capital, they arranged for 300 or 400 East End working-class women to travel to Westminster on the day of the opening of Parliament, 16 February, and process, carrying banners, to a WSPU meeting in Caxton Hall, where they joined an audience of middle- and upper-class suffragists. When news arrived that there had been no mention of 'Votes for Women' in the King's Speech, the meeting sent groups of women over to Parliament to lobby MPs. Newspaper reports of large crowds of women waiting outside Parliament in the cold, reinforced by a published photograph of marching East End women, ensured ample publicity for the WSPU. Although this demonstration was peaceful, as were those on 19 and 20 May (see Object 20), it was not long before 'militancy' began its inexorable escalation.

In March 1906, Kenney and others attempted on a couple of occasion to interview the Prime Minister, Campbell-Bannerman, at 10 Downing Street. This was at a time when Sir Charles Dilke's Adult Suffrage bill was before Parliament, a bill opposed by the WSPU, believing it unachievable and merely a distraction from their call for equal suffrage. On the second occasion Kenney was arrested but Campbell-Bannerman declined to press charges. However, on 19 June when she, Baldock and others doorstepped Asquith, Campbell-Bannerman's successor as prime minister, at his house in Cavendish Square, Kenney and two East End women were arrested and, in lieu of a fine, were sentenced to six weeks' imprisonment. Although Teresa Billington was sentenced to two months, her fine was, without her consent, paid. Of this incident Christabel Pankhurst later wrote, 'Militancy had now begun in London. The first prisoners for the vote were in Holloway Gaol.'[2]

During the rest of the summer, while Parliament was on recess, the WSPU left London in peace. In July Christabel Pankhurst joined Billington to campaign at the Cockermouth by-election, implementing her new policy of campaigning for any candidate who would 'Keep the Liberal Out', and in October harried Asquith at the East Fife by-election. However, by 20 October the WSPU leaders had regrouped in their new London office at 4 Clement's Inn, Holborn, to hold a conference at which a constitution was democratically adopted. Plans were also laid for a demonstration to take place in the Lobby of the House of Commons on the opening of Parliament on 23 October.

Object 21, a photographic postcard, published in Berlin, records the fracas that occurred on that day when only two small groups were allowed into the Parliament building and the remaining WSPU demonstrators were held outside in Old Palace Yard. The caption translates as: 'From the disturbances in London: The security forces prevent women's rights activists from entering the English Lower House'. The police were prepared. Cannon Row police station in Westminster had been informed that about thirty suffragettes were on the way from the East End by Tube train and the Metropolitan police, having studied photographs of the WSPU leaders, such as Mrs Pankhurst and the WSPU's new treasurer, Mrs Emmeline Pethick-Lawrence, were able to recognize them in the ensuing fray. The result was that a number of women, including Kenney, Baldock, Billington, Pethick-Lawrence, the youngest Pankhurst daughter, Adela, and Mrs Anne Cobden-Sanderson, a long-time suffragist, were arrested and went to prison, as was now established practice. Sylvia Pankhurst followed them to Holloway the next day, after committing a disturbance outside the court in which the others were being tried.

The postcard photograph of the group of women and policemen, with the statue of Oliver Cromwell in the background, is virtually identical to one that appeared in the *Daily Mirror*.[3] The paper, clearly apprised in advance of the demonstration, had sent along a reporter and a photographer. Although no British postcard of the event is known, the efficacy of the militant policy of creating publicity is evidenced by the fact that Hermann Hillger Publishers, of Berlin W9, who boasted they brought 'the latest from around the world on postcards', thought this image would sell in Germany and, as the printed date of 10 November attests, produced it barely two weeks later. Object 21 quickly found a buyer, who posted it in Pforzheim on 19 November to a recipient in the same city. As originally sent, the card did not carry any message, allowing the caption to speak for itself. The fact that a rough Italian translation of the German caption was later added on the reverse by an Italian dealer in second-hand postcards is proof of the ongoing international interest in 'suffragette' objects.

Object 22

Illustration of 'The Mud March', February 1907

Object 22 is an illustration of the National Union of Women's Suffrage Societies' (NUWSS) 'Mud March' by A. Michael for *Black and White*, 16 February 1907. (Lesley Mees Collection.)

When the members of the Women's Social and Political Union (WSPU) arrested outside Parliament on 23 October 1906 (see Object 21) were released from prison, in a gesture of solidarity Mrs Fawcett and the NUWSS organized a banquet in their honour, held at the Savoy on 11 December. Of the ex-prisoners Fawcett stated, 'The example which they had set of courage, endurance and self-sacrifice had fanned in every one of them a keener flame of idealism, a greater desire to serve, to spend and be spent in the cause which they had at heart.'[1] One of the prisoners, whom she had visited in Holloway, was an old friend, Annie Cobden Sanderson, whose father, Richard Cobden, was still revered as a leader of the campaign against the Corn Laws.[2] Cobden Sanderson had been the first prominent constitutional suffragist to defect to the WSPU and the banquet, at which she sat at Fawcett's right hand, may well have had a consequence, unintended by the NUWSS, of easing many constitutional suffragists into the militant camp.

While organizing this most traditional of political occasions, the NUWSS was also planning to mark the opening of the 1907 Parliament with a version of the procession with which the WSPU had observed its opening in 1906. However, instead of a raggle-taggle of East End women, on Saturday 9 February London would see the first large-scale street procession of aristocratic, upper- and middle-class women, each prepared to make of themselves a public spectacle for the sake of the cause. These were women belonging to the NUWSS and the Central Society for Women's Suffrage, its London affiliate, whose secretary, Philippa Strachey, was the procession's organizer. Also joining the procession was a contingent of northern mill workers, led by Eva Gore-Booth and Esther Roper of the Northern Franchise Demonstration Committee. Although often overlooked in discussions of this procession, these are the women who caught the eye of Arthur Michael, illustrator of Object 22.

The event soon became known as the 'Mud March' for, as the demonstrators assembled in Hyde Park at 2 pm, drizzle turned into heavy rain. Main roads, such as Piccadilly and the Strand, the route of the march, were still laid with woodblocks, the fibres of which, saturated with horse-dung and general waste, disintegrated over time, coagulating as sludge. As a journalist described, 'Whenever there is rain the Strand (laid with deal) is muddy, sloppy, greasy, and altogether unbearable. The walls of the houses and the shop windows are splashed with mud to a height of 15ft from the ground, and the glass of the windows has to be cleaned once every two days.'[3] But, despite the weather, it was an exciting occasion. One young Kensington woman, Kate Frye, described:

> The crowds to see us – the man in the street – the men in the Clubs, the people standing outside the Carlton – interested – surprised for the most part – not much joking at our expense and no roughness. The policemen were splendid and all the traffic was stopped our way. We were an imposing spectacle all with badges – each section under its own banners. I felt like a martyr of old and walked proudly along. It did seem an extraordinary walk and it took some time as we went very slowly occasionally when we got congested – but we went in one long unbroken procession. There were 3000 about I believe. The mud was awful.[4]

As on previous demonstrations, the sections from the North of England broke off from the procession at Trafalgar Square to hold an open-air meeting, addressed by Keir Hardie MP, Eva Gore-Booth and Sarah Dickenson, while the NUWSS contingent carried on to Exeter Hall in the Strand.[5] Although the WSPU was not officially included in the proceedings, Mrs Despard was photographed leading a WSPU group. In fact, the newspapers carried numerous photographs of the event, none of which did justice to the excitement felt by Kate Frye. Leafless trees and sodden winter costumes do not present a striking visual image, whereas Arthur Michael, in Object 22, while acknowledging the weather, communicates the spirit of those who were, for a few hours, the centre of London's attention.

The national gaze, however, swiftly moved on from the constitutionalists' display of dignified, if muddy, unity. For, on Wednesday 13 February, while members of the NUWSS were in Parliament, discussing with sympathetic MPs a possible private member's women's suffrage bill, the WSPU was sending successive groups of women from their meeting in Caxton Hall to lobby the House of Commons. After clashes with the police, fifty-six women, including Despard, Christabel and Sylvia Pankhurst, were arrested and given short prison terms.[6] The MP successful in the private members' ballot, W.H. Dickinson, did back a women's suffrage bill, but a month later it was 'talked out'. Although neither the tactics of the NUWSS nor of the WSPU had proved effective, their difference was becoming increasingly visible. However, at this stage the NUWSS had not yet formally condemned the militancy of the WSPU, an organization that at the beginning of 1907 still appeared united in aims and methods but which was soon to splinter.

Object 23

Press photograph taken on 31 October 1906

Object 23 is a photograph, credited to Barratt's Press Agency. A cropped version of the photograph was published on the front page of the *Daily Mirror*, 1 November 1906. (7JCC/O/02/109, The Women's Library collection, London School of Economics and Political Science.)

Object 23 shows the leading members of the Women's Social and Political Union, photographed on 31 October 1906, eight days after the events recorded on Object 21. From the left are Mrs Flora Drummond, Christabel Pankhurst, Jessie Kenney, Mrs Nellie Martel, Mrs Emmeline Pankhurst and Mrs Charlotte Despard, all important figures in the early years of the WSPU's London campaign. The woman on the right, who is excised from the *Daily Mirror* version, is unidentified, but may possibly be Miss Carolyn Hodgson.

Flora Drummond had come from Manchester with Annie Kenney at the beginning of 1906, launching the WSPU campaign amongst working women in the East End, Christabel had arrived in July 1906 as organizer-in chief, after completing her university degree, Jessie Kenney

(Annie's sister) was, from spring 1906, secretary to Emmeline Pethick-Lawrence, the WSPU's new honorary treasurer, while Emmeline Pankhurst, the WSPU's founder, finally moved from Manchester to London in 1907 (see Object 19). Despard was a very recent recruit, a Labour supporter, in favour of adult suffrage, who only joined the WSPU in the late summer of 1906, won over by Keir Hardie and Teresa Billington. Shortly before photographed at this meeting, she had taken over the honorary secretaryship from Edith How-Martyn, who had been imprisoned after the House of Commons fracas (see Object 21), sharing this role with Carolyn Hodgson.[1] The photograph was taken in the WSPU office at 4 Clement's Inn, rooms found for them by Emmeline and Frederick Pethick-Lawrence, who also lived in the building.

Another, different, photograph, taken at the same session, survives, focusing on Despard, who is speaking.[2] Although the reverse of this photograph carries apparently useful information, it serves as a lesson in keeping an open mind. For, in the top left-hand corner is written '1907 HRK', the initials being those of Harriet Kerr, the WSPU's efficient office manager who might have been thought to have dated the image correctly. If research had not discovered the photograph to have been published in 1906, it would be easy to be misled. Written in pencil, in a different hand, is a caption nearly identical to that printed in the *Daily Mirror*: 'A special meeting of the Committee of the Council was held today to consider the future policy of the suffragists. Held at the offices of the Women's Social and Political Union.' The names of the women are noted in sequence, as though to identify them. Is this annotation contemporary with the photograph? To complicate matters, the reverse also carries a date, '1934'. Could this be the date when the photograph was added to the Suffragette Fellowship Collection (see Object 96)?

Another matter to consider is the discrepancy between the names of those credited as photographers of the 31 October 1906 scene. The last image discussed, the one centring on Mrs Despard, carries on the reverse the stamp of 'Park, Fleet Street', a press agency run in partnership by photographers Alfred Barratt and Harry Park. But Object 23 (held by the Women's Library collection at LSE) and an identical photo (held by the London Museum) both bear the stamp of 'Barratt's Photo Press Agency, 8 Salisbury Ct, Fleet St, EC.', a firm only started by Alfred Barratt in April 1909 after the dissolution of his partnership with Park. Presumably Barratt later reissued Object 23 on his own account. He certainly had further contact with suffragettes, for seven years later he would be hiding in a van in the Holloway exercise yard, commissioned by the Home Office to take secret surveillance photographs of suffragette prisoners. Suffragette image making, of one kind or another, was all good business.

Barely a year after the Object 23 scene another, less harmonious, meeting took place at 4 Clement's Inn. As Carolyn Hodgson reported in September 1907,

> I was called with other members of the committee to a meeting at Clement's Inn on Tuesday last [10 September]. At this meeting Mrs Pankhurst made a statement to the effect that 'it had been decided' to take several important steps, which she enumerated. Mrs Pankhurst was asked upon whose authority this step had been decided. She replied that she alone was responsible, and added further that in future she would have no one at the committee meeting who was not in absolute accord with her views. She then gave a list of the proposed new committee. The names of Mrs Despard and Mrs How-Martyn were omitted, although they had been elected to their positions at the previous conference.[3]

The 1907 conference was to be cancelled, the organization's constitution ignored, and Pankhurst autocracy assured. The split in the WSPU was widely reported in the press, with both sides adding their own 'spin'. This time, however, there was no photographer to record the occasion.

Object 24

Women's Freedom League Minute Book
1907–8

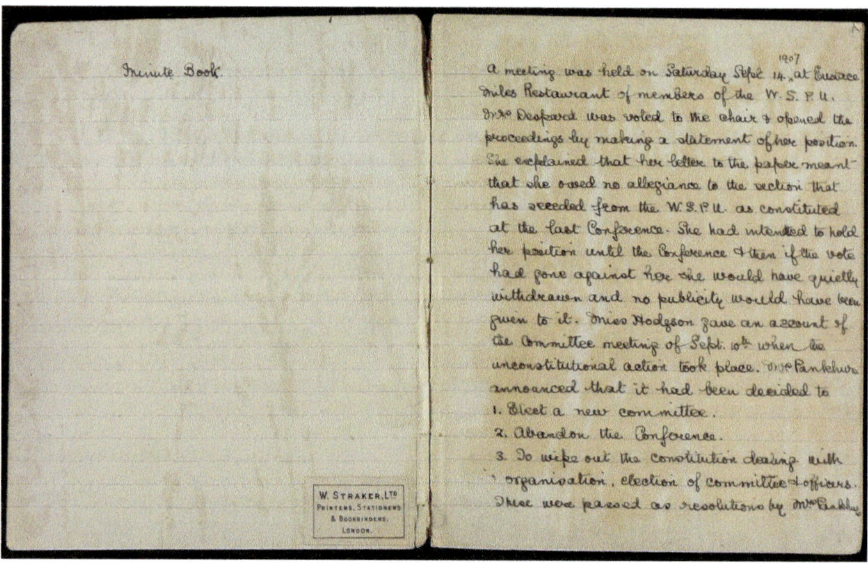

Object 24 shows the opening page of the Women Freedom League's first Minute Book, 1907. (Martin Last collection, Zurich.)

For well over 100 years this, the first Minute Book of the Women's Freedom League (WFL), was 'lost' until bought at an internet auction and lent to the Women's Library collection at LSE to join the WFL's main archive.[1] The entries cover the crucial first year of the WFL's existence and are important in allowing us to follow every step of the organization's development.

The opening page of the Minute Book is that of an organization whose members still believed themselves to belong to the Women's Social and Political Union (WSPU). We saw under Object 23 that at a meeting held in the WSPU office on 10 September 1907 Mrs Pankhurst's had unilaterally abolished the WSPU constitution. Now, on 14 September, someone, probably Miss Carolyn Hodgson, had bought an exercise book from a branch of W. Straker, a London stationer, in readiness to minute a small meeting held in the Eustace Miles, a popular vegetarian restaurant in central London. Mrs Charlotte Despard took the chair and among others present were Teresa Billington-Greig and Edith How-Martyn. All were strong individuals with strong views, in particular a belief in democracy and socialism. Despard, born into an Anglo-Irish family and long a widow, had since the 1890s devoted herself to social work with women and children in an impoverished area of Battersea. Teresa Billington-Greig had been a teacher before devoting herself to the WSPU suffrage campaign, while Mrs Edith How-Martyn, a young science graduate, was an effective and practical campaign organizer. The three leaders, all supporters of the Independent Labour party, had been particularly troubled by the Pankhursts' decision, announced earlier in 1907, not to support Labour candidates at elections. Prepared to give a lifetime commitment to campaigns for social justice for women, they did not take kindly to autocracy.

It took a little time for matters to resolve themselves, but in November 1907, having realized it would be impossible to wrest the WSPU from the Pankhursts, the new society was given a new name, the 'Women's Freedom League', chosen democratically by its members. Other suggested names were all associated with emancipation and rights, but 'Women's Freedom League' was a good choice, not tied only to suffrage but encompassing all kinds of freedom and appropriate to an agenda that changed over time to meet changing conditions. After a year in a temporary office in Buckingham Street, in September 1908 the WFL moved into four rooms on the first floor of 1 Robert Street, off the Strand, staying until 1915, when they moved to High Holborn.

Although considered a militant society, unlike the WSPU the WFL did not carry out acts of physical protest. Instead, they conducted campaigns of passive resistance, such as protesting in Police Courts, where, as they saw it, women were tried by laws made only by men (see Object 54), and in 1909 conducting a five-month continuous picket of the House of Commons (see Object 44). It was WFL members who attracted publicity by chaining themselves to the grille in the Ladies' Gallery in the House of Commons (see Object 36) and a WFL member, Australian Muriel Matters, who hired an airship from which to drop leaflets over London. It was the WFL who first had the idea of boycotting the 1911 census, and whose members set up the Tax Resistance League, refusing to pay taxes and creating publicity when their goods were seized and auctioned (see Object 70). Local WFL branches were set up throughout the country, the League being particularly strong in Wales and Scotland, but at both local and national levels it always struggled financially.

To support their work the WFL relied on generous donors and, on their own, time-consuming, fund-raising activities. Seen as of particular importance was raising enough money to ensure the publication of their weekly paper, *The Vote*, which ran from 1909 until 1933 and is an invaluable source of information on the changing nature of feminism in the first three decades of the twentieth century. Object 24 represents the first stitch sewn with the thread of equal citizenship, equal pay and equal opportunity that ran through the WFL's long, active life.

Object 25

A suffrage poster

Object 25 is an early suffrage poster, designed by Joan Harvey Drew for the Artists' Suffrage League. 73.6 cm x 97.8 cm. (Lesley Mees Collection.)

In October 1907, while the Despard contingent was vying with the Pankhursts for control of the Women's Social and Political Union (WSPU), the National Union of Women's Suffrage Societies (NUWSS) was working with a new organization, the Artists' Suffrage League (ASL), to promote its aims through a medium new to them, that of the political poster.[1] For in the years before the First World War this art form was a necessary accompaniment to two general and numerous by-elections. The street being the obvious place in which to catch the public eye, political posters, pasted onto wooden hoardings or brickwork, competed there with lavish consumer advertising.

The ASL had been founded in January 1907 by a group of women artists who, although professionally trained, had no experience of commercial poster work and it took a little time before members were able to balance the required ingredients of 'artistic merit, suitability of reproduction and excellence of idea' in order to create posters that could punch home the suffrage message.[2] Object 25 is one of the earliest of the ASL posters, probably dating from c.1908, but was still in use in 1911 (see Object 49). The artist, Joan Harvey Drew, an active member of the NUWSS Leith Hill Suffrage Society, depicts 'John Bull', the personification of England, beset by the governmental problems of the day, which include the 'Wife's Sister's Bill' [1907], 'Barmaids' [Employment of Barmaids Bill 1906] and 'Free Food for School Children' [Education (Provision of Meals) Act 1906], while a calm 'Jane Bull' figure asks, 'Won't you let me help you John?'

This poster, as with others issued by the ASL, was printed by commercial lithography; those issued by the other main suffrage artist organization, the Suffrage Atelier (SA), were bolder, using wood or lino-cuts, in black and white or with colour added by hand, giving a strong, urgent stamp to their message. All printing of SA posters was done by women, the Atelier being keen to teach its members the hand-printing processes necessary to produce its publications.

On posters, and in other media, suffrage artists employed a variety of tropes to ensure the campaign maintained the moral high ground.[3] Some posters communicated a social realist message, but in many others woman was personified as an angel or as a 'warrior, crusader, earth mother, virgin, hero, or pilgrim'.[4] All these would have been familiar to the reformers of the day, brought up on Walter Crane's *Cartoons for the Cause*, the cover of which features not only a bold young woman but also two other stalwarts of suffrage imagery, the broadcasting of seed and the rising sun.[5] While Crane's sun and seed were identified with 'socialism', suffrage artists linked the new dawn and seed-scattering to 'votes for women' (see also Object 99). As was Crane, some suffrage artists were influenced by the pre-Raphaelites, their style lending itself admirably to chivalric image, while the beatification of Joan of Arc in 1909 gave popular currency to the idea of the suffragette as 'the militant maiden out for vengeance'.[6] Artists could conflate this theme with that of the androgynous knight of medieval romance who, as rendered by one anonymous SA artist, rides with his 'Votes for Women' lance to rescue the fair maiden 'Justice'. Since ancient times 'Justice' had been personified as a woman and was another significant image in the morally uplifting section of the suffrage artist's arsenal. Amongst the more prosaic tropes, instantly recognizable to contemporaries if less so nowadays, were figures such as in Object 25, John Bull/Mrs Bull, but also Mrs Partington/Canute (who were both reputed to have attempted to hold back the sea) and Alice in Wonderland, whose various situations the suffrage artist could manipulate to communicate her chosen message.

The scope of the suffrage poster campaign is put into perspective when we discover that in the whole of 1910, the year of the two general elections, the ASL issued a mere 4,000 posters, while the Conservative party decorated Britain's streets with over a million word-only and 983,000 pictorial posters. Although the ASL pictorial posters would have been augmented by those of the SA and the WSPU, suffrage artists could not rely on the span of their poster coverage to put their message across to the public but had to create images every bit as clever and attractive as those ordered from commercial artists by the political parties. Finance, or lack of it, would have been a reason they did not commission well-established poster artists, such as John Hassall, who could charge £25 for a design and produced posters for the Anti-Suffrage League. But it is also likely that it was felt necessary for the message to be devised by someone totally committed to the Cause.

Of all items of political ephemera, the poster is surely the most ephemeral, torn down once its moment had passed and discarded without another thought. It is very rare for a suffrage poster to appear for sale, most surviving copies being ones that were preserved by the various suffrage organizations and are now held in public collections.

Object 26

Suffrage scrapbook compiled by Mrs Spencer Graves

Object 26 is a 'Woman's Suffrage' scrapbook, subtitled 'The Fight As I Saw It', compiled by Mrs Beatrice Spencer Graves. (10/05, The Women's Library collection, London School of Economics and Political Science.)

Many scrapbooks recording involvement in the twentieth-century suffrage campaign have survived, now held in archives, while yet others may still be awaiting discovery. Women created their personal histories of the movement by selecting, cutting out and pasting into albums a wide variety of ephemeral material; posterity has been reluctant to jettison testaments to such time-consuming enthusiasm. Object 26 is one such record, a green cloth-covered album holding a collection of newspaper cuttings, letters, flyers, pamphlets and other printed ephemera. The album consists of 114 pages, of which, in order, ten cover 1918–28, five 1914–18 and ninety-nine 1905–14. As the paper of the first two sections differs from that of 1905–14, it is clear Mrs Graves supplemented the original album by adding in at the front the pages that cover 1914–28.

Beatrice Spencer Graves was a daughter of Robert Leake MP, a Salford industrialist and Liberal MP, and in 1882 married William Spencer Graves, a retired Navy commander, later a stockbroker. Living at 20 Craven Terrace, Lancaster Gate, London, by 1908 she was honorary secretary of the Paddington branch of the London Society for Women's Suffrage (LSWS) and was one of the organizers of the suffrage shop in Westbourne Grove that proved such a success at the time of the June NUWSS procession (see Object 49). The double-page shown commemorates Graves' involvement in that event, thoroughly memorializing this first of the NUWSS summer rallies. Apart from the newspaper photographs, she also pasted in the flyer giving instructions to the marchers and her paper rosette, red and white still being the colours of the NUWSS, green not yet added to form their tricolour. On the following pages she included a large photograph of the inside of the Albert Hall, her ticket (Box 27 Loggia), many more news cuttings and a flimsy commemorative square issued by a commercial printer, Mrs S. Burgess, for sale by street vendors.

Although there is no mention of Graves in histories of the suffrage movement, Object 26 shows her to have been, from at least 1905, a valued member of the LSWS, of which, from 1913, she was for many years treasurer. Assiduously pasting in newspaper cuttings and suffrage printed ephemera, some items now rare, she covers many pre-1914 NUWSS occasions. Of note are a letter from Mrs Fawcett thanking her for help in organizing the 1909 visit to London of the International Women's Suffrage Alliance Congress and a July 1913 bill from the Hotel Ritz Budapest and annotated programme of the IWSA Budapest Congress, proof of her attendance as a member of the British contingent.

Throughout the First World War Graves dealt with the finances of the LSWS' various ventures. Pasted into Object 26 are two scarce items, evidence of LSWS war work: an extremely rare card advertising Bimbo Toys, made in the LSWS toy workroom, and a postcard of the 'London Suffragist' ambulance supplied by the London Committee of the Scottish Women's Hospitals, of which she was treasurer (see Object 82). Included is a January 1918 letter from Fawcett, who wrote of the final debate on the women's clause of the Representation of the People Bill, 'It has been a wonderful time. On Tuesday the 8th I was hopeful, on the 9th I was in despair, on the 10th intensely anxious until the end of Lord Curzon's speech when, of course I knew all was well' (see Object 83). Graves later pasted in, among other items, descriptions of Lady Astor's entrance into the House of Commons, December 1919 (see Object 85), reports of the 1922 election when a further two women MPs were elected and ended with the letter received from Fawcett in July 1928 to mark the achievement of the equal franchise.

Graves' album stands as a narrative history of the LSWS campaign. It is indeed 'the fight as I saw it', that is, from the suffragist viewpoint, with little mention of the militant agitation. Nor does she make much of her own involvement, her restraint the antithesis of Maud Arncliffe-Sennett's emotional record of suffrage campaigning that bulges from thirty-seven scrapbooks.[1] Unlike Graves, Arncliffe-Sennett annotated material, recording her thoughts and opinions, revealing the slights and wounds she sustained along the way. A member of most suffrage societies at one time or another, her scrapbooks are a rich source on all aspects of the campaign, whereas those compiled by Women's Social and Political Union (WSPU) members Isabel Seymour and Kitty Marion are confined to the work of that one society. Yet the scrapbooks of these two could not be more different. Isabel Seymour, from mid-1906 a paid employee in the Clement's Inn office, packed hers with flyers and other printed ephemera relating to demonstrations and meetings, formal and informal, providing an excellent record of this form of WSPU campaigning, whereas Kitty Marion's loose album concentrates on the militant campaign, including cuttings that point to her own involvement in particular arsons and bombings.[2]

As objects, suffrage scrapbooks are ripe for investigation, revealing individual personal and political beliefs, as well as, more prosaically, providing the researcher with a wealth of material they may not encounter elsewhere.[3]

Object 27

Suffrage newspapers

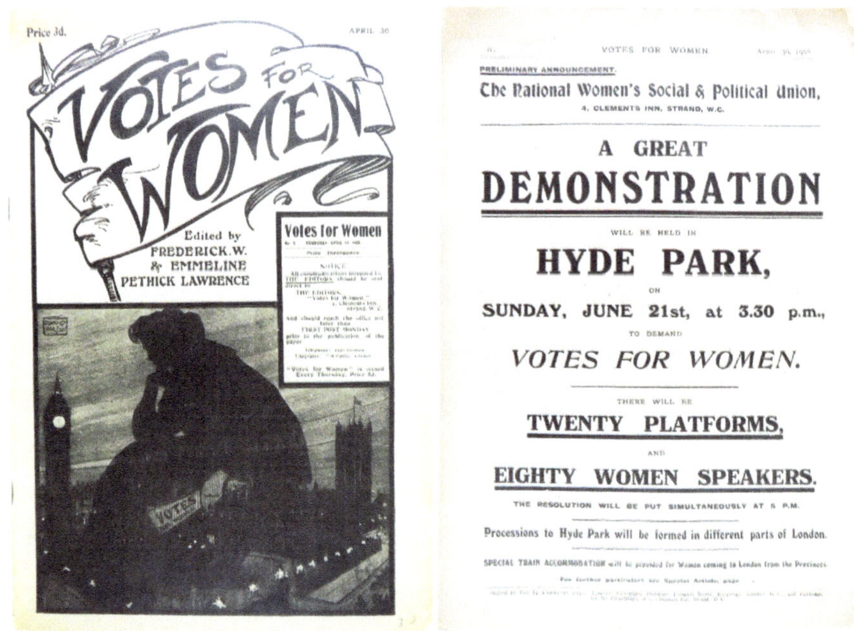

Object 27 is the cover of *Votes for Women*, the Women's Social and Political Union (WSPU) newspaper, together with an advertisement printed in the paper. (From the Collection of Dr Kenneth Florey. Photograph by Emilia van Beugen.)

After the demise of *The Women's Suffrage Journal* in 1890 (see Object 9), the suffrage movement had no paper solely devoted to the Cause until the launch in June 1903 of a quarterly, the *Women's Suffrage Record*, edited by Edith Palliser of the National Union of Women's Suffrage Societies (NUWSS). This paper was useful but short-lived, ceasing publication in November 1906. The baton was then taken up in June 1907 with the publication of a substantial weekly, *Women's Franchise*, featuring news of all the current suffrage societies, NUWSS, WSPU, Women's

Freedom League (WFL) and Men's League for Women's Suffrage. However, as the influence of the societies grew and their memberships increased, the first three societies made the decision to fund their own papers.[1]

The WSPU's paper, *Votes for Women*, was first issued in October 1907, published by Emmeline and Frederick Pethick-Lawrence, who had the will, the money and the Fleet Street experience to fund a campaigning paper. With a front page dominated by Fleet Street cartoonist David Wilson's compelling image of 'The Haunted House', a seated woman brooding over the Houses of Parliament, a demand for 'Votes for Women' in her hand, the first issues made a striking impression.[2] By June 1908, the time of the WSPU's first major London demonstration, as advertised in Object 27, the weekly paper, priced at 1d, had a circulation of 10,000 and a year later had passed 30,000. As membership of the WSPU and its range of activities expanded, so the size of the page and their number increased to accommodate the flood of reports and the paid advertising very necessary to the paper's success. From 5 March 1909 the front page carried a cartoon by Alfred Pearse, who signed himself 'A Patriot', and each annual run of issues was offered as a bound volume, its boards decorated with Sylvia Pankhurst's 'Angel of Freedom' design in the WSPU colours of purple, white and green (see Object 43).[3] When the Pethick-Lawrences were ousted from the WSPU in 1912 (see Object 57), they kept *Votes for Women*, which they ran until January 1914 as an independent militant paper before handing it over to the United Suffragists. However, after this, the paper's finances were always precarious and as soon as the Representation of the People Act was passed in February 1918, the paper ceased publication, its work accomplished.

After the 1912 split, the WSPU replaced *Votes for Women* with *The Suffragette*, a paper of similar design, edited by Christabel Pankhurst from her exile in Paris. 'A Patriot' stayed loyal to *Votes for Women*, but *The Suffragette* found other cartoonists, including Will Dyson, to grace their front pages. The content covered all details of increasing militancy, appeals for funds and, from 1913, discussions of prostitution and venereal disease based around Christabel's book, *The Great Scourge and How to End It*, which called for 'Votes for Women and Chastity for Men'. From 1913, as militancy increased, the Home Office made every effort to suppress the paper so that on occasion it appeared with blank columns where the printer felt at risk of prosecution if he printed the WSPU's text. The paper ceased publication on the outbreak of war in August 1914, was revived as a patriotic, pro-war paper in early 1915, before being renamed *Britannia* in October. Now the paper of the Women's Party (see Object 84), *Britannia* published its final issue on 20 December 1918.

The first issue of *The Common Cause* appeared on 15 April 1909, financed by Manchester suffragist, Margaret Ashton, but was soon adopted by the NUWSS. Initially edited in Manchester, the paper moved to London in 1911. A weekly, it ran until January 1920, when it became *The Woman's Leader*, first as the paper of the National Union of Societies for Equal Citizenship and then, until March 1933, of the Townswomen's Guild. Throughout its long life the paper campaigned vigorously not only for equal suffrage, but on a wide range of feminist issues, such as equal pay.

The third of the main suffrage newspapers was *The Vote*, the paper of the WFL, first published on 28 October 1909 and run by Marie Lawson, a young businesswoman who ensured it carried a good number of advertisements. A weekly, it was later edited for a time by Mrs Charlotte Despard, maintaining its selling price of 1d until the final issue, dated 10 November 1933. *The Vote* was less abrasive in tone than *Votes for Women* and *The Suffragette* and over the succeeding years espoused the WFL's increasingly 'constitutional' attitude to suffrage campaigning. As with the *Woman's Leader*, in the 1920s and early 1930s it campaigned not only for equal suffrage but on a range of feminist issues, while reporting on the work of WFL branches around the country.

Although these papers may be considered the principal conveyers of suffrage news, as new societies were formed, so they, too, issued their own publications. Originals of all suffrage newspapers are extremely scarce, but many have now been digitized, revolutionizing suffrage research, and are available through the British Newspaper Archive and the LSE Digital Library.

Object 28

Women's Social and Political Union 'Haunted House' buckle and belt

Object 28 is the Women's Social and Political Union (WSPU) 'Haunted House' brass-plated buckle and grosgrain belt. (From the Collection of Dr Kenneth Florey. Photograph by Emilia van Beugen.)

In the spring of 1908, Emmeline Pethick-Lawrence selected the combination of purple, white and green as the colours with which to brand the WSPU, the 21 May issue of *Votes for Women* carrying an announcement that ribbons and badges in the 'colours' were now on sale. By the 4 June issue it was clear that these colours would dominate the procession organized for 21 June that was to culminate in a rally in Hyde Park (see Object 27). Known as 'Woman's Sunday', this was the most ambitious public event yet staged by the WSPU and received wide praise in the press for the style in which it was conducted. As the *Daily News* reported, this was 'a beacon day in the women's movement ….a white demonstration, touched with the green and purple that have become the emblem of the Women's Social and Political Union'.[1]

The WSPU lost no time in monetizing the colours, an advertisement for one of its earliest items of merchandise, the 'Haunted House' buckle and belt, appearing in the 30 July 1908 issue of *Votes for Women*. The manufacturer is unknown, but the buckle was presumably directly commissioned by the WSPU, taking David Wilson's image, used on the front page of early issues of *Votes for Women*, and combining it with a ribbon belt in the colours (see Object 27). The buckle and belt were priced at 2s 6d, were stocked for only a year and are now extremely scarce. A year later the WSPU had for sale a wide range of goods in the colours, including brooches, handkerchiefs, ribbon badges, neck cords, ties, silk rosettes, leather belts, hatpins, motor scarves and even copies of *Omar Khayyam*.[2] In *Votes for Women* Christabel Pankhurst lauded the success of the colours and heralded the WSPU fund-raising Exhibition, to be held in May at the Prince's Skating Rink in Kensington, as a magnificent opportunity for buying the myriad of purple, white and green objects ingeniously devised by the WSPU.[3] In the programme for the Exhibition, Emmeline Pethick-Lawrence provided a soulful gloss on the derivation of the colours (white for purity, green for hope and purple for dignity).

Before the adoption of the purple, white and green, which, well over 100 years later, have come in the popular mind to be synonymous with the suffrage movement in its entirety, the basic combination of red and white had been used by both the WSPU and the National Union of Women's Suffrage Societies (NUWSS) on flags and badges. It was only in November 1909 that the NUWSS added green, a tricolour later glossed as the colours of the standard of the Italian Risorgimento, and used, therefore, in memory of Garibaldi and Mazzini, heroes to the founders of the suffrage movement in the mid-nineteenth century.[4]

The Women's Freedom League (WFL) was a little quicker than the NUWSS to recognize the power of 'colours' and by February 1909 had adopted green, white and gold as their brand, using them to promote a Caxton Hall 'Green, White and Gold' fund-raising fair in early April, a tradition they maintained into the 1930s. Like the WSPU, the WFL issued a range of merchandise in their colours.

In the years leading up to the First World War, it became a prerequisite of each new suffrage society to sport their own combination of colours on their badges, flags and publications, ranging from the pink and green of the Actresses' Franchise League to the black, white and gold of the Women Writers' Suffrage League. We shall see these put to good use in, for example, Objects 29, 43, 45, 52 and 71.

Object 29

Women's Freedom League 'Dorothy bag'

Object 29 is a 'Dorothy bag', hand-made using a dark-green cotton with a smooth finish, its carrying straps a gold satiny material, decorated with the badge of the Women's Freedom League (WFL). (SC/29, The Women's Library collection, London School of Economics and Political Science.)

A 'Dorothy bag', a drawstring handbag with handles to loop over the wrist, was a very popular accessory in the years before the First World War, easily made at home, fashioned to meet the need of the moment.[1] Object 29 originally belonged to one of three sisters, Edith, Florence or Grace Hodgson, two of whom were teachers and one a telegraphist, living in Gospel Oak, Hampstead, and from *c.*1908 until the 1930s active members of the WFL. We do not know if one of the sisters made the bag or whether it was bought at a WFL 'Green, White and Gold Fair', for this is just such an object as might have been on sale, appropriately coloured, at any fund-raising suffrage society event. Miss Louisa Chapman of 11 Bristol Gardens, Maida Vale, a London member of the Women's Social and Political Union (WSPU), possessed a similar bag, crocheted in purple, lined in cream silk and adorned with a WSPU 'Votes for Women' silk ribbon badge. That one was decorative, but we do know that, in March 1912, other, necessarily stouter, versions of the 'Dorothy' were used by WSPU activists, resulting in news reports such as 'the Suffragettes have given the "Dorothy" bag its death-blow. A few days ago thousands of women were to be seen carrying this very convenient form of handbag, but since the window-smashing Suffragettes concealed their weapons within its folds the very sight of a "Dorothy" in the streets is sufficient to make its owner an object of suspicion'.[2]

While Object 29 is defiantly home-made, commercial retailers soon realized there was a market for items of dress and accessories 'in the colours' and that the suffragette press (see Object 27) was the obvious medium in which to advertise. There was a certain synergy between the suffrage movement and the dress trade in that it was felt necessary to combat the perception of campaigners as 'the shrieking sisterhood' or, perhaps, even more damaging, as 'frumps'. *Votes for Women* encouraged every WSPU member to be 'dainty and precise in her dress ....whether she is to appear on a public platform, in a procession, or merely in house or street about her ordinary vocations'.[3] In advertorials the suffrage papers endorsed favoured advertisers, for instance *Votes for Women* described 'the new Suffragette coat, made specially for the WSPU by Mr Charles Lee of Wigmore Street'. Made up in purple, green or white, with facings in the other colours, it is hoped that members of the WSPU will wear this coat in processions and on official occasions.[4] In November 1910, when leading a deputation to Asquith and Lloyd George, Christabel Pankhurst wore a coat with wide satin lapels in purple, white and green, of which the journalist Henry Nevinson commented in his diary, that it was 'fine – but a little overdone for the morning'.[5] The needs of WFL members could be satisfied by visiting, for instance, William Owen's store in Westbourne Grove, London, where 'blouses, golf-jerseys, coats and hats in the colours of the League' were available.[6] The NUWSS was considerably less prescriptive on matters of dress, with the exception of outfits for the Pilgrimage (see Object 74), and received a flurry of letters, for and against when, in August 1913, it was suggested that *Common Cause* should include articles on dress. No 'dress' articles appeared, *Common Cause* having clearly decided its readership did not desire guidance.

But for susceptible suffragettes, there were many temptations. For instance, as, at that time, no woman could leave the house without a hat, this was an item that, visible, yet relatively inexpensive, lent itself to a declaration of suffrage allegiance. In *Pages from the Diary of a Militant Suffragette*, the heroine tells a woman, who is interested in joining the WSPU but reluctant to fight with the police, that the fashion store 'Derry and Toms have charming hats in the colours – they are really most becoming', thereby suggesting she could participate in the fight for the vote by merely wearing a sympathetic hat.[7] 'Hats and toques (ready to wear) trimmed in the Colours of the Union. 4/11' were advertised by Mrs Clara Strong, a WSPU member and self-styled 'Suffragette Milliner'.[8] The toque, a round, brimless hat with no strings or fastening ribbons, heralded a more streamlined style, for in the years before the First World War women's dress did alter decisively, from a curvy, fussy outline, topped by a large hat, to a more tailored look. It is perhaps not coincidental that the change occurred as the suffrage campaign became increasingly physically militant.

While larger items of suffrage-related clothing have not survived, lacking both material resilience and societal value, even small dress items such as Object 29 are rarely found and, being easily faked, require a credible suffrage provenance to be accepted as authentic. See Objects 48, 49 and 74 for more ways the suffrage societies, militant and constitutional, used 'dress' as a means of fostering an image that would both charm the public and unite their followers.

Object 30

'Susan B. Anthony' suffrage banner, 1908

Object 30 is the 'Susan B. Anthony' banner, designed by Mary Lowndes, made by the Artists' Suffrage League (ASL) for the National Union of Women's Suffrage Societies (NUWSS) 13 June 1908 procession. (TWL.1998.19, The Women's Library collection, London School of Economics and Political Science.)

Although few items of suffrage-related clothing have survived (see Object 29), another form of textile, the suffrage banner, has been more assiduously conserved, with many now held in public collections.[1] Valued by their creators both for what they represented and for their intrinsic beauty, many banners were preserved by the societies or individuals who inherited them until, in time, they were presented to local or national institutions.

Although the banners displayed at the Grand Demonstrations of the 1880s and at the 1907 NUWSS 'Mud March' (see Object 22) are lost, we are still able to admire many made for later suffrage occasions. Object 30 is typical of the banners designed for the 13 June 1908 NUWSS London procession by Mary Lowndes, founder and chairman of the ASL. Many of these banners, sewn, appliquéd, embroidered and painted by members of the ASL, together with Lowndes' designs, augmented by swatches of suggested materials, survive. One of these is Object 30, rendered in blue velvet, with alternating moiré satin and red velvet stripes, the stars painted in silver and the lettering in red.[2] Object 30 fittingly acknowledged the many years of cooperation between the British and the US suffrage movements, being one of a trio of banners dedicated to US suffrage pioneers, the others commemorating Elizabeth Cady Stanton and Lucy Stone. Anthony had been a correspondent of British campaigners such as Elizabeth Wolstenholme Elmy, had enjoyed lengthy visits to Britain and in 1904 was inaugurated as the first honorary president of the International Women's Suffrage Alliance (IWSA). Many IWSA members, passing through London in June 1908, on the way to their conference in Amsterdam, took part in the procession. One of them, Lucy E. Anthony, was photographed in front of her aunt's banner.[3]

The NUWSS banners recognized not only female pioneers, such as Anthony, Lydia Becker, Mary Wollstonecraft, Florence Nightingale and Mary Somerville, but the towns and cities of Britain represented by their members. Lowndes was ingenious in creating appropriate heraldry and slogans, the Leeds banner, for instance, includes a fleece, three stars and owls, all derived from the city's coat of arms, together with a motto 'Leeds for Liberty'. Lowndes' annotation on the design shows that the banner was 4' 4" wide by 6' 6" high [132 x 198 cm], [cost] 'with bamboo poles and cords complete £2. The lovely blue and gold strips are given by Mrs Herringham. The owls are silver'.[4] The banners received high praise, the journalist James Douglas reporting, 'They have recreated the beauty of blown silk and tossing embroidery. The procession was like a medieval festival, vivid with simple grandeur, alive with an ancient dignity.'[5] The latter was exactly the quality the NUWSS wished to project, to demonstrate how dignified, well-organized and united women could be in publicizing their claim to citizenship. They were optimistic, a suffrage bill had recently passed its Second Reading before being blocked, the greatest progress achieved by a suffrage bill since 1897.

In *Banners and Banner Making* (1909), Lowndes traced women's involvement in the craft to the 'warrior maidens' of a romanticized medieval past. While she lamented the use of commercial banners, the WSPU did commission some from manufacturers such as Thomas Brown & Co., makers of the 'First in the Fight' banner which the Manchester WSPU carried in the 'Woman's Sunday' rally in London on 21 June 1908.[6] However, WSPU banners were also made by their numerous artist members and sympathizers, such as in London, Edith Downing, Marion Wallace-Dunlop and Laurence and Clemence Housman; in Cardiff, Dorothy Salmon; and in Glasgow, Ann MacBeth.[7] The WFL was also well-endowed with banner-making members and enjoyed the support of the Suffrage Atelier, which designed its banners for the major processions of 1910 and 1911.

Although pageants did not persuade Parliament to pass a suffrage bill, banners were versatile marketing tools. They not only allowed suffragists and suffragettes to parade with a purpose and were used to decorate meeting halls but also provided a focus for further consciousness- and fund-raising efforts, subversively combining a forceful political message with a demonstration of womanly skills. Immediately before the 1908 NUWSS procession, eighty ASL banners were displayed in Caxton Hall, Westminster, while, on 17 June, at London's Queen's Hall, the WSPU 'unfurled' their 'Woman's Sunday' banners, which included 'Prison to Citizenship' by Laurence Housman and some designed by Sylvia Pankhurst.[8] The NUWSS then decided to tour their banners around the country, realizing that 'undoubtedly we have here an opportunity of presenting an artistic feast of the first order under circumstances that make it in itself, and in all attendant conditions that may be grouped around it, a unique act of propaganda'.[9]

In fact, as the centrepieces of many national and local exhibitions, the original banners not only have proved an excellent means of memorializing the suffrage campaign, but have also been the inspiration for contemporary creations, as evidenced by the spectacular '100 Banners' project that in 2018 marked the centenary of the passing of the Representation of the People Act.[10]

Object 31

The train and the suffrage movement

Object 31 is a photographic postcard of a steam train bearing a 'Votes for Women' placard, the location not identified. (Lesley Mees Collection.)

Although there is no documentary evidence, it is likely this train was hired by a local Women's Social and Political Union (WSPU) society to bring members to London to take part in a procession. For instance, for the 21 June 1908, 18 June 1910 and 17 June 1911 processions such trains travelled from all parts of the country. Of 'Woman's Sunday' in June 1908, *Votes for Women* commented, 'Another remarkable feature of the day were [*sic*] the enormous numbers of women who came in by the special trains from the various parts of the country. Many of these trains were filled to overflowing, women standing all down the corridors.'[1] For these special occasions the local suffrage societies negotiated reduced fares on the 'excursion trains' run by the various railway companies. Thus, in advance of the June 1910 London procession the WSPU advised that, for instance, Manchester suffragettes could take a midnight train on 17 June, returning from London the following midnight, for a probable fare of 12s, in carriages reserved for WSPU members. Or, if travelling from Liverpool in a saloon carriage reserved for forty WSPU members, suffragettes could catch the recommended train at 9.15 am and return at midnight.[2]

While these occasions marked the peak of suffrage train travel, the railway had since the beginning of the campaign been one of its main agents. For, by 1870, the railway network already covered about 15,000 miles, its stations, many more numerous than in the twenty-first century, allowing activists access to all areas of the country.[3] For instance, over a couple of weeks in March/April 1871 it was by train that Miss Taylour (see Object 4) would have travelled between the towns of Kelso, Hawick, Galashiels, Selkirk and Dalkeith, in each of which she gave a lecture and garnered a petition for presentation to Parliament.[4] Although too mundane to be recorded, very occasionally an early train-related scene is crystallized, such as Lilias Ashworth's remembrance of her first meeting with Millicent Fawcett, 'I can always recall her girlish figure when she stepped out of the train at Bath station'.[5] It was March 1871 and the two young women were about to embark on a suffrage lecture tour. Forty years later Kate Frye's diary is packed with details of the trains that carried her between small towns as organizer for the New Constitutional Society for Women's Suffrage. When setting out on these assignments she was able to forward a trunk to her lodgings using the services of 'Advance Luggage', and, if necessary, engage a station porter to help carry any other bags.

One train that played an important part in the creation of a WSPU legend was witnessed by Frye who, on 14 June 1913, walked in the procession through London that accompanied Emily Wilding Davison's coffin and, continuing to 'Kings Cross station …. went on the platform and there was the train – the special carriage for the coffin. Lots of the processionists were in the train, which was taking the body to Northumberland for interment. To think she had had to give her life because men will not listen to the claims of reason and of justice'.[6] Some months later, on the same line, the driver of a southbound train stopped at Loudoun Road (South Hampstead) station, just north of King's Cross, with the front portion of the long train in a tunnel, thereby trapping inside a number of vociferous suffragettes and allowing her police escort to whisk Mrs Pankhurst, who had been arrested in Scotland, straight to Holloway.

For, in 1913/14, Mrs Pankhurst was constantly imprisoned and, among the objects at which, in retaliation, the more intemperate suffragettes directed their attention, were trains and railway stations. The first arson attack came soon after Mrs Pankhurst's arrest in March 1913 when Hugh Franklin, a member of the Men's Political Union for Women's Enfranchisement, was caught setting fire to a railway carriage at Harrow station. Sentenced to nine months' imprisonment, he went on hunger strike and was forcibly fed more than a hundred times before being released under the 'Cat and Mouse' Act and escaping abroad. Although in the next eighteen months there were at least another dozen attacks on stations and trains, most took place at night, the damage was relatively slight, and no other arrests were made. But, as the militant campaign reached its peak, one of the last attacks, in July 1914 at Blaby, Leicestershire, gutted the station. Around the same time, a bomb was found in a goods train at Wellingborough and mailbags on a train were set alight after an explosion.[7] Nor were politicians safe while travelling. In November 1913 a suffragette entered the compartment of an Irish MP, John Redmond, and questioned him about forcible feeding before throwing two bags of flour over him. Reported in the press, the incident doubtless caused other politicians to reconsider their travel plans.[8]

Despite the ubiquity of suffrage train travelling, Object 31 is the only known photograph of a 'Votes for Women' train, the unknown photographer clearly feeling this image worth capturing.

Object 32

The bicycle and the suffrage movement

Object 32 is a photographic postcard of bicycling suffragettes. Photographed at Faversham, Kent, in December 1910, during that year's second general election. (Martin Last collection, Zurich.)

In the 1890s the bicycle was an emblem of freedom for the 'New Woman'. As Dora Montefiore, an early supporter of the Women's Social and Political Union (WSPU) and Women's Freedom League (WFL), recalled,

When the bicycle came in we women pioneers in the new method of transport were often hooted in the villages by other women, more especially if, for the sake of safety, we wore what was known as the divided skirt, but we held on our way, and the bicycle took us through home and Continental highways and byways, enlarged our mental outlook, and strengthened our mental aspirations, preparing women in some sort of way for their new duties and responsibilities as citizens.[1]

It is unsurprising, therefore, that in the late nineteenth century many suffragists were also bicyclists.

Although the machine had not yet become an active agent in the campaign, it had prompted new thinking as to what was appropriate dress for a woman cyclist, resulting in many intriguing designs for the garment known to Dora Montefiore as the 'divided skirt' and much discussed by the Rational Dress Society, who in 1885 had awarded a prize for a 'Ladies' Cycling Costume' to Lydia Becker's dressmaker (see Object 2). Taking a political turn, in 1895 the cycling craze was harnessed to the Labour movement with the formation of the Clarion Cycling Club, among whose early members were Christabel and Sylvia Pankhurst.[2] By 1907 women were so much part of the cycling scene that Mrs Rose Lamartine Yates was elected to the council of another organization, the Cycling Touring Club; the following year she became a leading member of the Wimbledon WSPU.

By the summer of 1907 bicycles had been adopted as vehicles of propaganda. For the WSPU Mrs Flora Drummond organized a brigade of 'Suffragette Scouts' to meet each week in Sloane Square, Chelsea and cycle to an outer suburb, such as Harrow, Redhill, Woolwich and Wimbledon, while a few months later the Women's Freedom League (WFL) stressed that, as their funds were so limited, they relied on volunteers with bicycles to campaign for them at by-elections.[3] It is their WSPU counterparts that we see in Object 32, cycling down Court Street, Faversham, in support of the Unionist candidate, Granville Wheler, during the December 1910 general election. His opponent was a left-leaning Liberal, George Nicholls, but, as it was WSPU policy to oppose the Liberal, government, candidate, the cyclists are displaying 'Wheler' placards. Wheler was elected, although with a reduced majority.

It is possible that among that array of bicycles in Court Street could have been one of the special 'Votes for Women' bicycles, 'enamelled in the well-known Elswick Green, lined in the colours of the Union – mauve, emerald, and white, the gear-case bearing the medallion of Freedom'.[4] They were made by the Elswick Company, which had shown a prototype at the May 1909 Women's Exhibition. Although it was stated that the WSPU would receive a commission from sales, the price of ten guineas compared unfavourably with that of five guineas for a regular bicycle. Research indicates that the 'Votes for Women' Elswicks may have been slow to sell, all mention of them dropping from *Votes for Women* after September 1910.

In the following four years, the use of the bicycle was advocated ever more urgently by all suffrage societies as a means of spreading their propaganda and selling their newspapers. Holiday campaigns were organized around cycling tours, the WSPU supplying 'colours' for attaching to bicycles. As *Votes for Women* reported, 'The decorated bicycle seems to play an important part in the Holiday Campaign this year', noting, at Keswick 'Miss Crook rides about on a decorated bicycle and sells many papers in that way to both villagers and to tourists'.[5] In early 1914, in the aftermath of their 1913 Pilgrimage, which had featured many bicyclists, the National Union of Women's Suffrage Societies (NUWSS) formed an Active Service League to undertake 'Saturday Afternoon Tramps and Bicycling Parties to villages and hamlets' to raise funds by selling *The Common Cause*, distribute suffrage literature and attract new members to the Friends of Women's Suffrage scheme (see Object 74).[6] The latter, a concomitant of the setting up by the NUWSS of the 1912 Election Fighting Fund in support of the Labour party, was aimed at working-class women.

However, the bicycle was a means not only of peaceful propaganda, as shown in Object 32, but was implicated in many acts of suffrage militancy, such as providing the means for Ethel Moorhead's escape after attempting to set fire to Burns' cottage at Alloway in July 1914. In

March 1912 Olive Hockin, suspected of setting fire to Roehampton Golf Club, attempted to escape on a bicycle as the police were uncovering the 'suffragette arsenal' in her London flat. However, it was difficult to regard a bicycle, even in the hands of a convicted suffragette, as other than benign and it may have been with the same machine that the following year, after four months in Holloway, Hockin took second prize in the 'Decorated Bicycle' competition at a Berkshire fair. Her decoration was 'a suffragette arrangement' that 'came in for some good-humoured banter'.[7]

Object 33

The car and the suffrage movement

Object 33 is a photograph of the Women's Social and Political Union (WSPU) car, driven by Vera Holme in her chauffeur's uniform. Photographer, date and location **unknown.** (7VJH/5/2/03, The Women's Library collection, London School of Economics and Political Science.)

In 1895, when bicycles were all the rage, they were competing with no more than fifteen motor cars for space on Britain's roads. By 1905, as the suffrage campaign gathered pace, the number of cars had increased to around 700, one of which was owned by the Lancashire and Cheshire Women Textile and Other Workers' Representation Committee (see Object 20), purchased with funds given by, among others, the National Union of Women's Suffrage Societies (NUWSS). Its purpose was to take the suffrage campaign into towns and villages around Lancashire and Cheshire, but it was also used on the night of 20 October to take Christabel Pankhurst and Annie Kenney to the Free Trade Hall, Manchester, to celebrate their release from prison (see Object 19). Over the next few years cars became increasingly important as, decorated with flags and placards, they transported both constitutional and militant suffrage campaigners to all manner of meetings, being especially in demand at general and by-elections.

Naturally, as cars were expensive, ownership was confined to the wealthier members of suffrage societies. Thus, when the Women's Social and Political Union (WSPU) acquired Emmeline Pethick-Lawrence as treasurer in early 1906, she came with her car and Mr Rapley, her chauffeur. Soon nicknamed 'La Suffragette', the car was used to campaign in London in June 1906 when Emmeline Pethick-Lawrence, Annie Kenney, Mrs Pankhurst and Mrs Baldock, accompanied by Alderman Sanderson, secretary of the London Independent Labour party (ILP), and 'luncheon', drove 'with the aid of this fast-travelling vehicle to a large number of ILP meetings in various parts of the Metropolis, at each of which one or more of the visitors made a brief speech and submitted a resolution'.[1]

Three years later, in May 1909, the car shown in Object 33 was presented to Emmeline Pethick-Lawrence by the WSPU to mark the end of her prison sentence. It was a fifteen-h-p Austin, painted and upholstered in the 'colours', with white wheels and a green body lined with a narrow purple stripe. Costing over £400, it was supplied by Messrs Paddon and Sopwith of 1 Albemarle Street, Mayfair, had a landaulette body 'of superior taxicab type, fitted with a front extension and wind screen, combination Stepney wheel, Lucas lamps, pump, horn, etc, the tyres Continental steel armoured, non skid'.[2] It also carried an 'Automobile Association' badge and two WSPU flags, a small pennant on the bonnet and a larger one at the back. The car's registration number was W.S. 95, with 'W.S.' standing, presumably, for 'Women's Suffrage'. As, at the time, those letters were registered to Leith, this may be considered an early 'personalized' number plate. The car was paid for by donation and set to work immediately, driven around London advertising the WSPU Women's Exhibition. Mrs Pethick-Lawrence dedicated the car to the general use of the WSPU and in August Vera Holme drove Mrs Pankhurst to Scotland for a lecture tour.

Holme was succeeded as a, self-described, 'lady chaffeuse' by Aileen Preston, the first woman to qualify for the AA Certificate for Driving. She, too, drove Mrs Pankhurst to Scotland, but this time in a Wolseley, given to the WSPU by Mary Dodge, heiress to a US copper-mining fortune. In a radio interview Preston describes what it was like to drive the WSPU leader and her associates, together with vast quantities of suffrage literature, over untarmacked roads during the hot summer of 1911.[3] It was nothing to experience several punctures daily and there was always the danger the low-slung petrol tank would rupture, caught by a stone on the rural roads, or that the brakes, which worked directly onto the tyres, would cause a blow-out while driving down a steep hill. With garages few and far between, the 'lady chauffeuse' had to be resourceful, with nerves of steel, while helping to spread the suffrage message.

A supporter who owned a car was treasured by the foot soldiers of the suffrage campaign. While organizing meetings for the New Constitutional Society, Kate Frye never fails to record in her diary the blessing of a lift in a motor. For instance, during that hot summer of 1911, after an exceptionally trying day in Hatfield Peverel, Essex, with the Chappelows, a very militant mother and daughter ('Good kind people but so peculiar and so unwashed. Very emancipated – no servant and lots of animals not very fresh and all kinds of weird theories'), she was relieved to be rescued at the end of the evening by Mrs Sadd Brown, her hostess, who motored her home, noting 'A wonderful ride through the hot night'.[4]

By 1928, when all women received the right to vote, there were more than a million cars in Britain, although inequality in income ensured that women owners were in a minority. But, as a signifier of emancipation, to mark the passing of the Equal Franchise Act the National Societies for Equal Citizenship chose to reproduce as a postcard a photograph of Ray Strachey at the wheel of her open-topped car, with Millicent Fawcett in the passenger seat and Philippa Fawcett and Agnes Garrett in the back (see Object 91).

Object 34

The caravan and the suffrage movement

Object 34 is a photograph of the horse-drawn caravan in which Ray Costelloe and friends travelled from the Scottish Borders to Oxford in the summer of 1908, campaigning for the vote. Location unknown. The photographer was presumably one of the caravanners. (7BSH/5/2/04, The Women's Library collection, London School of Economics and Political Science.)

In the early twentieth century, although less ancient forms of locomotion, such as trains, bicycles and cars, were available, suffrage campaigners were still happy to employ the horse to carry their message around the country. Political caravanning was already well established, the Independent Labour Party having introduced their Clarion Van in 1896, and in 1908 members of both the National Union of Women's Suffrage Societies (NUWSS) and the Women's Freedom League (WFL) hitched horses to their vans and sallied forth. 'Caravanning', along with 'tramping' or rambling, and bicycling, was an aspect of open-air culture favoured by a section of the Edwardian middle class.

Object 34 shows the NUWSS caravan in which Ray Costelloe (later Strachey), Elinor Rendel and friends from Newnham College travelled from Beattock in southern Scotland to Oxford, holding meetings along the way. Rendel recorded, 'The van is a great attraction, and helps us to collect our audiences. It gets much admiration and attention, and when it is covered with posters and planted in the middle of a market-place it is a really wonderful sight. We speak from the front which is a very good platform.'[1] The poster decorating the caravan is 'They Have a Cheek', by Emily Ford. As Ray Costelloe wrote of the caravan tour, 'It really is the greatest possible fun and the least possible bother. Our horse stands like a stone, and our house is large and roomy'.[2] The caravan has been identified as 'Curlew', lent by Louisa Lumsden, a Scottish suffragist, together with a big grey horse, 'Jock', driven by a Scotsman. Some of their meetings attracted very large crowds; in Derby marketplace 'over 1,000 people came to hear'. 'While one answered questions, the others went round collecting money in a hat, distributing pamphlets, selling postcards and badges, and exchanging remarks. We always had a good collection, and we sold a great number of brooches.'[3]

In May the WFL had launched their new purpose-built caravan around Surrey and Sussex, hitched to a horse named 'Asquith'. The van had 'Women's Freedom League', 'Votes for Women' and 'Women's Suffrage' painted on its sides; there was no mistaking its message. Muriel Matters and Mrs Lilian Hicks were in charge for the first three months, succeeded in August by Mrs Charlotte Despard. In subsequent summers that caravan toured other parts of England.

Caravans also played their part in the 1911 census boycott, a civil disobedience campaign that encouraged women to withhold their details from the government. From a Paddington firm, Rickards, Arthur Marshall, the WSPU's solicitor, with his wife, Kitty, and nine others, rented what were described as 'smart Pullman caravans'. These horse-drawn caravans were then driven in the dark from Paddington, into and round Trafalgar Square, where the main suffragette protest was taking place, and then down Whitehall and out to the west, eventually coming to a halt on Putney Common. Having evaded census enumerators at their home addresses, the WSPU members refused all information to the police who turned up to take their particulars. In the morning, they decorated their caravans with placards stating, 'If we don't count we shall not be counted.' and, thus adorned, travelled back into London. It was a novel protest, one among many.

Caravans were used again by the NUWSS in 1913, as an adjunct to their Pilgrimage (see Object 74). For instance, the Oldham Women's Suffrage Society deployed at least one caravan on their journey, although it was not always possible to find a suitable pitch in a town and when parked at Thame attracted an irate mob. There had also been a difficulty further north at Buglawton, where it could not get down the lane to honour Elizabeth Wolstenholme Elmy (see Object 15), as had been intended. Once in London the horses were put on a train at St Pancras to travel back to Oldham.

Although in its earlier years the WSPU appears to have been less keen on caravanning than the other societies, by 1913, as part of its fund-raising Holiday Campaign, it launched two caravan tours, one in the Lake District and another band of 'Gypsy Wanderers' to 'spread the knowledge of our splendid paper, *The Suffragette*, through the highways and byways of Kent'.[4] One August night eight WSPU members dressed as gypsies climbed in an odd-decorated cart and made seats for ourselves on our bundles of luggage and provisions. The crowd collected outside Lincoln's Inn House and made a way for us as the gypsy queen took her seat in front and we flicked the old horse up. We had commenced our journey from the Kingsway to carry our message to the women of Kent.[5]

As had the WFL caravanners in 1908, these WSPU 'gypsies' named their horse 'Asquith'. *The Suffragette*, 7 August 1914, suggested that, following the success of the previous year, a 'Gypsy Caravan' tour might be staged 'this August'.[6] But by then Britain was at war and there was to be no more suffrage caravanning.

Object 35

Suffrage offices

Object 35 is a photographic postcard of one of the WSPU offices at 4 Clement's Inn, Holborn, 1910.[1] (TWL.2002.479, The Women's Library collection, London School of Economics and Political Science.)

Of all the offices from which the long suffrage campaign was conducted, it was those of the Women's Social and Political Union (WSPU) that are now most well-known. For, recognizing they would draw their members closer by allowing them to see behind the scenes, in *Votes for Women* the Pethick-Lawrences published photographs such as Object 35, showing 'the editorial staff in the main editorial office' in which 'the large table in the foreground plays an important part in "making up" the paper, each page having a special place on the table'.[2] More photographs were taken in other WSPU offices at 4 Clement's Inn, including ones of Emmeline and Christabel Pankhurst at work in their respective rooms. Also reproduced as postcards, every image rewards a careful study, noting the work being done and the photographs, posters and personal items on display.

The Pethick-Lawrences ensured that all equipment necessary for a modern office was available; one Japanese visitor particularly mentioned 'the large telegraph exchanging-box at the entrance', operated by two very young women. As Christabel Pankhurst exclaimed, 'You see, everything is done by women here.'[3] H.G. Wells, a frequent visitor to the Fabian Society office at 3 Clement's Inn, had surely the WSPU offices in mind when, in his 1909 novel *Ann Veronica*, he furnished the Woman's Bond of Freedom office with 'notice boards bearing clusters of newspaper slips, three or four posters of monster meetings and a series of announcements in purple copying ink, and in one corner a pile of banners'.[4] Here, in Object 35, we can see two posters on the walls and in the window embrasure a banner proclaiming 'Fiat Justitia' ('Let There Be Justice'), a relic of the 23 July 1910 WSPU procession.

These scenes are far removed from those in which the suffrage campaign was conducted in its early years. It was then mainly confined to the 'private sphere', operating out of the homes of its honorary secretaries, their only business equipment being notepaper headed with the society's name. It was only Lydia Becker who chose to rent an office, first in Manchester and then in 1871 in London for the Central Committee. The latter office was at 9 Berners Street, north of Oxford Street, in a 'feminine' area, close to shops, dressmakers and a growing number of women's clubs. It was not until 1885 that the Central Committee moved into the male preserve of Westminster, where its successors, the National Union of Women's Suffrage Societies (NUWSS) and the National Union of Societies for Equal Citizenship, remained for the rest of the campaign, albeit in a succession of different offices. That at 22 Great Smith Street, where from 1910 to 1918 the NUWSS was based, is now marked with an English Heritage Blue Plaque.

The WSPU had settled in Clement's Inn because it was offered a home there by the Pethick-Lawrences (see Object 23) and, being so close to the newspaper world of Fleet Street, it proved an ideal position for their type of campaign. After the 1912 break between the Pankhursts and the Pethick-Lawrences (see Object 57), the WSPU moved close by, as first tenants of a monumental new building in Kingsway, designed, by Edwin Lutyens, to impress.

After separating from the WSPU (see Object 24) in 1908 the Women's Freedom League took an office at 1 Robert Street, Adelphi, their presence there also now commemorated by a Blue Plaque. Here they remained until 1915 before relocating to Holborn. Some other smaller suffrage societies were also based in the Adelphi area, south of the Strand, midway between Westminster and Fleet Street. All these societies were operating in 'business' areas, unlike the New Constitutional Society for Women's Suffrage which, when it was formed in 1910, opened its office at Park Mansions Arcade, between Knightsbridge and Brompton Road, a distinctly 'shopping' area, a milieu appropriate to its membership (see Object 69).

As the suffrage campaign gathered momentum in the years before the First World War, although many local societies did continue to be run from the homes of their honorary secretaries, the main societies opened offices in Britain's cities and provincial towns, in some cases incorporating a 'shop' section (see Object 49). The commercial reality of renting office space can be traced through the accounts that most suffrage societies published in their Annual Reports (see Object 7). But neither in London nor in the rest of the country did any other society reveal its working life so openly as did the WSPU in images such as Object 35. As the Pethick-Lawrences perceived in 1910, the possibility of peeking behind the scenes is ever an attractive prospect, proved by the popularity of this series of photographic postcards with collectors today.

Object 36

Women's Freedom League 'Proclamation' banner, 1908

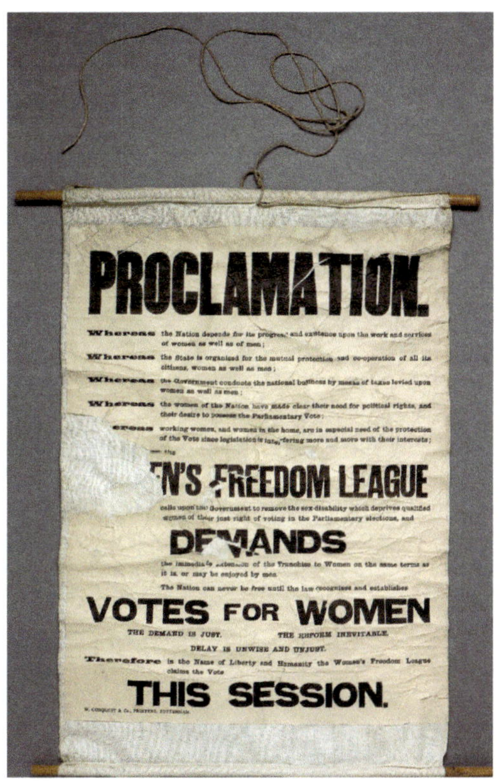

Object 36 is the banner dropped into the chamber of the House of Commons from the Ladies' Gallery by members of the Women's Freedom League (WFL) on 28 October 1908. (Parliamentary Archives, London, HC/SA/SJ/3/1.)

Very soon after moving into their office on the first floor of 1 Robert Street in September 1908 the WFL, still barely a year old, put into effect a campaign that resulted in the 'Grille Protest'. To mark the opening of the new session of Parliament on 12 October, Teresa Billington-Greig had composed a 'Proclamation', setting out why the 'Women's Freedom League Demands Votes for Women'. The text was printed in large black type on a white poster, gummed on the reverse and requiring only a wipe with a wet sponge to adhere to the chosen surface. Then, in the early hours of Monday 12 October, members of the WFL 'set out on foot and on bicycles, and stealthily placarded Cabinet Ministers' houses, several public buildings, and even the House of Commons, with a "proclamation" demanding the immediate extension of the parliamentary franchise to women'. [1] At the same time other members of the WFL posted the 'proclamation' on public buildings throughout England and Scotland. 'In all over 5,000 "proclamations" were posted, close upon 1,000 members of the League being engaged in the work.'[2]

The fragile posters were easily torn down by the authorities but not before the London News Agency, presumably alerted by the WFL, had photographed two young women, Barbara Duval and Helen Fox, pasting the 'Proclamations' onto Cleopatra's Needle, Gatti's restaurant in the Strand and the offices of the Metropolitan Police. At least one poster was retained by the WFL and pasted onto cloth that at the top and bottom was sewn around bamboo sticks to create a banner. On the evening of 28 October this banner was taken into the Ladies' Gallery of the House of Commons by Muriel Matters, Helen Fox and Violet Tillard. A 'Gallery protest' had been mooted by the WFL as early as May 1908; this was the night. While other demonstrations took place, from men in the public gallery and from women in St Stephen's Hall, at 8.30 pm Matters and Fox chained themselves to separate sections of the grille of the Ladies' Gallery and Tillard lowered the banner down on strings into the House of Commons chamber. For decades women had reviled the brass grille which ran the length of the Gallery, set within stone gothic arches and divided into eighteen sections. Offering women only a limited view of the proceedings on the floor of the House, it was a symbol of women's exclusion and a site ripe for protest.

Matters and Fox had worn 'long, dark cloaks, which concealed wound round their waists a long and heavy chain. To these chains were attached spring padlocks, and the ladies made their way to the front seats close to the Grille, to which latter they attached the padlocks'.[3] While one shouted, 'we have listened behind this insulting Grille too long; get to the women's question', the other exclaimed, 'We women demand the vote'. 'Seizing hold of the two sections of the grille to which the women were chained, the attendants attempted to wrench them from their fastenings. With additional force the metal-work was loosened, and finally broken away from its stone casement.'[4] Fox and Matters were removed to a committee room, while 'attendants marched behind carrying the broken pieces of the grille and the chains, which were still locked around the women's waists'. The chains were filed off and Fox and Matters ejected from the House. 'But they immediately went to another entrance, and tried to push their way in again, with the result that Miss Matters – who is an Australian – was arrested.' [5] Fox 'was delighted when they wrenched away two pieces of the grille, each as big as a door. We never thought they would really break the absurd old grille, and when I got back and told Mrs Billington Greig she danced for joy'.[6]

The Protest was widely reported in the press, the combination of young women, heavy chains and the 'insulting grille' lending itself to vivid descriptions of the scene. The immediate result was that for several months both the Ladies' and the Strangers' Gallery were closed to visitors and Matters, and other women arrested at the House of Commons that evening, spent a month in prison.

The grille remained in place until in August 1917, at a time when the Representation of the People Act was passing through Parliament, it was removed after a petition from the London Society for Women's Suffrage. One section was given to the London Museum, much of the remainder placed in windows around the Central Lobby in the Palace of Westminster with, in 2010, one section lent to the South Australian Parliament to honour Muriel Matters.[7] For a short time on 28 October 1908 the 'Proclamation Banner' hung from the grille, but was then removed and lay forgotten in the Serjeant at Arms' department until rediscovered in the 1990s. It is now one of the objects listed in the UNESCO Memory of the World UK Register.[8]

Object 37

Bow Street Police Court, 1908

Object 37 is Bow Street Police Court, photographed during the October 1908 trial of (from the left) Christabel Pankhurst, Mrs Flora Drummond and Mrs Emmeline Pankhurst. (7JCC/0/02/060, The Women's Library collection, London School of Economics and Political Science.)

Bow Street Police Court, Covent Garden, London, was the scene of numerous suffragette trials, one of which, recorded in this photograph, took place shortly before the 'Grille Protest' (see Object 36). The three leaders of the Women's Social and Political Union (WSPU) were in the Bow Street dock in consequence of speeches they had made at a WSPU rally in Trafalgar Square on the afternoon of Sunday 11 October, a few hours before members of the Women's Freedom League (WFL) placarded London with their 'Proclamation' posters. Incensed to learn from Prime Minister Asquith that no time would be given in the new session of Parliament to H.Y. Stanger's women's suffrage bill that had passed its Second Reading in February, both the WFL and the WSPU decided to focus their attention directly on Parliament.

Warned that the WSPU planned to hold a demonstration at Westminster on 13 October, the day after the opening of Parliament, Superintendent Wells of the Metropolitan Police paid a couple of visits to Clement's Inn. On the second occasion, on 3 October, Christabel showed him the wording of a handbill inviting the public to 'rush' the House of Commons alongside members of the WSPU. She explained that, because Parliament would not consider a bill for women's enfranchisement, they intended to force their way into the building to make their case. Despite Wells' cautions, the 'Rush' handbills, some printed on green and some on purple paper, were handed out at the Trafalgar Square meeting, resulting in Drummond and the two Pankhursts being summonsed to appear at Bow Street Court the following day, charged with causing a breach of the peace. The women ignored the summonses and, instead, attended a WSPU meeting, informing the police they would be available for arrest in Clement's Inn at 6 pm the next day, the 13th. This baiting of the authorities maximized both publicity and donations. The WSPU ensured that a press photographer, Arthur Barrett, was in the office to record Inspector Jarvis arresting the three women, an image they, within a week, reproduced as a postcard.[1] With the women confined overnight in police cells, Emmeline Pethick-Lawrence conducted the meeting in Caxton Hall, Westminster, sending a deputation to the House of Commons through throngs of supporters, onlookers and more than 5,000 police.

The following morning Bow Street Court was 'besieged by crowds of men and women, most of the latter being members of the WSPU. Nearly everyone in the crowd wore the colours of the union in various forms – scarves, hat-bands, ties, rosettes, etc, together with "Votes for Women" brooches'.[2] Although other suffragettes, arrested the previous evening, were also to be tried, the case of the Pankhursts and Drummond was the first heard and Object 37 shows this scene, one of several images taken from different angles. It is likely the work of Arthur Barrett, one of whose photographs, taken that day, notes on the reverse that it was 'taken by small camera hidden inside a top hat fitted with a flap to allow the lens to see the picture'.[3] Although discouraged, it was only after 1925 that it became illegal to sketch or photograph inside a courtroom.

Even in a black-and-white photograph it is not difficult to visualize the purple, white and green of the cockade in Emmeline's hat and of Christabel's belt (just seen). In another of the images Christabel is clearly wearing the WSPU necktie she sported for her arrest the previous evening and doubtless other signifiers of loyalty adorned the dress of supporters in the court. Frederick Pethick-Lawrence is clearly recognizable sitting in the front row behind the dock.

For this first hearing and the subsequent trial on Saturday 24 October, Christabel conducted the case for the defence, cross-examining as witnesses two Cabinet ministers, Lloyd George and Herbert Gladstone. From a sympathetic press she earned the soubriquet 'Portia', the spectacle of a woman acting in a legal capacity being most unusual. Courtrooms were male spaces. The women were, however, all found guilty, choosing imprisonment rather than paying the imposed fine. Emmeline Pankhurst and Flora Drummond were sentenced to three months' imprisonment, Christabel to ten weeks'.

The WSPU took every advantage of this publicity, raising £3,000 at a rally a few days later and publishing within a couple of weeks *The Trial of the Suffragette Leaders,* a pamphlet containing Christabel's examination of witnesses and the final speeches from the dock. Bow Street Court became familiar territory to the hundreds of suffragettes who stood in its dock over the next six years, although it was more usual for them to be photographed outside the building, waiting for their trial, than inside the courtroom itself. That was an honour reserved in the future by the undercover press photographer for only a few.[4] Christabel was careful never to face trial again.

Closed in 2006, Bow Street Police Court and part of its adjoining police station have been converted into a hotel, the Courtroom now the Ballroom. Another section of the police station now houses the Bow Street Police Museum.[5]

Object 38

Photograph of women wearing replica prison dress, 1908

Object 38 is a photograph of women wearing replica prison dress during the Chelmsford by-election, November/December 1908. Exact location and photographer unknown. (TWL.2009.01.4, The Women's Library collection, London School of Economics and Political Science.)

While Christabel and Emmeline Pankhurst remained in Holloway after sentencing on 24 October 1908, Mrs Flora Drummond was soon released; she was three months' pregnant but miscarried.[1] However, in late November she returned to the fray, leading the Women's Social and Political Union (WSPU) campaign at the Mid-Essex by-election, for which polling day was Tuesday 1 December. WSPU by-election policy was to campaign against the return of all Liberal candidates, even though, as in Mid-Essex, he had declared he would, if elected, vote for the inclusion of women in any Reform Bill. The local newspaper approached WSPU headquarters for an explanation of this policy, reporting, 'They are at war with the Liberal Government because the Liberal Government is at war with them, and persistently refuses to listen to and deal with their claims for enfranchisement.'[2]

With their leaders, and many followers, in prison, WSPU members drew public attention to their predicament by demonstrating while wearing replica prison garb. The precedent had been set by crusading journalist W.T. Stead, an active supporter of the WSPU. Each year since 1885, by donning his prison uniform, he had commemorated the anniversary of the conviction he received in consequence of his intrepid investigative reporting into child prostitution. Similarly, the WSPU recognized that by publicly flaunting prison dress they transformed what might be considered a badge of shame into one of honour. It seems likely that in October/November 1908 a band of seamstresses produced these garments, described as 'coarse green prison dress of the second division, sprinkled with broad arrows, and smart white caps'.[3] Wearers then pinned to the front of the dress a large, round leather badge bearing a prison cell number. Thus robed, on 7 November some ex-prisoners had taken part in a procession to Holloway to demand that the Pankhursts be treated as political prisoners. This demonstration had little effect, but Sylvia Pankhurst declared that within two days of the 20 November announcement of the Mid-Essex by-election, the Home Office had relaxed its treatment of Mrs Pankhurst, the implication being it was worried about the effect of the WSPU campaign. Pankhurst had been denied visitors and had been held in solitary confinement but was now allowed an hour a day exercise and conversation with Christabel, her fellow prisoner.[4]

It is likely that Object 38 was photographed no earlier than the afternoon of Saturday 28 November because two of the women, Ada Flatman (back left) and Winifred Bray, had only that morning been released from Holloway, after serving their sentence for taking part in the 13 October Westminster affray (see Object 37). As they would have had no opportunity to make themselves the replica prison dress, it seems safe to assume they, and others, were able to borrow from a selection of ready-mades, just as prisoners had to take from the prison store any garment that approximated their size and shape. Of the other five women, Flora Drummond (front centre), Maud Joachim (front left) and Amelia Kern had been imprisoned during 1908, and Mary Keegan was to be in 1909. Only Elsa Gye, a long-term WSPU organizer, escaped ever being incarcerated.[5] For the 28 November demonstration

> five motor buses were chartered to take several parties of Suffragettes through the constituency. The first was an electric car and started from Chelmsford carrying among its freight ten of the released prisoners in prison dress and an excellent band – that of the Mid-Essex Prize Band. The other four started at various times from Kingsway. This new method of 'invading' the constituency was received with no small favour by the electors, and hearty cheers greeted the women wherever they went, the purple, white, and green lending colour and charm to the proceedings.[6]

Although the meetings held by the National Union of Women's Suffrage Society in the town came under attack, all reports indicate that the WSPU campaigners were well-received in Chelmsford. *The Standard* reported, 'They undoubtedly share the popularity of the town with the Tariff Reformers.'[7]

Replicas of prison dress and prison cells were employed by the WSPU on subsequent occasions, for instance, as a feature at the May 1909 Women's Exhibition (see Object 43), with Elsie Howey posing as a 'prisoner'.[8] Christabel and Emmeline Pankhurst, Annie Kenney and

Charlotte Marsh are among those who modelled for the camera in prison costume, while a Women's Freedom League (WFL) member, Mrs Borrmann Wells, who had served a Holloway sentence, donned the garb to be photographed scrubbing a 'cell' floor. As 'A Suffragette at Work in Prison', the image was published as a WFL fund-raising postcard. Although W.T. Stead's prison uniform is preserved, believed to be the one originally handed to him in 1885, the suffragettes' replica prison dresses are no more, memorialized only in photographs.

Object 39

Record of a speech made by Christabel Pankhurst, 1908

Object 39 is a record of a speech made by Christabel Pankhurst for the Gramophone Company in December 1908. (Image courtesy of Forum Auctions.)

On orders from the Home Office, Emmeline and Christabel Pankhurst were released from Holloway on the evening of Saturday 19 December 1908, shortly before the end of the full term of the sentences given them at Bow Street Court on 24 October (see Object 37). On regaining her freedom one of Christabel's first engagements was at 21 City Road, Islington, the recording studio of the Gramophone Company Ltd, founded in 1898 by an agent for Emil Berliner, the inventor of the gramophone record. The label of the 12-inch 78rpm shellac record states it 'was made within a few hours of her release from Holloway', suggesting it was possibly recorded on Monday 21 December, it being unlikely the studio was working on the Sunday. Such a speedy appointment also indicates that arrangements for the recording were likely to have been made while Christabel was still in Holloway, giving her plenty of time to compose her speech.

In this she hammers home, in three minutes and thirty seconds, all the obvious points. They are, to paraphrase: that women taxpayers had a right to the vote. That, as Parliament discussed matters important to women, they should have a say. That for forty years women had campaigned peacefully, now they had to bring pressure. That men got the vote not by persuading but by alarming the legislature. That the tactics of the WSPU are clearly thought out. That deputations involve arrest and imprisonment. That the Liberal government must be compelled to do justice. She ends by declaring, 'We are resolved that 1909 must and shall see the political enfranchisement of British women.' Christabel is clear and direct. This is the voice that, two months earlier, speaking from the Bow Court dock, cross-examined Lloyd George and Herbert Gladstone.

In 1909 the majority of the Gramophone Company's products were musical, Harry Lauder and Enrico Caruso being among Christabel's fellow artistes, and it is rather surprising that this speech recording appears to have gone unmentioned in the press, not even advertised in *Votes for Women*. But it was not forgotten and was re-released in 1925, when *The Woman's Leader* commented:

> There was a time when one might have prophesied that Christabel Pankhurst, with her youth, her shrewd wit, and her fierce energy would have contributed something to that post-suffrage phase of feminism which she did so much to bring into being. Nevertheless, in hearing again that familiar voice, and visualizing imaginatively those familiar gestures, how vividly should we be reminded of the magnitude of our stride in 1918.[1]

Excerpts from the recording were included in the BBC's 'Scrapbook for 1909', broadcast on 7 February 1939, which also included 'live' interviews with Inspector Jarvis and Muriel Matters. In 1959 the record was played at a party to celebrate the unveiling of the memorial to Christabel that had been added to Emmeline Pankhurst's statue. A reporter present described hearing the 'voice from the past declaring crisply and decisively: "Imprisonment will not deter the women of this country from getting the vote … "' as the 'elderly ex-suffragettes nodded approvingly'.[2]

Research indicates that recordings were made by other suffrage activists, although none appear to have survived. For, eighteen months before Christabel recorded her speech, Women's Freedom League (WFL) leaders, including Mrs Charlotte Despard, Lady Grove and Mrs Billington-Greig, had made Pathéphone recordings that were for sale, 1d each, at the WFL Fair at Caxton Hall, 31 March–1 April 1908.[3] At the eventual conclusion of the suffrage campaign, for the 1929 'Flapper Election' (see Object 94), the Columbia Graphophone Company produced recordings made by three women MPs, the Duchess of Atholl speaking for the Conservatives, Mrs Wintringham for the Liberals and Margaret Bondfield for Labour. Newspapers reported a 'phenomenal demand' for the records, deducing that 'undoubtedly the flapper is keenly aware of her new power'.[4] In 1947, Emmeline and Frederick Pethick-Lawrence were recorded together, reminiscing about the suffrage campaign for a disc made for the Suffragette Fellowship by Gui de Buire, a private studio in New Bond Street, London.

Although we can listen to the Emmeline Pethick-Lawrence recording and to an excellent series of interviews with a wide range of suffrage campaigners made by Professor Sir Brian Harrison in the 1970s–80s, when recorded all these speakers were elderly.[5] But, thanks to Object 39, we can hear the voice of Christabel as it sounded when she was at the peak of her powers, although originals of the record only very occasionally appear on the market.[6]

Object 40

Tea rooms and the suffrage movement

Alan's Tea Rooms,
263, OXFORD STREET (near JAY'S).
LUNCHEONS, 1/-, 1/6.   TEAS, 6D., 1/-
OPEN ON SUNDAYS, 4 to 6 p.m.

Object 40 is an advertisement for Alan's Tea Rooms, *The Vote*, 2 December 1909, 62. (JK1880, Women's Library collection, London School of Economics and Political Science.)

In the nineteenth century, although women could attend suffrage meetings in the public halls of Britain's towns or, if of the right sort, could attend 'drawing-room' meetings in the houses of the better-off, it was difficult to meet informally outside the home, the coffee houses, chop houses, ale houses and public houses that enabled men to congregate, do business and eat and drink being socially barred to respectable women. When it did become acceptable for middle-class women to move around independently outside the home, one practical, material element that facilitated this freedom was a new type of business, the café, tea room or restaurant suitable for women to visit, either alone or in company, where their presence was not seen as an invitation to molestation, where they could eat and drink and, most importantly, use the lavatory, without breaking any social taboos.[1]

While chains of cafés, such as the ABC, founded in the 1880s, and Lyons in 1894, catered for upper-working-class and lower-middle-class women, the first decade of the twentieth century saw a proliferation of tea rooms aimed at a more middle- and upper-middle-class female clientele, often run by women of that class who, although they may have had no training in anything other than 'home responsibilities', now seized the opportunity of running a business.

'Alan's Tea Rooms' was one of the tea rooms that advertised regularly in the suffrage press, offering not only refreshments but also rooms that could be hired for meetings. The owner was not a man, as the business name might lead one to expect, but Marguerite Alan Liddle, daughter of a Shropshire solicitor, who had opened her Tea Rooms in November 1907 in a building on the south side of London's Oxford Street, slightly to the west of Oxford Circus and, as stressed in advertisements, 'three doors away from Jays', a large fashion store. It was described as

> the cosiest and prettiest of snuggeries for lunch or tea, just like a club, with its quaint oak-settled dining-room and its dainty smoking-room, prettily-appointed dressing-room and handy little writing-room adjoining, with telephone. Its dining-room, with the parquet floor, oak settles, brown wainscot and casement curtains suggests a country-house parlour. The 'ladies in waiting' wear sweet blue linen frocks, and the china, silver and glass and beaten copper coffee trays are all bright and shining.[2]

As a business, 'Alan's' was centrally placed but on the first floor, which, with so much competition nearby, was a disadvantage. Recognizing this, Liddle may have considered it necessary to carve out a niche market, over and above passing trade, appealing to suffrage sympathizers by advertising regularly in *The Vote, Women's Franchise* and *Votes for Women*, always mentioning that a private room was available for hire, free of charge to members of the Women's Social and Political Union (WSPU).[3] She did not advertise in journals of more general interest. Although there is no evidence that Liddle was a member of the WSPU, her sister, Helen Gordon Liddle, was the author of *The Prisoner*, which, describing a month in 1909 spent in Strangeways prison, Manchester, is one of the more sought-after WSPU memoirs.

The room for hire, a glass-roofed studio a floor above the tea room, was where, every Saturday in 1909 the Young Hot Bloods, a group of younger members of the WSPU, met; where the London WFL held its first meeting of the autumn season in 1909; where, in October 1909, members of the Church of England founded the Church League for Women's Suffrage (see Object 76); where in November 1910 the Tax Resistance League (see Object 70) held its first members' conference; where the Catholic Women's Suffrage Society held its inaugural meeting in March 1911 and where, *c.*1912, the Forward Cymric Union, a militant Welsh suffrage society, held monthly meetings. Although visits of individual women to 'Alan's Tea Rooms' are more elusive to pinpoint, we do know that Marjory Lees and her companions dined there in July 1913 at the end of their National Union of Women's Suffrage Societies' Pilgrimage (see Object 74). 'Alan's Tea Rooms' remained in business until *c.*1916, closing only when Liddle offered her services as a cook to the British Committee of the French Red Cross.

Some other London tea rooms and restaurants, for instance, the Gardenia, the Tea-Cup Inn, the Eustace Miles (see Object 24) and the Criterion, were particularly favoured by suffrage campaigners, as were their equivalents in provincial towns. In Newcastle, Fenwick's was the chosen venue, in Nottingham, Morley's Cafe, in Glasgow, Miss Cranston's famous tea rooms, while in Edinburgh the Cafe Vegetaria was the choice of the local WFL. As the WSPU campaign became ever more desperate, tea rooms and restaurants occasionally became sites of protest, such as on 20 December 1913 when diners at the Eustace Miles listened to a suffragette delivering a long speech castigating the government's treatment of suffragette prisoners, while her companion distributed leaflets.

Although 'Alan's' and the other tea rooms are long defunct, by researching in newspapers and company files it is possible to recreate the materiality, the fittings, style and menus, that appealed to suffrage sympathizers, while diaries of the period can reveal the lived experience.

Object 41

Suffrage medals

Object 41 (Left) The Women's Social and Political Union (WSPU) hunger-strike medal, given to WSPU prisoners who went on hunger strike. (Right) The Women's Freedom League (WFL) 'Holloway' brooch, a reward to imprisoned WFL members. (From the Collection of Dr Kenneth Florey. Photograph by Emilia van Beugen.)

The WFL was the first militant suffrage society to commemorate the imprisonment of its members by awarding them with an object to honour their experience. At a first ceremony, on 5 March 1908, Mrs Charlotte Despard presented ten newly released WFL prisoners with silver 'Holloway' brooches.[1] The brooch, the designer of which is unknown, takes the form of a stylized representation of Holloway prison and is inscribed on the reverse with the name of the recipient, in the case of Object 41 (right-hand image) that of Elsie Cummin, the daughter of a Sussex vicar. As relatively few WFL members were imprisoned, these brooches are very scarce.

It was over a year later that the WSPU rewarded imprisoned members with its 'Holloway brooch'. Designed by Sylvia Pankhurst and commissioned from Toye & Co., a London maker of regalia, it takes the shape of a portcullis, flanked on each side by a short, fine chain. This, the symbol of Parliament, has superimposed on it the broad arrow stamped on prisoners' outfits, signifying government property. It was made in silver, the arrow enamelled in purple, white and green. Unlike the WFL 'Holloway brooch', those of the WSPU do not carry the recipient's name. Contained in a small, hinged cardboard box, the lid striped in purple, white and green; they were first presented, together with an illuminated address, on 29 April 1909 at a WSPU meeting in the Albert Hall. Such ceremonies were perfect opportunities for raising emotion and funds; £800 was taken that day.[2] By then WSPU members had served 451 prison sentences, some more than one term, and the brooches, pinned to dress or blouse, can be spotted in many suffrage-related photographs. If every WSPU prisoner did receive a 'Holloway brooch', it might be expected they would now be more common than they are, but it is possible that in the past such a small piece of jewellery was disregarded on the death of its owner.

In April 1909 the WSPU referred to their 'Holloway brooch' as 'the Victoria Cross of the Union', that is, the highest honour for bravery they could bestow. However, the 'Holloway brooch' was soon superseded in the WSPU hierarchy of reward by the 'hunger-strike medal', also made by Toye & Co. During 1909 the form of the medal evolved, the first presentation of what was described as 'a commemorative medal' being held in London on 29 July.[3] The thirteen recipients had been tried at Bow Street Court (see Object 37) after taking part in a WSPU deputation on 29 June, had gone on hunger strike in Holloway, but were released without being forcibly fed. Two of these medals are known; on both the top bar is engraved 'For Valour' and the medallion with 'Holloway'.[4]

It was only at the next medal ceremony, held in Birmingham Town Hall in November 1909, that medals with 'Hunger Strike' engraved on one side of the roundel and the recipient's name on the other, and with 'Fed by Force', accompanied by a date, on a purple, white and green enamelled bar, were presented to WSPU ex-prisoners.[5] After protesting at a meeting held by Asquith in Birmingham, the recipients had gone on hunger strike in Winson Green prison and had then been the first suffragette prisoners to be forcibly fed. As with the earlier 'commemorative medal', the top bar of the 'hunger-strike' version is engraved 'For Valour'. Additional clasps would be added for further imprisonments and force feeding. Henceforward it was the 'hunger-strike medal', rather than the 'Holloway brooch' that the suffrage press referred to as the suffragettes' 'Victoria Cross'.

As seen in Object 41, the WSPU hunger-strike medal came in a purple case, lined with green velvet and personalized with details of the recipient, printed in gold on white silk inside the lid. Although very few of the little cardboard boxes that held the WSPU 'Holloway brooch' have survived, the brooches are often found, together with the owner's WSPU 'hunger-strike' medal, in this rather more impressive case. The medal and case in Object 41 had been presented to Lavender Guthrie, known as 'Laura Grey' in suffrage circles, imprisoned for taking part in the March 1912 window-smashing campaign. The purple, white and green enamel bar records she had been forcibly fed.

Adept at creating mementos of involvement in militancy, in July 1909 the WSPU presented stone-throwers arrested after the 29 June deputation with small brooches set with a sliver of flint. However, such items seem insignificant unless attached to a WSPU provenance and are now all but unknown.[6] Similarly, tiny (381mm) brooches in the shape of a hammer, engraved 'March 1912', were commissioned to reward the WSPU window smashers (see Object 63). They are now extremely scarce, their significance overlooked in the past and, being so small, easily lost.

The existence of the items shown as Object 41, besides providing their recipients with evidence of their society's appreciation, is also material evidence of the increasing harassment of the authorities by the WFL and WSPU. Unsurprisingly, the constitutional societies had no need to institute any similar system of rewards for their members.

Object 42

Postcard advertising the NUWSS 'Pageant of Women's Trades and Professions', April 1909

Object 42 is a postcard advertising a 'Pageant' and meeting held in the Albert Hall by the National Union of Women's Suffrage Societies (NUWSS) for delegates to the fifth congress of the International Woman Suffrage Alliance (IWSA), held in London, April/May 1909. (TWL.2000.33, Women's Library collection, London School of Economics and Political Science.)

The IWSA was formally constituted in 1904 to act as an international body to encourage the work of individual national suffrage societies. Among its co-founders was Millicent Fawcett, who was elected first vice-president of the organization during the fifth congress, held, at her invitation, in London in 1909. It was thought that the publicity engendered by this international gathering would help to bring public attention to the British suffrage campaign. Attended by women from twenty-one countries, the congress allowed both the constitutional and the militant wings of the British suffrage movement the opportunity of staging spectacular displays, even though the Women's Social and Political Union (WSPU) had in 1906 been refused membership of the IWSA on account of its militant policy. On 29 April the international delegates attending the WSPU meeting in the Albert Hall saw militancy lauded as the first 'Holloway brooches' were ceremoniously presented to those who had suffered imprisonment for the Cause (see Object 41).

The same delegates, sitting on the platform in the same hall, had two days previously watched an impressive 'Pageant of Women's Trades and Professions' organized by the London Society for Women's Suffrage (LSWS). Extolling the wide range of women's work and its contribution to the nation, the NUWSS indicated that its efforts towards enfranchisement would not be restricted to any one class. It was for the cover of the programme of this event that the portrait of Mary Wollstonecraft had been selected (see Object 16). A working writer, she was now internationally recognized and adopted as the foremother of the suffrage movement.

To advertise the Pageant, the LSWS produced Object 42, displaying the prices for seats in the Albert Hall and stressing that the society was 'Constitutional and Non-Party', finding it now necessary to distinguish it from the militants. Rather surprisingly the artist whose work the LSWS selected to decorate the postcard was not a member of the Artists' Suffrage League (ASL), with whom they were designing the Pageant, but David Wilson, the *Daily Chronicle* cartoonist whose image of the 'Haunted House' was closely identified with the WSPU (see Objects 27 and 28). For the postcard artwork he depicts the upward path of 'Constitutional Methods' along which the woman must travel to reach the 'Suffragists' Goal – Excelsior'. The LSWS Albert Hall meeting is marked as a waypoint and 'Misunderstandings' and 'Misrepresentations' have been cast aside. As the militant campaign was increasing in intensity, the NUWSS was keen to emphasize that their aim could be achieved by uniting behind a constitutional campaign.

In the evening of 29 April a thousand women walked through Knightsbridge in a lantern-lit procession to the Albert Hall, carrying devices indicating the nature of their work. These were made by the ASL and, although none has survived, many of the designs, ranging from 'Political Speakers' to 'Charwomen', can still be viewed in the Album of the ASL's founder, Mary Lowndes.[1] Of the evening, 31-year-old suffragist, Kate Frye (see Object 69), has left us an honest appraisal, writing in her diary,

> Had my commands given to me and then helped with odd jobs for the Committee and got my money bags, programmes etc and went on the Orchestra. I was so glad to be there – quite the nicest place amongst the delegates, who were most interesting, and I enjoyed the meeting. I made £1-9-6 selling programmes and took the collection later. The procession was the best part – 1,000 women of all kinds of Trades and Professions who came marching from Sloane Square carrying symbols of their craft designed by the Artists League. It was quite thrilling – but for them I must own the meeting was a little dull and there were a great many empty seats. Mrs Fawcett in the Chair, Mrs Chapman Catt, Miss Frances Sterling, that wonderful orator Mrs Philip Snowden, Dr Anna Shaw and Mr Ramsay McDonald M.P. spoke and Madame Marie Brema sang.[2]

The empty seats might indicate that the advertising postcard had not been sufficiently compelling. However, a commentator in the NUWSS paper, *Common Cause*, was in sympathy with Kate, writing that the Pageant was the most enthusiastically received of all the events organized during the Congress.[3] It was obvious that spectacle trumped speeches.

With its headquarters in London, Millicent Fawcett and other members of the NUWSS continued to play leading roles in the IWSA, which, for the duration of the First World War, reconstituted itself as the International Women's Relief Association and in 1926 became the International Alliance of Women for Suffrage and Equal Citizenship.

Object 43

China and the suffrage movement

Object 43 is part of a tea set designed for the Women's Social and Political Union (WSPU) by Sylvia Pankhurst, 1909. (Lesley Mees Collection.)

Among the goods produced for sale by the WSPU were tea sets for use as propaganda, elegantly promoting the movement and converting 'anti' visitors, while eliciting a feeling of solidarity amongst comrades. It was not a novel idea, having been adopted in the early nineteenth century by women who set their tea tables with 'anti-slavery' china. Ironically, it was not the constitutional National Union of Women's Suffrage Societies that adopted this most pacific style of campaigning, but the militants.

To keep up momentum after the end of the International Woman Suffrage Alliance Congress (see Object 42), the WSPU planned a major fund-raising bazaar, the Women's Exhibition, opening on 13 May 1909 at Prince's Skating Rink, Knightsbridge, London, and in a spirit of exuberance decided to commission china for use in its Tea Room. To link the various elements of the Exhibition's publicity, Sylvia Pankhurst had created the motif of the 'angel of freedom' and it was this that was transfer-printed onto a standard pattern of china from H.M. Williamson of Longton, a Staffordshire pottery. No documentary evidence survives to explain why this firm was chosen, although Pankhurst could have viewed the pottery's range at its London showroom in Thavies Inn, Holborn, not far from Clement's Inn. It is likely she selected the shape for its strikingly clean, straight lines, merely rimming the edges and angular handles in dark green, keeping the design uncluttered so that the 'angel of freedom' motif would be shown to best effect. Each piece of the white bone china carries this motif; behind the angel and accompanying banner and trumpet are the initials 'WSPU' set against dark prison bars and dangling chains, surrounded by the national emblems of thistle, shamrock and rose. At the end of the Exhibition, the china was sold, made up into sets of twenty-two pieces, priced at 10s 6d. A cup and saucer could be bought separately for 1s; a jug and basin 1s each; plates came in two sizes, 9d and 1s each, as did teapots, 2s 6d and 3s. Of all the stalls at this profitable exhibition, the refreshment stall raised the most money, £600, to which the sale of the china contributed. It is possible a further order was placed with Williamson, as the china was advertised again in 1911.[1] One photograph survives showing guests at a garden party, held by Mrs Rose Lamartine Yates, taking tea from the china. The little tables at which they sit are laid with the white tablecloths, banded in purple and green, made for the Exhibition refreshment room and afterwards sold.[2]

In 1910 the Scottish WSPU commissioned china from another Longton pottery, the Blyth Porcelain Co., for use at the refreshment stall at their exhibition, held in Glasgow at the end of April. The pieces are less angular in shape than those produced by Williamson, the design delicately allying the Scottish thistle with a simple 'angel of freedom' motif, hand-painted in purple and green, inside transfer outlines. Sold after the exhibition, this china is now very scarce. A little more expensive than the English version, it was priced at 'a breakfast set for two, 11s; small tea set 15s, whole tea set £1'.[3] Pieces were also sold singly as souvenirs.

Four years after the London exhibition, the WSPU placed another order with Williamson, using the same style of china but now with Pankhurst's 'Holloway brooch' motif (see Object 41) applied, rather than the 'angel of freedom'. This range was made for sale at the WSPU Summer Festival, 3–13 June 1913, described as 'breakfast sets for one or two persons'. At a time when militancy was increasing in frequency and violence, it was suggested, perhaps wryly, that this 'portcullis' design would have an especial appeal to WSPU prisoners.[4] Certainly pieces with this design were owned by at least one WSPU ex-prisoner, Nellie Hall.[5] The current scarcity of this pattern would suggest it was produced in far smaller quantities than the 'angel of freedom' version.

Although the Women's Freedom League (WFL) had held a three-day 'Green, White and Gold Fair' in Caxton Hall, Westminster, in mid-April 1909, a month before the WSPU Women's Exhibition, it had not then been sufficiently ambitious as to commission china for its tearoom. However, although it never appears to have been advertised or mentioned in *The Vote*, tea sets decorated with the WFL shield, containing within it 'Votes for Women' and 'WFL' in gold, white and green, with the League's motto, 'Dare to be Free', underneath, were made. The surviving pieces are marked with the name of a London retailer, 'J. Abrahams, 133 Oxford Street', who was one of the first tenants at this address after the building was erected in 1911, suggesting that the china was unlikely to have been commissioned any earlier.[6] Although there is no mention anywhere else of this design of WFL china, a variation was later produced for use in the WFL's offshoot, the Minerva Club (see Object 87).

While items of china commissioned by the suffrage societies are now very scarce, ceramic figurines of suffragettes, originally sold by commercial retailers, are rather more common (see Object 68).

Object 44

Women's Freedom League petition badge, 1909

Object 44 is the petition badge issued by the Women's Freedom League (WFL), 1909. (From the Collection of Dr Kenneth Florey. Photograph by Emilia van Beugen.)

Object 44, a celluloid badge, carries the message, 'It is the Right of the Subjects to Petition the King and all Commitments and Prosecutions for such Petitioning are Illegal', while the outer rim tells us it was issued by the 'Women's Freedom League 1909'. Displaying the League's colours of green, white and gold, the badge rewarded those who took part in the 'Great Watch', WFL's 'picketing' of Parliament. Although there was usually a lull in active campaigning during the summer, between 5 July and 27 October 1909, 250 women stood, day and night, outside the St Stephen's entrance to the House of Commons, holding brown cardboard cylinders containing a petition they hoped to present to the Prime Minister, Asquith. Their intention was to be as conspicuous as possible, patient and immovable in this male space. However, as Asquith refused to meet them, they also appealed to King Edward VII, asking him for an audience. This policy was a continuation of that of the previous year when, to draw attention to the fact they had no voice in the House of Commons, WFL members instigated the 'Grille Protest' (see Object 36).[1]

On 23 July 1909, the Home Secretary, Herbert Gladstone, wrote to Mrs Charlotte Despard that the petition must be presented to the secretary of state, who would present it to the King and informing her that there was no right of audience, whether with king, home secretary or prime minister. In her reply Despard contested this, concluding that, from a reading of the Bill of Rights, 'women have no representatives to voice their views in the House of Commons, and if further they are denied a hearing by His Majesty and His Majesty's Ministers, it is evident that that they have a very real grievance, one which calls for speedy redress'.[2]

By the end of August, 6,700 woman hours had been expended on the WFL picket, yet the authorities were obdurate.[3] Eventually, recognizing it was impossible to contact the prime minister at the House of Commons, eight WFL members, including Annie Cobden Sanderson and Despard, moved to Downing Street, guarding all the entrances of no.10, waiting for Asquith to emerge. The police allowed them to remain for one day, arresting them on the second and charging them with obstruction. The ensuing court case, held first at Bow Street (see Object 37), where the defendants were found guilty and sentenced to a fine of 40s or seven days' imprisonment, then proceeded to appeal in January 1910, the sentence being upheld. All chose prison, although Despard and some others were indignant to discover their fines had been paid without their consent. The legal decision was also dispiriting; women might have a right to present a petition but could not force the prime minister to receive a deputation.

The 'Great Watch', however, had ended earlier, after 14,000 hours of silent demonstration. For, on 28 October, a stronger protest had been made, when two members of the WFL attempted to destroy the contents of ballot boxes at the Bermondsey by-election by splashing them with chemicals, slightly injuring an election official in the process. The plan had been instigated by the National Executive Committee because, as a leading member of the WFL told a reporter, 'they had been standing for weeks outside the House of Commons, and no notice was taken of their constitutional efforts' and so 'Members of the League have begun today a new militant policy at Bermondsey and have invalidated the by-election by destroying the recorded votes of the electors. This was done as a strong protest against your inaction and the unworthy treatment which has been accorded to our question in the House of Commons'.[4] After a trial, during which every effort was made to exclude members of the WFL from the public gallery, Mrs Alice Chapin, whose action had caused damage to papers and official, was sentenced on two counts to terms of three and four months, to run concurrently. Alison Neilans, the other protestor, received a three-month sentence. Both women made use of their experiences, Chapin as the author of *At the Gates*, a one-act play based on the 'Great Watch', while Neilans published *The Ballot Box Protest* as a WFL pamphlet.[5]

Object 44 was made for the WFL by the Merchants' Portrait Co. of Kentish Town, who produced many postcards and badges for the League. Not available for purchase, it was a 'reward' given by the WFL for a 'militant' action and, as such, is an extremely rare item. Originally owned by one of the Hodgson sisters (see Object 29), it was possibly presented to her by Despard at a meeting held in 'a crowded drawing-room at 60 Onslow Square' on 23 September 1909.[6]

Object 45

Suffrage society badges

Object 45 comprises a representative selection of suffrage society badges. (The Women's Library collection, London School of Economics and Political Science.)

While Object 44 is a badge issued by the Women's Freedom League (WFL) as a reward for a particular suffrage-related activity, all the early-twentieth-century suffrage societies produced badges that could be bought by their members to demonstrate allegiance. As the suffrage movement gathered momentum, so the number of suffrage societies increased, offering those with religious, occupational, national or political loyalties scope to campaign in a manner that appealed. Creating an identity was essential to attracting members, with the production of a badge the obvious first step.[1]

Although none of the nineteenth-century suffrage societies had a badge, women's groups supporting the main political parties, such as the Primrose League, did encourage their members to wear emblems. The earliest suffrage badge is likely to have been one made for the Women's Social and Political Union (WSPU) *c.*1906; it is very simple, round, white, printed with 'Votes for Women'. After the adoption of the purple, white and green colours in June 1908, the number of WSPU badges multiplied, some bearing designs by Sylvia Pankhurst. Many badges are unmarked, but among the known regular suppliers of enamel badges to the suffrage societies were two Birmingham manufacturers, Arthur Fenwick of Vyse Street and W.O. Lewis of Howard

Street, and, in London, Toye, the makers of the WSPU hunger-strike medals. The Merchant's Portrait Company in north London produced many of the cheaper celluloid badges.

Of the seven badges shown as Object 45, six advertise specific suffrage societies. The seventh, on the top left, was created by the WFL for their campaign of civil disobedience, urging women to boycott the 1911 census, the argument being that, because women had no vote, they should not be counted.[2] It was unusual for a suffrage society to produce a badge as part of a specific campaign and this 'census' badge is very scarce.

Taking the other badges in turn, we see that each society has adopted a symbol and combination of colours indicative of its allegiance. On the top row, second from the left, the Catholic Women's Suffrage Society, founded in 1911, chose for its colours white, gold and blue which, with the central fleur-de-lis, are symbolic of the Virgin Mary.[3] Next is the badge of the Irish League for Women's Suffrage, which originated as the London branch of the Dublin-based Irish Women's Franchise League (see Object 8) but, with alteration to its constitution, changed its name in December 1911. Green and gold had been representative of Irish resistance since the seventeenth century, while the woman-harp and the surrounding shamrocks symbolize Ireland. On the right is the standard badge of the WFL, which had adopted its colours by early 1909.

On the bottom row, from the left, is the badge of the Jewish League for Women's Suffrage, founded in 1912, open to both men and women. Its colours were purple and blue, both with ancient Israelite associations, and the badge, celluloid over a metal base, has the star of David in the centre, containing the initials JLWS, surrounded with a Hebrew quotation from Proverbs, 'It is the Joy of the Righteous to do Justice'. Next to it is a red, white and green NUWSS badge, which incorporates elements used on other of their badges, the Tudor rose being a common device. This enamelled example, finer than the more usual metal versions, is the work of William Mark, an Australian who in 1911 was living at The White House, Chipping Campden, Gloucestershire, and had, from 1900, been a member of Ashbee's Guild of Handicraft. In 1913 NUWSS headquarters exhorted its members to always wear a badge and, as encouragement, even reduced the price of a common enamel version from 9d to 6d.[4] On the right of the bottom row is a very scarce badge, that of the Cymric Suffrage Union, formed in 1911 to campaign in London and in Wales.[5] 'Cymric' means 'Welsh' in Welsh and the colours of the badge are yellow and red, which may be a reference to Wales' Liberal (yellow) and Labour (red) politics. The motto across the centre, 'Etholfraint I Doynes', translates as 'Votes for Women'.

Although the NUWSS may have felt it necessary to emphasize the importance of badge-wearing, many campaigners needed no encouragement. Kate Frye often writes in her diary that she was wearing a suffrage badge. Like many women, she had a range to choose from, having changed societies during the campaign. On occasion, a badge spoke for itself. Present in Parliament Square on 18 November 1910, 'Black Friday', a witness to the most violent of the WSPU demonstrations and to the many men watching suffragettes being assaulted, Frye reported,

Several spoke to me – many indignant: 'What good do you suppose this will do?' 'What else would you suggest?' said I. Then he began the usual – that the militant methods had disgusted all nicely feeling people etc. I turned his attention to my two badges – constitutional societies, as I told him – and asked, 'What help have you ever given us?' He walked away.[6]

Kate would have been wearing her NUWSS badge and that for the New Constitutional Society for Women's Suffrage (see Object 69). That no badge for the latter society appears to have survived is evidence of how very scarce such emblems of the smaller societies can be.

Object 46

Designs for emblems of the federations of the National Union of Women's Suffrage Societies

Object 46 is a sheet of emblems for the new federations of the National Union of Women's Suffrage Societies (NUWSS), designed by Mary Lowndes of the Artists' Suffrage League (ASL). (2ASL/11/18-20, The Women's Library collection, London School of Economics and Political Science.)

In the first decade of the twentieth century NUWSS membership expanded rapidly, benefitting from the publicity generated by the more vociferous Women's Social and Political Union (WSPU). For many women who became interested in the Cause were not prepared to break the law but, instead, joined their local constitutional society. These, too, had multiplied, the number of societies affiliated to the NUWSS rising from 33 in 1907 to 180 in 1910. To keep control of this expanding organization, in March 1910 the decision was taken to decentralize control from the London headquarters to new regional federations. The editor of the NUWSS paper, revealing an awareness perhaps born of experience, commented, 'Federations only work well when they are formed with the full consent and understanding of the units, and that, not only have complicated questions of geography, of railways, and mountain ranges to be considered, but so have the far more complicated questions of local feuds and sympathies, jealousies, and interests.'[1]

Object 46 shows one sheet of the designs for shields, created by Mary Lowndes of the ASL to decorate the Albert Hall's Grand Tier Boxes for a NUWSS meeting, addressed by the Chancellor of the Exchequer, Lloyd George, on 23 February 1912.[2] They are: top row (left to right), the shield for Oxford, Berks and Bucks, which incorporates the chained swan, the emblem of Buckinghamshire, with a variation on the coat of arms of Oxford University and a blue band for Berkshire; the North-Western Federation, represented by the red roses of Lancashire; the Manchester and District Federation bears the ship indicating the city's trading history, with the bee symbolizing an industrial community. In the middle row are: the East Anglian Federation, represented by the crowns and arrows of St Edmund; the Midlands (West) Federation, by the chimneys of the Potteries; and the West Riding Federation, by the white rose of York. Bottom row are: the South-Western Federation, represented by a red bull (for Devon) above ten bezants (a heraldic ornament) relating to Cornwall; the North of Scotland Federation (formed from three counties in August 1910), represented by the thistle emblems; and the Scottish Federation by the red Scottish lion. Apart from the nine represented on this sheet, Lowndes also created similarly ingenious devices for the London Society and the North-Eastern; Midlands (East); West Lancashire, West Cheshire and North Wales; South Wales; Surrey, Sussex and Hampshire; Kentish and West of England Federations. As Mary Lowndes laconically remarked in her pamphlet, *Banners and Banner-Making* (1909), 'In all decorative matters a little knowledge of heraldry is of value.'

By 1914 the NUWSS had over 50,000 members and was organized into eighteen federations, to which over 500 local societies were affiliated. These societies were to be found throughout England, Scotland and Wales, extending from Shetland in the north to Falmouth in the south.[3] NUWSS finances were well-managed, Mrs Fawcett calculating that by 1914 the NUWSS was spending £45,000 a year on the campaign to enfranchise women. To this end the NUWSS employed federation organizers, young women, often university graduates, who travelled throughout their district, educating the public in the arguments for giving women the vote.

Object 47

Photograph of Millicent Fawcett planting a tree in Annie's Arboretum, Batheaston, 1910

Object 47 Millicent Fawcett planting a tree in Annie's Arboretum, Eagle House, Batheaston, Somerset, 3 July 1910. Photograph by Col. Linley Blathwayt. (TWL.2009.02.083, The Women's Library collection, London School of Economics and Political Science.)

Col. Linley Blathwayt and his family were for some years active supporters of both the constitutional and the militant wings of the suffrage movement. Blathwayt, a keen entomologist, botanist and photographer, had retired from the Indian Army in the 1880s, settling with his family in Eagle House, a large early-eighteenth-century house at Batheaston, on the outskirts of Bath. Caught up for a while in admiration of the WSPU, the family offered suffragettes rest and recuperation both in their home and in the 'Suffragettes' Rest', a summerhouse built in the grounds. In 1909 they conceived the novel idea of creating 'a living monument to the suffragettes' fight for political equality' by inviting visiting suffragettes and suffragists to plant a tree in a two-acre field adjacent to the house. The area was named 'Annie's Arboretum' in honour of Annie Kenney, the WSPU West of England organizer and, devotion crossing the class barrier, a Blathwayt family favourite.[1] It is thought that sixty-eight trees were planted, each marked by a lead plaque indicating the name of the planter, the date and the tree variety, with Blathwayt photographing each occasion.

As part of a long family tradition, Blathwayt, his wife Emily, and their daughter, Mary, kept extensive daily diaries, excellent sources of information on grassroots suffrage campaigning.[2] While her mother's diary shows a degree of political awareness, Mary reveals herself ingenuous to a fault. Described by her mother as 'slow with her head but very quick with practical things', she was the diligent, kind, uninspiring helper so necessary to all causes.[3] She joined the National Union of Women's Suffrage Societies (NUWSS) in May 1907 and in November, at a Women's Social and Political Union (WSPU) meeting in Bristol, met Annie Kenney, Christabel Pankhurst and Emmeline Pethick-Lawrence. Soon, as joint honorary secretary of the Bath branch of the NUWSS, she was also organizing a meeting for the WSPU. She continued as a member of the WSPU until June 1913, resigning after a local house had been burned in a suffragette arson attack.

Object 47 is a photograph taken by Blathwayt, signed and dated across the corner; the annotation on the mount ('In Col. Blathwayt's garden, July 3 1910') is in Millicent Fawcett's handwriting. The planting took place the day after Fawcett had been the guest speaker at a meeting organized by the local NUWSS society in the Bath Assembly Rooms. Alongside her on the platform was Mrs Lilian Ashworth Hallett, whom she had first met in Bath in 1871 (see Object 31). These hardy campaigners were hoping that real progress was about to be made, for, as Fawcett explained, the government had granted two days of parliamentary time, on 11 and 12 July, for a Second Reading of a suffrage bill proposed by an all-party Conciliation Committee of thirty-six MPs. If passed this would give the parliamentary vote to the million women who were already qualified to vote in municipal elections.

It was at this hopeful point that Fawcett was invited to 'Annie's Arboretum' and photographed planting a holly tree, *Ilex acquifolium 'Macropara'*. In the Blathwayt taxonomy, varieties of holly represented anyone working for suffrage, varieties of conifers those who had been imprisoned. On the left is Dr Mary Morris, Bath's first female medical inspector of schools, who had also been on the platform of the Assembly Rooms meeting, and slightly behind her is Mary Blathwayt, wearing the 'Boadicea' brooch given to her by Annie Kenney on 10 December 1908. Illustrative of the eclectic nature of the suffrage movement, the photograph shows that also watching this planting ceremony, conducted by the leader of the NUWSS, were three WSPU members, from the left, Annie Kenney, her sister Kitty and Adela Pankhurst, Emmeline's youngest daughter.

Apart from emotional and practical support, the Blathwayt contribution to the suffrage cause produced, besides the diaries, a rich collection of material objects, photographs, plaques and trees. Object 47, given by Blathwayt to Fawcett, remained among her papers and is now held in the Women's Library collection at LSE, but it is entirely fortuitous that any other items survive. In 1938 former suffragettes were apparently hoping to preserve the arboretum, but nothing was done.[4] The end came after Mary's death in 1961. Eagle House was eventually saved from demolition, but in 1964 four acres of its estate were sold and 'Annie's Arboretum' felled.[5] The only tree remaining is a 30-metre-high Austrian pine planted by Rose Lamartine Yates (see Object 43), saved because it had already been incorporated into a private garden. Although the contents of Eagle House were sold by auction, among them 'a suffragette sash and a string bag, and five volumes of *Votes for Women*',[6] one object thus dispersed, Blathwayt's album of suffragette photographs, was later retrieved from a junk shop. The album led the new owner, Antonia Raeburn, to Eagle House where she discovered a pile of photographic glass plates, among them the original of Object 47.[7] These inspired her to undertake the research for *The Militant Suffragettes* (1973) for which she interviewed many former members of the WSPU, introducing a new era in suffrage studies (see Object 97).

Object 48

Photographic postcard of the Prisoners' Pageant, 23 July 1910

Object 48 is a postcard of a scene from the Women's Social and Political Union (WSPU) procession, 23 July 1910, photographed by Mrs Christina Broom. (Lesley Mees Collection.)

While the Conciliation Bill championed by Millicent Fawcett at the Bath meeting on 2 July 1910 was under discussion (see Object 47), the WSPU and the Women's Freedom League (WFL) had organized a demonstration in its support in London on 18 June. This took the form of a 'Prison to Citizenship' procession, the first large-scale rally since 1908.[1] As the WSPU declined to call a truce on militancy until a date for a Second Reading of the Conciliation Bill was fixed, the NUWSS had felt unable to participate but, instead, held a public meeting in Trafalgar Square on 9 July. Here their local societies displayed banners showing the number of electors who had signed the NUWSS petition in favour of 'votes for women' during the January 1910 general election. Newsreels captured a few moments from this and from the WSPU 18 June demonstration.[2]

Once the Conciliation Bill had passed its Second Reading on 11–12 July with a majority of 110, the WSPU and WFL put into action plans for yet another spectacular demonstration in the hope of keeping up the momentum of the bill's progress through the parliamentary system. Although, with the Second Reading successfully achieved, many suffragists wished to take part, it still proved difficult for the constitutional and militant societies to reach an agreement. Therefore, the 23 July event went ahead without NUWSS participation. For the militant WSPU, the day and place chosen, while being convenient, also had a particular resonance, being the anniversary of the day in 1867 on which men demonstrating for their inclusion in the 1867 Reform Bill pulled down the railings to Hyde Park.

The 23 July WSPU demonstration was designed as two processions, one coming from the west and one from the east, culminating in a meeting in Hyde Park.[3] Object 48 shows the leaders of the 617 women who took part in the Prisoners' Pageant at the head of the eastern procession. From the left they are Emmeline Pethick-Lawrence, Sylvia Pankhurst and Emily Wilding Davison. The latter, a university graduate, is wearing her academic robes, complete with mortar board, such marks of distinction being always encouraged, while Sylvia Pankhurst holds a representation of the portcullis/prison gate, one of the motifs of the Prisoners' Pageant. It was particularly requested that those taking part in the Pageant should 'wear white, with no regalia, and with small white hats if possible'.[4] As we can see, Mrs Pethick-Lawrence, most elegantly dressed in white, is not entirely observant as to her hat. The fringed satin insignia that she and Pankhurst wear denote each as 'Chairman', that is chairman of one of the forty platform meetings held in Hyde Park. Pethick-Lawrence chaired Platform 3 and Pankhurst Platform 28. The young woman on the right is clearly wearing a WSPU purple, white and green tie. Behind them we can see that a woman holds one of the arrow-shaped wands that was held aloft while processing, indicating she has been a prisoner. The pennant towards the back carries the WSPU motto, 'Deeds not Words'. Police, both mounted and on foot, are in evidence; the afternoon passed without incident.

The event was considered a triumph both by the WSPU and by the press. As the *Manchester Guardian* reported, 'In mere size this demonstration of the Women's Social and Political Union was certainly the most momentous thing of the kind that London has seen. It takes something important to keep half a million people quiet. There is now really no taunt left, even for the most loose-lipped London loafer.'[5] Although no newsreel of this procession survives, present with camera and tripod to capture the image that is Object 48 was Mrs Christina Broom, generally credited as Britain's first female press photographer. Using her coal cellar as a darkroom she then printed postcards from the glass plate, able to monetize, while publicizing, suffrage. Her suffrage images have a particular clarity, a reality, and the postcards are eminently collectible in the twenty-first century. In 2024 Mrs Broom was commemorated by the award of an English Heritage Blue Plaque to her former home, 92 Munster Road, Fulham, London.[6]

There was no doubt that the London procession was spectacular, but however many the participants and however sympathetic the audience in London and at contemporaneous meetings in Edinburgh, Bristol, Liverpool, Nottingham, Manchester, Birmingham and Glasgow, the fact remained that votes for women could only be achieved in Parliament and it quickly transpired that Asquith and his government were not willing to grant further facilities to the Conciliation Bill. As Parliament broke up for the summer recess, Christabel Pankhurst threatened, 'If they fail to get rid of the Government's veto upon the Conciliation Bill, women themselves must act. Unless Members of Parliament have in the meantime secured the necessary facilities, a great concourse of women will, immediately after Parliament reassembles in the autumn, proceed to Westminster to demand of the Government that the Suffrage Bill be forthwith carried into law.'[7]

In November the pageantry of Object 48 would seem a distant memory. The bill was lost when Asquith called a general election and Christabel's threat was put into action in Parliament Square on 'Black Friday' (see Objects 55, 56 and 75).

Object 49

Suffrage shops

Object 49 is a photograph of the Oldham National Union of Women's Suffrage Societies (NUWSS) shop, published as a postcard, November 1911. (TWL.2000.49, The Women's Library collection, London School of Economics and Political Science.)

As the twentieth-century campaign gathered momentum, the suffrage societies developed increasingly sophisticated methods of waging their propaganda campaigns. Spectacular processions, such as shown in Object 48, was one tactic, launching high street shops was another.[1] Object 49 is typical of the many combined shops and committee rooms opened as centres of campaigning for a few weeks during elections, both general and local. Here the leading members of the Oldham NUWSS pose for a local photographer outside their shop at 30 Yorkshire Street, opened for a by-election, held on 13 November 1911.[2] From left to right the women are: Margaret Robertson BA, the Manchester and District Federation organizer; Marjory Lees, president of the Oldham NUWSS; Mrs Mary Siddall; Mrs Margaret Aldersley, the local by-election NUWSS organizer; and Mrs Rachel Bridge. Siddall and Bridge were joint honorary secretaries of the Oldham Women's Suffrage Society.

Although the fleeting existence of these shops generally went unrecorded, the Oldham organizers arranged for William V. Garner to come from his studio in nearby Clegg Street and document their efforts. That the purpose of the photograph was to highlight the window, rather than the personalities, is obvious from the way the women have positioned themselves, leaving a clear view of the display. For the by-election all three candidates, Conservative, Liberal and Labour, had pledged to support the Second Conciliation Bill (see Object 58) and in the window the Oldham suffragists have pasted 'a gigantic bill: – we have, side by side, three upright bills, one in blue, one in yellow, one in red; the blue one announcing Mr Denniss' pledge, the yellow Mr Robinson's, the red Mr Stanley's. Below is a strip, saying "Whoever wins, the women win". And there is a green border to bring the whole thing together'.[3] Also in the window is the lithographed poster, 'Won't You Let Me Help You, John', designed by Joan Harvey Drew for the Artists' Suffrage League (see Object 25), together with a rougher, block-printed poster, perhaps the work of the Suffrage Atelier, showing a widow with young children and carrying the message that, despite being a sole breadwinner and taxpayer, she is voteless. The display also includes the latest issue of *The Common Cause* and a sheet of NUWSS badges, all of which were on sale inside, and an array of NUWSS pamphlets, these being free. This photograph was published in the suffrage press, as were a few others of suffrage shops, but, unusually, this original postcard has survived, the records of Marjory Lees and the Oldham WSS having been carefully preserved.[4]

It is likely the Women's Social and Political Union (WSPU) had been the first society to open a shop, in September 1907 at 64 Nicolson Street, Edinburgh. It was 'emblazoned with posters' and praised as 'an excellent centre and advertising medium' for the forthcoming procession through the Scottish capital on 5 October.[5] In 1908 both wings of the movement took to shopkeeping to publicize their June processions in London. The NUWSS shop, the initiative of the Kensington branch, proved a great success, the organizers commenting, 'From the first hour a kaleidoscopic crowd has gazed at our posters and derived instruction and amusement from them. Where should we be without our Artists' League who has made this method of conversion possible?'[6] For the WSPU 'Woman's Sunday', the Chelsea WSPU opened a shop at 400 King's Road, displaying in the window 'Votes for Women bills and photographs of the speakers for June 21'.[7] By early 1909 the Kensington WSPU had opened a more permanent shop at 143 Church Street, Notting Hill Gate, later described by one member as 'tiny, wedge-shaped, you sidled round purple, white and green posters of Mr Two-Faced Asquith, brassards, badges, buttons, scarves, pamphlets, hatpins made of stained fish-bones, portraits of the leaders of the WSPU and the current number of *Votes for Women*'.[8]

WSPU marketing strategy was well in advance of that of the NUWSS. Not only did the WSPU create more merchandise, but in May 1910 opened a permanent London shop at 156 Charing Cross Road, 'only three doors from Oxford Street', from which to sell their wares. Emmeline and Frederick Pethick-Lawrence were the lessees, the premises also housing the offices of the Woman's Press. The shop was close to Tottenham Court Road tube station, its exterior soon adorned with a large clock, the face of which, spelling out 'Votes for Women', was visible to shoppers in Oxford Street. *Votes for Women* reported,

The shop is a blaze of purple, white and green. Just now the Woman's Press is showing some beautiful motor and other scarves in various shades of purple, as well as white muslin summer blouses, and among the almost unending variety of bags, belts, etc, are noticeable the 'Emmeline' and the 'Christabel' bags, and the 'Pethick' tobacco pouch. In addition to books, pamphlets, and leaflets, stationery, games, blotters, playing cards, and indeed almost everything that can be produced in purple, white and green, or a combination of all three, is to be found there.[9]

Similar, if smaller, suffrage shops were opened around the country, although no other society could emulate the panache of the WSPU.

Object 50

Suffrage postcards

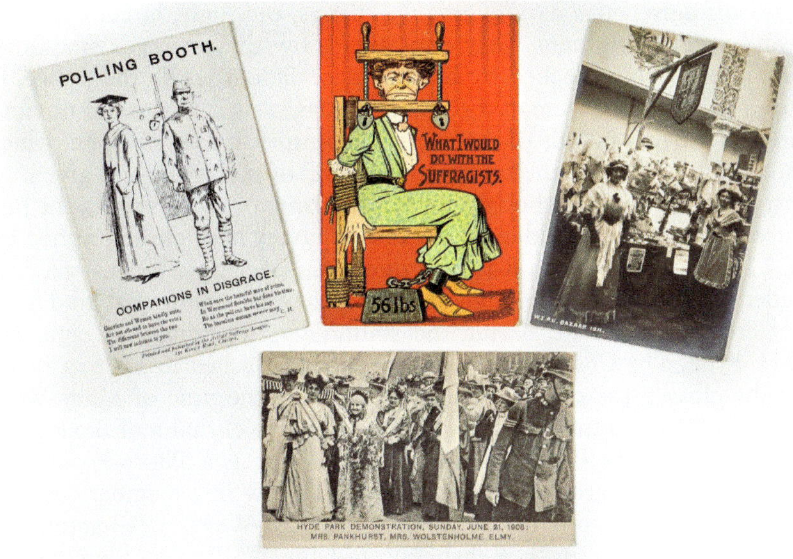

Object 50 is a selection of suffrage postcards. (7JCC/O/1/113 polling booth; 7JCC/O/1/145 anti-suffrage; 7JCC/O/1/49 Bazaar; 7JCC/O/1/16 EWE, The Women's Library collection, London School of Economics and Political Science.)

Among the range of goods sold in suffrage shops (see Object 49), particularly those of the Women's Social and Political Union (WSPU), were postcards, at the time enjoying their golden age. Frequent posts, the paucity of telephones and the affordability of a halfpenny stamp meant that a short message on a postcard was a favoured method of communication. In addition, the post-1905 revitalization of the suffrage campaign coincided with a 'craze' for postcard collecting; cards were bought to arrange in albums as well as to be posted. In their shops both the WSPU and the Women's Freedom League (WFL) sold albums, each decorated with their own motif, to encourage the collection of postcards of suffrage activists and events.[1]

Suffrage-related postcards can be roughly divided into two types, those featuring real photographs and those with hand-drawn illustrations. Most of the former were photographs of suffrage personalities and occasions and were sympathetic to the Cause; these were sold in suffrage shops. Most of the hand-drawn postcards were published by commercial firms and, intended to be comic, are generally judged as antagonistic; these were sold by newsagents and stationers. However, a relatively small number of the illustrated postcards were the campaigning work of members of the Artists' Suffrage League (ASL) and the Suffrage Atelier. An example of this type of postcard may be seen top left in the Object 50 collection. Captioned 'Polling Booth – Companions in Disgrace', it plays on a popular trope, contrasting the position of women with male convicts. As the verse accompanying the illustration emphasizes, although a convict while in prison is voteless, once released he may once more be enfranchised and yet a woman, however highly educated, can never vote. This illustration, which first appeared in the *Women's Franchise*, 26 December 1907, was published as a postcard by the ASL.

By way of contrast, the postcard next to it, issued by an unknown commercial publisher, is at the more extreme range of misogynistic depictions of suffrage sympathizers. Many commercial postcards portray suffragists/ettes as unwomanly, that is, old, ugly, large, equipped with big feet, umbrellas and unflattering hats. They may also show these viragos smoking, bicycling, haranguing an audience, being mocked by little boys or fighting with the police, but do not, as here, resort to illustrations of woman torture. But images such as this did obviously pass as acceptable humour in the first decade of the twentieth century. It may not be a coincidence that the artist has chosen for his palette the suffragist 'colours' of red, white and green.[2]

While that last postcard might be bought from a stationer or a newsagent, the photographic card on top right would have been sold in WSPU shops, having been photographed at the WSPU Christmas Bazaar, held at the Portman Rooms, London, in December 1911. Two young women stand beside a laden stall, the decorative sign indicating they are selling soap and handkerchiefs. Sylvia Pankhurst created the event, basing the stallholders' costumes on eighteenth-century designs from W.H. Pyne, *The Costume of Great Britain*, published in 1808, a book given her by Keir Hardie. She glossed the choice of dress as evoking the time of Mary Wollstonecraft. The photograph was taken and the postcard published by 'F. Kehrhahn of Bexleyheath', a two-brother firm, with Ferdinand as 'Photographer' and Frederick as a 'Photo Postcard Producer'.[3] 'F. Kehrhahn' published photographic portraits of leading WSPU members as well as cards of events, such as the 1911 'Coronation Procession' and the WSPU 1913 summer exhibition. It is likely the association between 'F. Kehrhahn' and the WSPU was ideological as well as commercial; after the First World War Ferdinand Kehrhahn (now 'Kerran') was, with Sylvia Pankhurst, a leading member of the British Communist party.

The card on the bottom row is a photograph of Emmeline Pankhurst and Elizabeth Wolstenholme Elmy (see Object 15), together at the WSPU's Hyde Park Women's Sunday, 21 June 1908. This is an important image, symbolizing the link between the first suffrage society (founded by Wolstenholme Elmy in Manchester in 1865) and the militant WSPU. Wolstenholme Elmy is carrying a bouquet of ferns, purple lilies and lilies of the valley, for it was for this rally that Emmeline Pethick-Lawrence had devised the WSPU 'colours', with (purple, white and green) 'Votes for Women' sashes much in evidence. Behind floats the banner honouring Mrs Pankhurst, 'Famed Far for Deeds of Daring Rectitude', and in the foreground is a large WSPU flag. The card was photographed for and published by Sandle Bros, a firm that produced all manner of stationery from its extensive premises in Paternoster Row, London. Clearly believing that WSPU personalities and events were commercially profitable, its postcard department produced a wide range of cards for the WSPU.

Now popular with collectors, photographic suffrage cards and those produced by its artists' societies are less common than those issued by commercial publishers. However, 'comic' commercial postcards were more likely to have been used to communicate messages, often with a quip at the expense of the campaigners. Thanks to the facilities afforded by internet genealogical sites, addressees can often be identified, allowing the researcher a fleeting view of the person to whom a card, whether pro-suffrage or 'comic', was deemed appropriate to send.

Object 51

Suffrage games

Object 51 is Pank-a-Squith, an example of a suffragette game. (Lesley Mees Collection.)

From October 1909 all Women's Social and Political Union (WSPU) shops (see Object 49) stocked 'Pank-a-Squith', promoted as 'a splendid advertisement for our cause. It illustrates beautifully all the important public events of our movement'. Most importantly, it was 'brimful of fun'.[1] Selling for 1s 6d, 'Pank-a-Squith' was a board game, following 'the attempt of a suffragette to get from her home to the Houses of Parliament. She has to cross fifty sections and meet with all sorts of opposition. It consists of six figures of suffragettes, witty rules, dice, and clear instructions – all printed in purple, white and green'.[2] Played on the 'Snakes and Ladders' principle, the squares represent scenes and incidents from the suffrage movement. The game was invented by a suffragette, its production probably commissioned by the Pethick-Lawrences' Woman's Press, and was available from toy dealers as well as from WSPU shops.[3] Mary Blathwayt bought 'Pank-a-Squith' in December 1909 and in July 1910 noted in her diary that she and Annie Kenney played the game to pass an anxious time while Annie's sister was undergoing an operation (see Object 47). Although uncommon, some of the decorative 'Pank-a-Squith' boards have survived into the twenty-first century, although usually long separated from the six suffragette figures that acted as counters.

When playing 'Pank-a-Squith' at Eagle House, Mary and Annie were already united in their support for the Cause but, in the guise of games, discussions of suffrage could be introduced into less committed domestic circles where more rabid propaganda might not have been welcomed. The Kensington branch of the WSPU had been the first to recognize this proselytizing potential, by November 1907 inventing and seeing into production 'The Game of Suffragette'.[4] This comprises fifty-four cards divided into thirteen sets, each of four cards, one of the odd ones being known as 'The Bill' and the other a spare. All the sets have names, e.g. Prominent Supporters, Arguments, Freewomen, Voteless Women, etc., and each card poses a series of suffrage-related questions. On the reverse of each card is David Wilson's image of the 'Haunted House' (see Objects 27 and 28), with photographs of leading suffrage personalities, such as Christabel Pankhurst, Annie Kenney and Mrs Fawcett, on the front of some cards. The rules describe in detail the various ways in which this very inventive game could be played. It was probably only produced in small numbers and is now rarely found, whereas another card game, 'Panko', is not uncommon. This was produced in time for Christmas 1909 by a commercial manufacturer, Peter Gurney, from premises very close to the WSPU offices. The artwork on the cards was by E.T. Reed, a *Punch* illustrator, showing the suffrage leaders, policemen, lawyers, politicians, etc., and was played between suffrage supporters and opponents. Advertisements declared, 'Not only is each picture in itself an interesting memento, but the game produces intense excitement without the slightest taint of bitterness.'[5] It was obviously thought necessary to make that final claim; 'Panko' would not disturb the family circle.

Several other board and card games were developed, particularly with a view to Christmas sales, but, as they are now all but unknown, were probably manufactured in small quantities. 'Suffragettes in and out of Prison', a board game by Whitworth Hird Ltd of Norwich and London, was described as a 'Game and a Puzzle'. With Holloway at the heart of a labyrinth, the aim was to find a way out.[6] 'Suffragetto' was a board game for two players, the conceit being that the suffragettes were attempting to outwit the police at the House of Commons and the Albert Hall.[7] Although no copies of 'Rushing the House', launched in late 1908, are now known, it was presumably inspired by the events of that October (see Object 37) and, priced at 6d, was likely to have been a card rather than a board game.[8] Also dating from Christmas 1908, 'The Suffragette Puzzle', made by F.H. Ayers, a leading games manufacturer with premises at Aldersgate Street, London, was a wooden dexterity game, the aim of which was to manipulate a tin 'suffragette', attached to a thin metal rod, in such a way as to get the 'Bill' (a pin) through the door of the House of Commons.[9]

Although the last 'Puzzle' might indicate a nod to constitutional methods, we can see that it was the ideas and methods of the militants that captured the imagination of games makers and players, evidence of the soft power wielded by the WSPU in 1908/9. That no similar games were developed in later years perhaps indicates that, as militancy increased, manufacturers considered suffrage-themed amusement less of a commercial proposition.

Object 52

Suffrage jewellery

Object 52 is an enamel brooch made by Ernestine Mills. (Lesley Mees Collection.)

This brooch is the work of Mrs Ernestine Mills, daughter of a signatory to the 1866 suffrage petition (see Object 1) and an enameller of renown. Mills joined the Women's Social and Political Union (WSPU) in 1907 and this brooch, and another similarly enamelled in the colours of the WSPU, was made either as a private commission or for sale at a suffrage bazaar. These, and another in the green, white and gold of the Women's Freedom League (WFL), all proclaim, in Mills' distinctive lettering, 'Votes for Women'.[1] Although other craftswomen, such as Annie Steen of Birmingham, made jewellery 'in the colours', it is impossible now to identify such pieces without corroborating evidence. This is important. No area of suffrage material culture is more prone to misrepresentation than that of jewellery. There is no reason why accepted rules of historical evidence and provenance should be suspended for this category of goods and yet items of jewellery are commonly described as 'suffragette' merely because their stones approximate to the WSPU 'colours' of purple, white and green. Jewellery can only be credited as produced with 'suffrage' intent if it is possible to identify the piece as commissioned by a suffrage society or for an individual associated with the suffrage movement.[2]

The distinction between a 'badge' and a 'brooch' is somewhat arbitrary, but we tend to think of brooches as made of better-quality material. For instance, the WSPU produced an oval silver brooch banded in purple, white and green guilloche enamel and a square one, enamelled in purple and green, with 'Votes for Women' on a middle white strip, both of which could be classed as jewellery. Two of Sylvia Pankhurst's designs featuring her 'Angel of Freedom' certainly fall into the jewellery category. Made by Birmingham firms, one is a silver and enamel brooch by Henry Morton and the other a silver pendant, enamelled in purple, white and green, bearing the 1908 hallmark for Joseph Fray.

In 1910 the Woman's Press shop (see Object 49) advertised four styles of brooches, the most expensive, at 3s 6d, being its 'Boadicea', depicting the warrior queen in her chariot. Annie Kenney gave one of these large, impressive pieces to Mary Blathwayt in December 1908 (see Object 47). The other WSPU brooches were a Bow (9d), made by W.O. Lewis of Birmingham, and a Shamrock (6d), both enamelled in the colours, and one in the shape of a Broad Arrow, made either in silver (1s 6d) or silver-plated (1s).[3] The latter were commissioned from J.R. Gaunt, another Birmingham firm.

Although there may have been commercial firms who, on their own account, created jewellery 'in the colours', only two advertised in the suffrage press. In December 1909 the firm of Mappin and Webb issued a catalogue of 'Suffragette Jewellery' and advertised five pieces mainly made of gold, set with amethysts, pearls and emeralds. While the Mappin family were committed members of the WSPU, the attitude to suffrage of the Wholesale Service Company, Birmingham, who in 1913 advertised an enamelled pendant and brooch in the WSPU colours, is unknown.[4] If there were other commercial firms producing jewellery for the suffrage market, it is surprising they did not advertise occasionally in the suffrage press.

The National Union of Women's Suffrage Societies (NUWSS) produced a variety of badges but there are only two sufficiently decorative to be classed as 'jewellery'. One is the enamelled, rose-shaped, badge shown in the centre of the bottom row of Object 45, the other, a 'Tudor Rose' in silver plate and enamel, was designed for the NUWSS by the Artists' Suffrage League. It is a cinquefoil shape with a red-enamelled centre, green enamel tips to the leaves and the initials 'NUWSS' set into the petals.[5]

While all these could be bought, other items of jewellery were made for presentation. In May 1909 the Kensington WSPU commissioned Mills to make a silver and enamel pendant, representing the winged figure of Hope singing outside prison bars, to celebrate the release from prison of Louise Eates, one of the branch's founders.[6] For a similar commemoration, on 14 January 1909 Mrs Pankhurst was presented with a 'necklace and pendant wrought in gold with amethysts, pearls, and green agates by a special expert in artistic jewellery'.[7] After being forcibly fed in prisons in Birmingham and Manchester, Mrs Mary Leigh was honoured with a pendant, edged with three stones, white, green and purple, holding a miniature portrait of Mrs Pankhurst, the reverse inscribed, 'presented to Mrs Marie Leigh Drum Major by the N.W.S.P.U. Drum and Fife Band in memory of her courageous fight for woman's freedom December 1909'. Although the NUWSS was less inclined to this type of commemoration, in 1913 they demonstrated their loyalty to Mrs Fawcett by commissioning Object 71.

As with so many material manifestations of the suffrage movement, alongside the uplifting iconography there were more comic renderings. One such, described as 'The Latest Novelty', was a little suffragette figure, hanging from a pin fitting and holding a 'Votes for Women' placard. She is enamelled in blue and red, the maker clearly unaware of suffrage colours. Although doubtless produced in greater quantity, trifles such as this, their novelty so ephemeral, are now even rarer than jewellery created for the suffrage societies.

Object 53

Suffrage plays

Object 53 is a photographic postcard of a scene from *How the Vote Was Won*, a play by Cicely Hamilton and Christopher St John. (TWL.2002.621, The Women's Library collection, London School of Economics and Political Science.)

This production of *How the Vote Was Won* was performed in the Paget Rooms, Penarth, south Wales on 13 December 1909 by the local Women's Freedom League (WFL), with Muriel Matters, then the WFL's organizer in Wales, as stage manager. A notable local photographer, Henry Corn (né Cohn) trading as C. Corn of Metropole Chambers, 3 The Hayes, in central Cardiff, was present to create Object 53, memorializing the event.[1] The humorous one-act play, first performed that April by members of the Actresses' Franchise League (AFL) at the New Royalty Theatre, London, was very popular with societies both militant and constitutional; it had been staged the previous week at an event in aid of the London Society of the National Union of Women's Suffrage Societies (NUWSS).[2] The sketch had originated as a story by

Hamilton, published at Christmas 1908 by the Women Writers' Suffrage League, telling how women of all sorts and conditions decided that 'every woman was to cease work until such time as her work was recognized by the State, and that, until the State did recognize it, she was to demand support and the necessities of life from her nearest male relative, however distant'. With sardonic humour, the play subverts all the stereotypical representations of suffragettes and was an immediate success, staged at the WFL's Green, White and Gold Fair in April and in May at both the Women's Social and Political Union (WSPU) Women's Exhibition and for NUWSS societies in Surrey. In July it was published as a 3d pamphlet by the WSPU's Woman's Press.

Between 1908 and 1914 at least 120 suffrage plays were staged in the UK. A very popular means of propaganda, they created cohesion among sympathizers, while hoping to convert antis.[3] The AFL, founded in November 1908, worked with both militant and constitutional societies, running a publishing programme that concentrated on one-act plays suitable for slotting into a suffrage society's evening entertainment and requiring only a small cast. Many of the plays were written by its members, issued in little booklets, the cover bearing the AFL colours of pink, white and green. A monologue, such as *The Mother's Meeting* by Mrs Harlow Phibbs, or a duologue, such as *A Chat with Mrs Chicky* by Evelyn Glover, were always popular, offering short, sharp entertainment.[4]

Suffrage activists, however, also wrote and produced three-act plays, one of the most popular being Elizabeth Robins' *Votes for Women!*, first staged at the Royal Court Theatre, Chelsea, in April 1907. On seeing it on 16 April, Kate Frye, then a member of the NUWSS, wrote in her diary, 'I loved the piece – it is quite fine – most cleverly written and the characters are so well drawn. Needless to say the acting was perfection as it generally is at the Court Theatre and the second act – the meeting in Trafalgar Square – ought to draw the whole of London. I was besides myself with excitement over it.'[5] Cicely Hamilton's *The Pageant of Great Women* was similarly uplifting, combining high moral tone with fund-raising opportunity. It was first performed at the Scala Theatre, London, on 10 November 1909, with a cast that included Hamilton, Ellen Terry, Edith Craig, Marion Terry and Winifred Mayo. *The Pageant* brought over fifty 'great women' of the past from many countries into a court setting in which, before the figure of 'Justice', 'Woman' and 'Prejudice' presented the case for and against women's enfranchisement. *The Pageant* was published as a book by Edith Craig's 'Suffrage Shop', a business venture stocking all manner of suffrage literature, then in Covent Garden, later moving to Adam Street, south of the Strand. The book included photographs of fifteen of the *Pageant* characters, represented by, among others, Hamilton (cross dressing as Christian Davies), Craig (as artist Rosa Bonheur) and her mother, Ellen Terry (as actress Nance Oldfield). Mounted, these were sold individually and are objects that still appeal to twenty-first-century collectors of both suffrage and theatrical memorabilia.

Women were by no means alone in staging suffrage-related plays; suffrage-sympathizing male writers produced some notable successes. Bernard Shaw gave the rights of London performances of *Press Cuttings*, his topical sketch in which women develop 'manly' characteristics of pugnacity and insolence while men are timid and indecisive, to the London Society of the NUWSS. Laurence Housman contributed both a parody, *Alice in Ganderland*, in which Alice attempts to take her seat at a Mad Hatter's Tea Party that closely resembles the House of Commons, and a translation of Aristophanes' *Lysistrata* in which he inserted contemporary suffrage jokes and references.

Although as productions, suffrage plays were ephemeral, they have left behind tangible objects, not only their texts, but theatre programmes, photographs and reviews, both published and private.

Object 54

Suffrage novels

Object 54 is *Outlawed: A Novel on the Woman Suffrage Question* by Mrs Despard and Mabel Collins, published by Henry J. Drane Ltd, Danegeld House, 82a Farringdon Street, London EC. (Lesley Mees Collection.)

In the later nineteenth century, a stream of novels used support for, or antipathy to, the suffrage cause as a shorthand by which to delineate characters or to put plot machinery into gear. However, after the WSPU brought militancy to London, novelists discovered they could now take their readers into places they might not previously have thought to enter, such as the prison cell, and were given legitimate reason to describe the indignities inflicted on women's bodies, whether through the horrors of force-feeding or at the hands of policemen in battles outside the House of Commons. The result was a spate of novels, some of which, such as Elizabeth Robins' *The Convert* (a novelization of her play, *Votes for Women!* – see Object 53) and Philip Gibbs' *Intellectual Mansions*, were supportive of women's suffrage and others that were more ambivalent or, indeed, antipathetic. For a few years there was a market for suffrage novels and publishers, such as H.J. Drane, obliged.[1]

Object 54 is unusual in that it still retains its illustrated cover, allowing us to view it as seen by its first readers. Suffrage novels of the period are now rarely found outside libraries and, if held in such institutions, have invariably been rebound or otherwise lost their dust wrappers. From the cover of Object 54 we can see the book was priced at 1 shilling, which, as well as being its cost, also denoted a class of popular fiction, cheaply printed and bound with an illustrated cover that aimed to attract attention. The artist, Frederick Coles, illustrates one of the main scenes in the book, the heroine being committed for trial on a charge of murder. The point was made in the novel that in such cases, apart from spectators in the public gallery (if the judge or magistrate did not ask women to leave, as he did in some types of cases), a woman prisoner was likely to be the only one of her sex in the court. Here we see her, majestic, in the dock, surrounded by policeman, clerks, magistrate and lawyer, with rows of men in the background. As she was taken to the cells, two voices from the public gallery cry out, 'I protest! Shame! Shame! Why are there no women there?' The Women's Freedom League made just such protests in courts to highlight the fact that women were tried by laws made only by men.

While the cover appears to confirm its classification as a 'shilling shocker', yet the novel combines a sensational plot with a lengthy and detailed description of the hard reality of life in Holloway. The authors describe this as 'a revelation on a subject almost unknown to the public', 'written by Mrs Despard from her own experiences and observation, when imprisoned as a Suffragist in Holloway gaol'.[2] Despard's experience did not include hunger-striking and forcible feeding, *Outlawed* is not that type of suffrage novel, but she wished to publicize the treatment meted out to common criminals, such as Beryl, her heroine. The plot that landed Beryl in Holloway was likely the work of Mabel Collins. Like Despard, Collins had long been a widow, was a vegetarian and anti-vivisectionist and had been a Theosophist; she earned her living as a prolific author of fiction, the occult often a speciality.

At the heart of *Outlawed* lies 'the conflict which exists in the centre of our social system which arises from the one sex being the ruler and the other the ruled'. As the heroine declares, 'We women are more than disenfranchised; we are outlawed. We are not protected by the law.'[3] However there is no overt mention of the suffrage campaign until all the complications of the plot are unravelled and the heroine is released from Holloway on 'Women's Suffrage day', encountering 'the great procession of women, that none who either saw it or took part in it will ever forget'.[4] The procession referred to was that of June 1908; *Outlawed* was published five months later. Henry J. Drane, a well-established London publisher of eclectic tastes, appears to have had a brief engagement with the suffrage movement, publishing in 1909 two more suffrage novels and an admirable collection of biographical essays, *Great Suffragists – and Why: modern makers of history*, edited by Ethel Hill and Olga Fenton Shafer.

Of the novels, Adrienne Mollwo's *A Fair Suffragette* is a febrile romance, set in 1907 at the time of the Mud March and Dickinson's suffrage bill, with discussion of the latter's clauses included in romantic speeches: 'I certainly believe in granting votes to women rate payers', says the hero, an anti-suffrage MP, as he at last proposes to Gipsie Grey, the fair suffragette.[5] This was a 6s novel, whereas H.J. Drane's other suffrage fiction offering, Napier Hawke's *The Premier and the Suffragette*, was, like *Outlawed*, issued at 1s, with a cover again illustrated by Frederick Coles. A combination of thriller and tract, the latter a long discussion of political philosophy, the audience for which may well have been at odds with the thriller element, *The Premier and the Suffragette* does, if nothing else, demonstrate how varied were the ways that the suffrage campaign could fire the imagination.

Object 55

Suffrage songs

Object 55 is the song sheet for 'The March of the Women', music composed by Ethel Smyth, dedicated to the Women's Social and Political Union (WSPU). Words by Cicely Hamilton. (Lesley Mees Collection.)

The music for 'The March of the Women', the anthem of the suffrage movement, was written by Ethel Smyth, an internationally renowned composer, towards the end of 1910 at a time when her burgeoning interest in the suffrage cause, intensified by meeting Mrs Pankhurst, had convinced her to set aside her musical career so that 'two years should be given to the W.S.P.U.'.[1] This coincided with a turning point in the 'Votes for Women' campaign, with the WSPU entering a new, albeit short, militant phase after the government announced on 18 November 1910 that Parliament was to be dissolved and a general election called, allowing no time for further discussion of the Conciliation Bill.

After the July Hyde Park procession (see Object 48) suffrage campaigning had continued peacefully in the hope that the all-party Conciliation Bill would continue to progress through Parliament, but the news of the dissolution resulted in a demonstration in Parliament Square where women were violently assaulted by the police (see Object 56). The event became known as 'Black Friday'. It was in this febrile atmosphere that Smyth resolved to put her individual talent to the service of the WSPU and compose for it a call to arms. The result was the rousing 'March of the Women', its source, apparently, 'an old tune Ethel had heard in the Abruzzi', a region of central Italy.[2] Smyth found her librettist in Cicely Hamilton, although she was a member of the Women's Freedom League (WFL) rather than the WSPU. As Smyth recorded, 'The poem was written after the music was composed, and that is about one of the most difficult things to do in this world. It is like asking somebody to move gracefully and easily in strait waistcoat and handcuffs.'[3] With its stirring chorus of 'Shout, shout, up with your song!/Cry with the wind for the dawn is breaking;/March, march, swing you along,/Wide blows our banner and hope is waking', the 'March' had its first performance at a gathering in London on 21 January 1911, celebrating the release that morning of WSPU prisoners, arrested in the aftermath of 'Black Friday'.

'The March' created unity and maintained the militant spirit at a time when the WSPU had once again put aside direct action while awaiting the outcome of the progress of a new private member's Conciliation Bill, introduced after the 1910 general election. If they were not to bond while taking part in acts of physical militancy, WSPU members could at least unite in singing their very own rousing chorus. By March 1911, cheap editions of 'The March' were on sale as well as a deluxe version, with a cover by Margaret Morris, artist and dancer, who depicted the women of the country, streaming over hill and dale in the wake of the 'Votes for Women' flag, her artwork rendered in the WSPU colours.[4] Although, when a piano was a commonplace item of furniture in homes throughout Britain, copies of 'The March' might have been found among a household's pile of sheet music, nowadays original versions are very scarce. However, such is the power of the anthem that 'The March' itself is still invariably used to introduce any staged or broadcast item featuring the suffrage movement.

Besides 'The March' there was an extensive repertoire of other suffrage songs, some issued as pamphlets by both the militants and the constitutionalists. Rather than compose new music, as Smyth did, many of these songs were familiar tunes to which apposite lyrics had been added. One such was 'The Women's Marseillaise', for which words written c.1908/9 by Florence Macaulay, a WSPU activist, were set to the tune of the French national anthem, another was 'Shoulder to Shoulder' by a NUWSS member, Miss S.J. Tanner, set to the tune of 'Men of Harlech'.[5] Such songs were sung while marching in processions or as part of a society's evening entertainment.

As with other examples of suffrage material culture, alongside inspirational songs appeared those with popular appeal, which, like commercial illustrated postcards, equated campaigning women with comedy. As early as the 1870/80s, Metzler & Co. published in London 'Bother the Men', written by Henry Walker, which includes the lines 'Only let the Government bring in a bill/To give us the franchise and have it we will!/Women we'll send into Parliament then./O ye shall see how they'll bother the men'. The sheet music cover depicts a mannish virago with her invariable accessory, an umbrella. In the twentieth century UK comedian/singers were successful with US ditties, such as 'That Ragtime Suffragette', recorded with a swing by Warwick Green for Phoenix in 1913.

Object 56

May Billinghurst's 'Velociman'

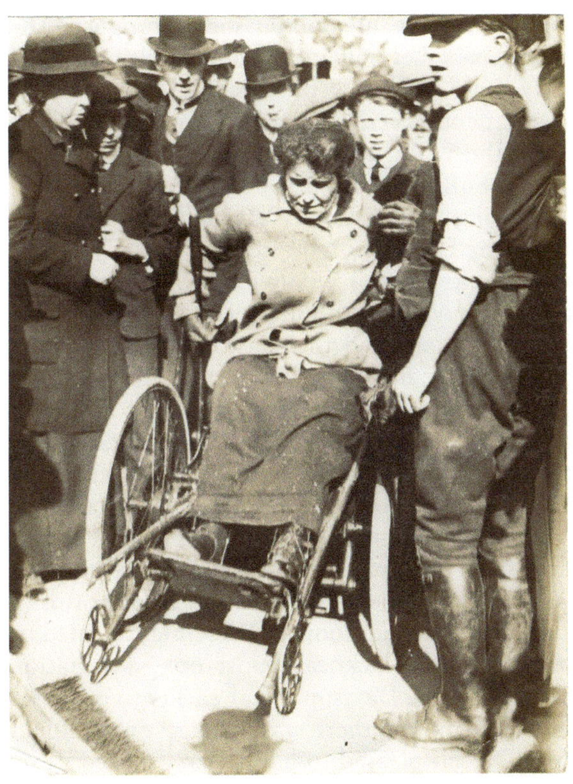

Object 56 is the hand-propelled 'invalid' tricycle in which May Billinghurst was photographed as she campaigned for the Women's Social and Political Union (WSPU). (TWL 2009 02 043, The Women's Library collection, London School of Economics and Political Science.)

A copy of Object 55, a flyer printed with the words and music of 'The March of the Women', was one of the items kept all her life by May Billinghurst, who never let physical disability prevent her from taking an active part in WSPU demonstrations, whether singing in a procession or engaging in the turbulence in Parliament Square on 'Black Friday' in November 1910.[1] That she was able to participate was due both to her determination and to her hand-propelled tricycle. This was described by her nephew as a 'Velocimain', probably a mis-rendering of 'Velociman', a vehicle produced from the early 1880s by the Singer company of Coventry.[2] This, the most popular vehicle of its type, was regularly commended by newspapers, describing how 'propulsion is effected by means of levers, which are pulled simultaneously, as in the act of rowing [and], for all who depend on their arms for the propelling power, the Singer Velociman can be driven with perfect ease at a speed of 8 miles per hour'.[3]

(Rosa) May Billinghurst was born in Lewisham, London, one of many children of a banker, Henry Billinghurst, who, with his wife, was supportive of the education and enfranchisement of women. One of her sisters attended Girton College, Cambridge, but little is known about May's early years other than that she suffered from paralysis as a child, perhaps as a result of polio. Her family always marvelled at the amount she accomplished, although, encased in leg irons up to her waist, crutches were her only means of propulsion until 1900 when she obtained the Velociman. In the early years of the twentieth century she volunteered at the Greenwich workhouse, an experience that convinced her that, to implement social reform, women needed the vote. In 1907 she joined the WSPU and, in her Velociman, took part in the 13 June 1908 National Union of Women's Suffrage Societies procession, using the occasion to distribute leaflets advertising the following week's Hyde Park WSPU demonstration. In July 1908 she campaigned for the WSPU at the Haggerston by-election and in July 1910 founded and became secretary of the Greenwich, Deptford and Woolwich WSPU. Four months later, in November 1910, she was thrown out of her Velociman during the 'Black Friday' demonstration, charged with obstruction, but, like others arrested that day, discharged. Newspaper reports mention how conspicuous Billinghurst was in her 'coloured' tricycle.[4] No specific colours are mentioned, but such a description does raise the question as to whether Billinghurst could have had the Velociman painted in the WSPU colours. She certainly did decorate it, for instance, with a 'Votes for Women' placard and flowers and greenery for Emily Davison's funeral.

Billinghurst was arrested again in Parliament Square in November 1911, later appearing in the dock on crutches, charged with attempting to force her tricycle through a police cordon. This time she was sentenced to five days' imprisonment for obstructing the police. In June 1912 she organized a large and raucous WSPU demonstration on Blackheath, with Sylvia Pankhurst as one of several speakers, and in December, from her Velociman, carried out a pillar box 'outrage', pouring a tar-like substance into a Blackheath post box, a variation on the 'incendiarism' campaign instigated by Emily Wilding Davison a year earlier (see Object 61). Other tubes of the liquid were found in the Velociman and there was a suggestion Billinghurst had been involved in similar acts. She declared herself pleased to have been arrested as the intention was to gain publicity for the 'Votes for Women' campaign. Despite her disability, she was sentenced to eight months' imprisonment, but, in acknowledgement of her physical condition, was placed in the first division; most WSPU prisoners were in the second (see Object 66). She immediately went on hunger strike and was forcibly fed but, after pressure behind the scenes, was released two weeks later by order of the Home Secretary.[5] Her account of her treatment in Holloway suggests she was held in an ordinary cell rather than the Infirmary. There is no mention in the reports as to how she navigated Holloway; presumably she had no Velociman, only leg irons and crutches.

Nor do newspaper accounts mention how Billinghurst travelled from her Blackheath home into central London to participate in the occasions mentioned, the last being the attempt by the WSPU on 21 May 1914 to petition the King, during which she chained her tricycle to the Palace railings. Object 56 forces us to consider how far the owner of a Velociman could travel in the first decades of the twentieth century? Surely Billinghurst could not have propelled herself all the way from Blackheath into central London before taking part in any suffrage, or other, activity? Did she hire a van to accommodate herself and the Velociman? Could the tricycle have been carried on a train? The solution to this problem was presumably so obvious that it occurred to no-one at the time to remark it.

Object 57

A *Votes for Women* poster highlighting male activism

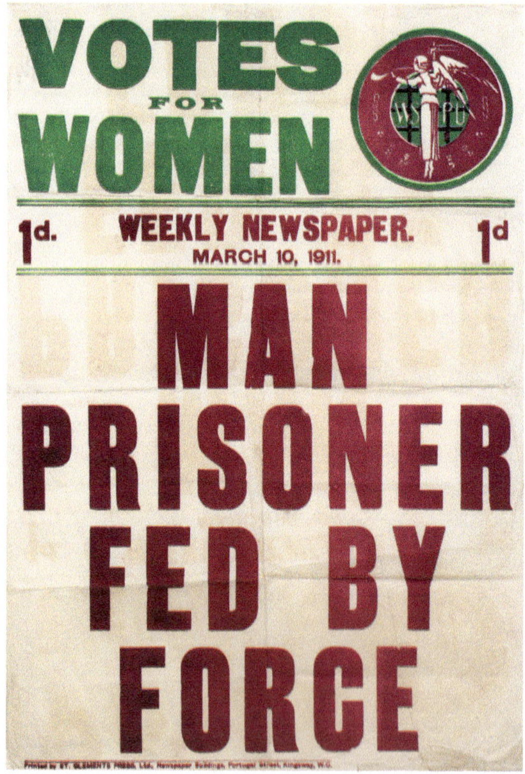

Object 57 is a *Votes for Women* poster advertising the issue of 10 March 1911 with the news that a member of the Men's Political Union was being forcibly fed. (TWL 7HFD/A/5/09, The Women's Library collection, London School of Economics and Political Science.)

In the early twentieth century, men not only offered support to the women's suffrage campaign by chairing and speaking at meetings but were also prepared to engage in militant activity.[1] The 'man prisoner' who featured on Object 57 was Alfred Abbey, a member of the Men's Political Union for Women's Enfranchisement (MPU), who had been arrested on 1 March 1911 after scaling the wall of the garden of 10 Downing Street with the intention of delivering a letter to the Cabinet by attaching it to a stone thrown at a window. Sentenced to three weeks' imprisonment in Pentonville, he went on hunger strike and was forcibly fed.

Founded in 1910 as the male counterpart of the WSPU, the MPU was one of two societies formed by men in the early twentieth century; the Men's League for Women's Suffrage (MLWS), formed in 1907, was the other. The MLWS was non-militant, though happy to work with the WSPU and the WFL on 'propagandist work', speaking at meetings and bringing pressure to bear, as electors, on MPs and parliamentary candidates. A 'Declaration of Representative Men in Favour of Women's Suffrage', issued by the MLWS in 1909, included the names of eighty-three officeholders, past and present, in the Liberal and Conservative parties, twenty-four high-ranking army and naval officers, eighty-six academics, and writers such as H.G. Wells and John Masefield. The president of the MLWS was the Earl of Lytton, chairman of the Conciliation Committee (see Object 58) and brother of one of the WSPU's leading members, Lady Constance Lytton. Both men's societies had branches in major UK cities, organizing demonstrations of their own, while also offering support to those arranged by women. By 1914, as the militant campaign became ever more dangerous, the MPU organized a Suffrage Speakers' Defence Corps.

Even though news of his case was confined to a short article on page four, there was shock value in selecting the forcible feeding of Alfred Abbey as the headline for that week's issue of *Votes for Women*. Ironically, a year later the paper's proprietor, Frederick Pethick-Lawrence, was also to endure forcible feeding in Pentonville (see Object 63). For the public might be immune to reports that women were subjected to this treatment, but it was 'news' that a man was prepared to endure it in the cause of women's enfranchisement. Abbey was soon joined in Pentonville by another member of the MPU, Hugh Franklin, who, in protest at Abbey's treatment, threw a letter wrapped round a stone at a window in Churchill's house. Franklin was a member of a Jewish family, many members of which were active suffrage campaigners, and had been imprisoned for six weeks the previous December after assaulting Churchill with a whip. This time he was sentenced to a month's imprisonment, went on hunger strike and was forcibly fed. In Bow Street Court he produced Object 57, declaring its wording, 'Man Prisoner Fed By Force' 'is my defence in a nutshell'.[2] Both men were denied the rights of political prisoners, despite claiming their offences were only committed with a political motive. These prison sentences did not deter Franklin who in 1913 was charged with arson, caught setting fire to an empty train (see Object 31). In 1915 he married Elsie Duval, a WSPU activist, sister of Victor Duval, the founder and organizing secretary of the MPU.

One of the most influential members of the MLWS was W.H. Dickinson, Liberal MP for St Pancras North, and a dedicated supporter of women's suffrage in the House of Commons. After his election in 1906 he voted in favour of every woman's suffrage bill and in 1916 was the member of the Speaker's Conference on Electoral Reform whose counterintuitive proposal that women electors should be subjected to an age limit was successful in carrying the first stage of women's enfranchisement into law (see Object 83).

Object 58

National Union of Women's Suffrage Societies flyer in support of the Second Conciliation Bill, 1911

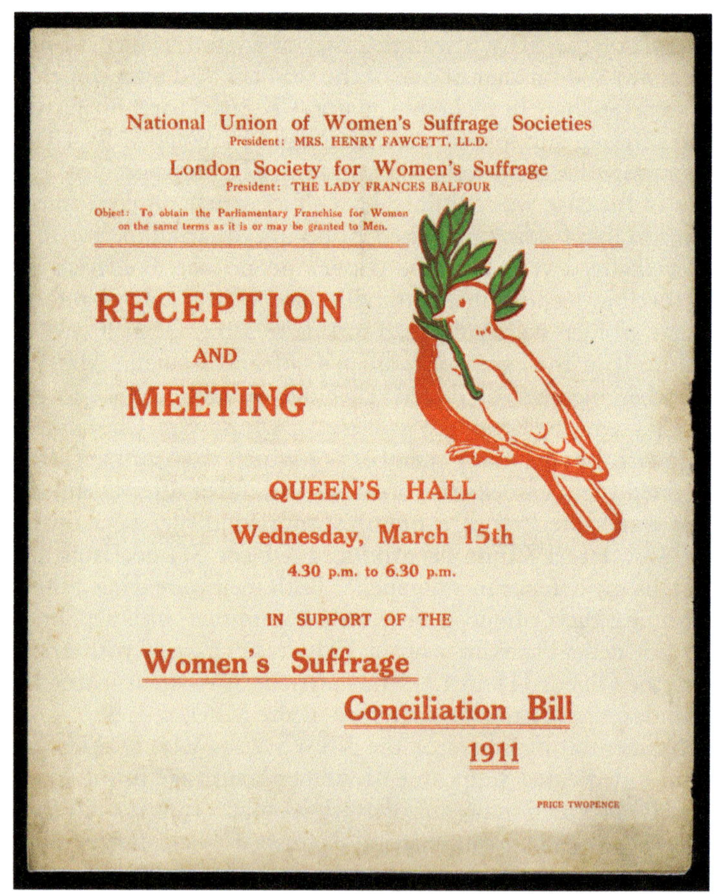

Object 58 is a flyer produced by the National Union of Women's Suffrage Societies (NUWSS), advertising a meeting in support of the 1911 Conciliation Bill. (2ASL/11/32, The Women's Library collection, London School of Economics and Political Science.)

After the December 1910 general election returned the Liberals to power, albeit now relying on the support of the Irish parliamentary and the Labour parties, the all-party Conciliation Bill was again presented to the House of Commons, passing its First Reading in February 1911 (for the earlier Conciliation Bill see Objects 47, 48 and 56). With the terms of the first bill very slightly revised, this private member's bill aimed to give the vote to women householders, enfranchising about 1 million women. Because there were numerous franchises other than the 'householder', this did not meet the NUWSS aspiration of obtaining the 'vote as it was or may be granted to Men', as printed at the head of the flyer, but it was recognized that the passing into law of any bill that removed the sex disqualification was well worth pursuing.

Both militants and constitutionalists campaigned vigorously in support of the Second Reading, due on 5 May. Featuring a dove and olive branch, symbolic of peace, and printed in the NUWSS colours, this flyer advertises a meeting on 15 March, organized by the London Society of the NUWSS in the Queen's Hall, Langham Place, London. Speaking in the hall, which was decorated for the occasion in red, white and green, Frances Sterling, the chairman, stressed that the meeting was held 'to back this particular bill with all possible strength and enthusiasm'.[1] One of the speakers was George Lansbury, newly elected as Labour MP for Bow, who stated he 'believed in votes for all women, but it would take a long time to convert the whole country to Adult Suffrage and in the meantime we must press for this small instalment'. In fact, analysis of the social status of women householders in a representative group of constituencies had proved that the overwhelming majority of those who would be enfranchised could be considered 'working-class'. To ensure the bill had the backing of Labour MPs, the NUWSS was keen to be seen as campaigning not only in the interests of its own, mainly middle-class, members. Millicent Fawcett was not present at the meeting but later stressed, 'The Bill gave no representation to property whatever. The only qualification which it recognized was that of the resident householder.'[2]

On 23 March the WSPU decked out London's Albert Hall in purple, white and green to hear Mrs Pankhurst urging members to support the Conciliation Bill. The proceedings opened with the presentation of a baton to Ethel Smyth, who at once used it to conduct a performance of the 'Women's March' (see Object 55). The WSPU had produced a leaflet, 'The Conciliation Bill Explained', which described how, under the terms of the bill, 'a duchess may get a vote for her palace, and a charwoman for her cottage, or (if she has full control) even for a single room. The household franchise is fair to all classes'. Further, although a wife would not get the vote unless the house was rented in her name, she would not be disqualified simply because she was married. This last eliminated a cause of discord that had plagued the nineteenth-century suffrage campaign.

Over the next couple of months, the Conciliation Bill was promoted around the country at meetings of all suffrage societies. Resolutions in its favour were sent to the government from fifty borough and city councils, numerous letters on the subject were printed in the press and MPs were bombarded with letters.[3] On 3 May the NUWSS held a national convention in London, chaired by Mrs Fawcett, to which all its federations sent delegates and from which a resolution was sent to the prime minister. With the Church League for Women's Suffrage (see Object 76) observing 5 May as a Day of Intercession, the Conciliation Bill passed its Second Reading with a majority of 167.

Hoping their goal was in sight, the WSPU maintained its truce and on 17 June all suffrage societies cooperated in producing the most spectacular of processions. Benefitting from the extravagant decorations erected in anticipation of the coronation of George V, it brought to the London streets every element of suffrage pageantry campaigners had ever contrived. On 23 August Lord Lytton, chairman of the Conciliation Committee, received a final promise from Asquith that in the next session of Parliament an opportunity would be given to proceed with the bill through all its stages. As in the previous year, with parliament in recess, suffragists and suffragettes removed their attention from Westminster, embarking on a 'holiday campaign' to keep the subject before the electorate.

Object 59

'Votes for Women' novelties

Object 59 is a 'novelty' figure, a crude representation of a suffragette, 150 mm high. (Lesley Mees Collection.)

In the summer of 1911, as the suffrage campaigners left Westminster and took to the seaside, parading with sandwich boards on the promenade or holding meetings on the beach, their holidaymaker audience might also be diverted by encountering in a local shop a novelty such as Object 59. For this little figure has still attached to its base a label revealing it was 'Sold by

Fred Franklin, Drapery & Fancy Stores, 11 High Street, Deal'. The Franklin family had been drapers, photographers and sellers of fancy goods in Deal, Kent, from the early nineteenth century; a surviving photograph shows Fred Franklin standing outside his shop, the window packed with goods.[1] The head of the figure is made from a ping pong ball, with the spectacled face hand-painted. The body is stuffed canvas, with pins for the hands, around the crown of the hat, and with another pin in the middle of the chest; its likely function was as a pin cushion. However, the same object, though rather more dishevelled and stuck through with more pins, held by the National Museum Wales, has been interpreted as an 'anti-suffragette voodoo doll', with a legend attached that it was sent anonymously, with ill intent, in the early twentieth century to a woman in west Wales. While there is no doubt that generic 'comic' humour did not favour the suffrage movement, it is difficult now to know whether actual malicious intent can be attributed to the creation of an object such as this.

A similar novelty, without even the function of a pincushion, was described in a 1907 press report as 'tiny and wooden and to all intents and purposes a doll. It is sold by the gutter merchants and holds, extended in its travesty of a hand, a legal-looking scroll bearing the legend "Votes for Women"'.[2] So, while standing in the gutter, as was the law, attempting to sell copies of *Votes for Women*, a suffragette could be competing with a street seller peddling her image.

At the other end of the novelty market, in 1908 the jewellery firm of Saunders and Shepherd produced in silver a figure of a woman draped with a sandwich board on which one side declares 'Votes for Women' and the other 'We can make things hot for you'. She is, in fact, a 'muffineer' – unscrew her head and insert the spices or sugar to be shaken out onto a muffin through the perforations in her large bonnet. Similarly, comic figures displaying a 'Votes for Women' placard or sash are to be found decorating metal mantel clocks that date from 1910–11.[3] It is necessary, however, to be suspicious of many silver items with ostensible 'suffrage' connections for there are on the market objects such as cigarette cases on which the unscrupulous, in the hope of increasing their value, have engraved suffrage mottos or figures or inserted a printed suffrage motif.

There is no doubt that the idea of a 'Votes for Woman' woman was an incentive to all manner of novelty makers, who were happy to place a flag in her hand and make her dance (as a 'jig doll'); or, working on clockwork, move in circles, pamphlet in hand, while ringing her bell; or pop up as a 'fright' in a Jack-in-Box; or be 'run in' by a policeman when a pneumatic bulb is pressed.[4] Expressing rather more sympathy for the Cause, 'suffragette' dolls were popular objects for purchase at the many fund-raising bazaars organized by all suffrage societies. While most will by now have suffered the depredations of the nursery and of time, the occasional 'suffragette' doll has survived, such as the one, made by Edith New and bought by Alice Singer, WSPU members both, that appeared on the Antiques Roadshow in 2004. Fittingly named 'Christabel', she had been cherished down the generations. One might, though, wonder what became of the 500 dolls dressed by a Mrs Stern 'in the suffrage colours of green, white, and mauve', arranged as a suffragette meeting and submitted to the Doll Show organized by the journal *Truth* at the Albert Hall in December 1912.[5] It is likely the message of 'Votes for Women' was directed at the Doll Show audience rather than at the poor-law school pupils for whom they were destined as Christmas presents. Again, care must be taken; proven provenance is imperative when assessing the authenticity of an object such as a 'suffragette doll'.

Object 60

Diaries and suffrage

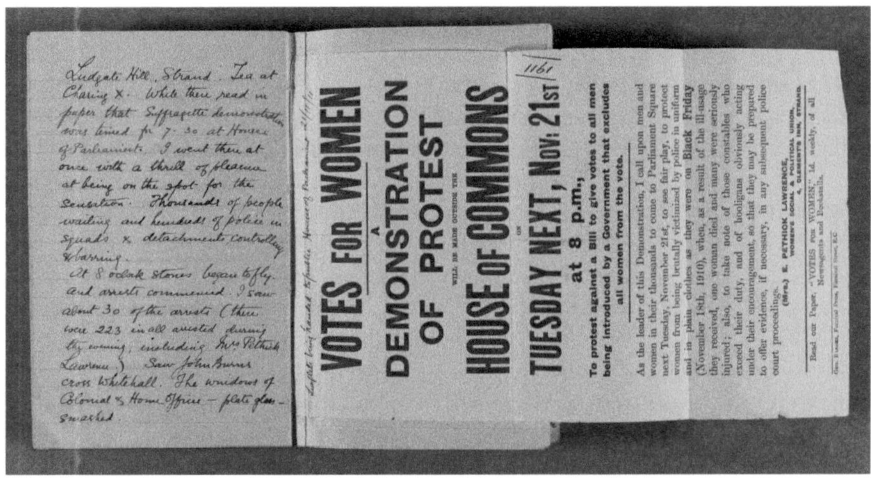

Object 60 Entry for 21 November 1911 from the diary of Harold Le Messurier (1874–1959). (Martin Last collection, Zurich.)

A page from the diary of Harold Le Messurier, a Guernsey bank clerk, tells us what it was like for a passer-by to witness a WSPU demonstration. On 21 November 1911, in London on business, Le Messurier was taking his tea at Charing Cross when he read in the evening paper that a demonstration was soon to take place at the Houses of Parliament and 'went there at once with a thrill of pleasure at being on the spot for the sensation'. This is what the militant campaign meant to the man in the street, 'sensation'. Le Messurier duly recorded what he saw: the crowds ('thousands'), police ('hundreds'), stones, windows smashed (Colonial and Home Offices), arrests ('30') and personalities recognized (John Burns, a government minister, and Mrs Pethick-Lawrence). From news later reported he was able to include in his entry the fact that a total of 223 arrests had been made. Early the next morning he set off back to Guernsey, having carefully preserved the handbill he had accepted from a campaigner.

This handbill explains the reason for the demonstration. As we have seen under Object 58, the suffrage societies had been promised that when Parliament returned in the autumn, the Conciliation Bill would continue its progress. However, on 7 November the prime minister announced that the government would be introducing in the next session an Electoral Reform Bill that would sweep away the existing complicated franchises and substitute a single one of residence. This was to be confined to adult males; women were again to be excluded. As Mrs Fawcett wrote of Asquith, 'If it had been his object to enrage every woman suffragist to the point of frenzy, he could not have acted with greater perspicacity.'[1] The Women's Social and Political Union (WSPU) resumed militancy and, as Le Messurier witnessed, while Mrs Pethick-Lawrence led a deputation from Caxton Hall to Parliament Square, hundreds of women attacked government buildings with stones and hammers. After Lloyd George complacently declared, at a Liberal Federation meeting on 24 November, that the Conciliation Bill had been 'torpedoed', the WSPU prepared for war. The National Union of Women's Suffrage Societies (NUWSS), however, while hoping that the proposed Electoral Reform Bill (later known as the Franchise and Registration Bill) might be amended to include women, still had hopes for the Conciliation Bill, which was duly reintroduced, but defeated at its Second Reading in March 1912.

In his diary, in a few sentences, Le Messurier sketches the 'sensation' behind which lay myriad political motivations, complications, strategies, hopes and doubts. His was an outsider's view. Researchers can experience the suffrage campaign from the inside through the daily diaries kept by suffrage activists such as, for the WSPU, the Blathwayts of Bath (see Object 47); actress and novelist, Elizabeth Robins;[2] and for the Women's Freedom League (WFL), Eunice Murray, a prominent Scottish member.[3] One of the most detailed diaries covering the suffrage years was that kept by Kate Frye who in the later years of the campaign was an organizer for the New Constitutional Society for Women's Suffrage (see Object 69), but who had previously been a member of the NUWSS and then of the WSPU, and, from its formation, was a member of the Actresses' Franchise League. She was present at all the great suffrage occasions, such as 'Black Friday' in November 1910 and Emily Davison's funeral in 1913 (see Object 73), while also recording the minutiae of daily involvement in the campaign, from reading palms at a WFL 'Green, Gold and White Fair' to organizing train journeys to deepest Norfolk.[4]

Some suffragettes kept diaries of the highlights of their involvement, particularly of their experience in prison. Among these diarists were Annie Cobden Sanderson,[5] Emily Wilding Davison,[6] Katie Gliddon,[7] Mary Anne Rawle[8] and Elsie Duval.[9] With writing materials forbidden, some were forced to record their daily lives on sheets of HM Prison toilet paper, while Katie Gliddon made use of the white spaces in a copy of *The Poetical Works of Shelley*. For NUWSS members the experience of the Pilgrimage (see Object 74) was in peculiarity, if not in hardship, comparable to prison, inspiring Marjory Lees and Annie Ramsay to keep diaries of their journey.[10]

While diaries focusing on close involvement in the suffrage movement are more likely to be preserved and to be mined by researchers, items such as Object 60 that reveal a fleeting glimpse of the intrusion of the campaign into daily life are most certainly worthy of attention.

Object 61

'The Pillar Box and the Suffragette' money box

Object 61 is a papier-mâché money box in the form of a pillar box, the base of which can be removed to retrieve the savings. When a coin is 'posted', the lid opens and, with a screech, up jumps the suffragette, wearing a purple dress and 'Votes' necklace. Most definitely not a lady, she is sticking out her tongue and waving a flag inscribed 'Votes for Women'. A label inside the lid describes this as a 'Militant Souvenier' [*sic*] and another, underneath the posting slot, reveals it was made for 'Xmas 1913'. This 'suffragette' novelty, like so many others, was made in Germany. 180 mm high. (Lesley Mees Collection.)

While the attack on government buildings in Westminster on 21 November 1911 represented an organized resumption of Women's Social and Political Union (WSPU) militancy (see Object 60), there were individual members of the WSPU who were prepared to work without instruction from headquarters, adopting destructive new campaigning methods. One such was Emily Wilding Davison who, three weeks later, embarked on a new militant method, described by her as 'Incendiarism'.[1] On 14 December 1911 she was arrested in Parliament Street, Westminster, in the act of stuffing a flaming piece of linen, saturated with paraffin, into a post box. She admitted setting fire to two pillar boxes in the City of London earlier in the day and declared, 'I did this entirely on my own responsibility.'[2] Davison, a university graduate, had worked at WSPU headquarters for a time, had contributed articles to *Votes for Women*, had secreted herself overnight in the House of Commons on several occasions, including on Census Night 1911, and had been imprisoned and on hunger strike in both Manchester and London. In court she explained that she

> called upon the Government to put Women's Suffrage in the King's Speech on 14 February 1912. As the proposal was meant to be serious, I adopted a serious course. In the agitation for reform in the past the next step after window-breaking was incendiarism, in order to draw the attention of the private citizen to the fact that this question of reform is their concern as well as that of women.[3]

After an Old Bailey trial, Davison was sentenced to six months' imprisonment. She did not go on hunger strike, but, as the Holloway authorities thought she was not eating enough, she was forcibly fed for a week. Later, still in prison in June 1912, she joined the mass hunger strike undertaken by other WSPU prisoners (see Object 66).

Through 1912 there were sporadic attacks on pillar boxes, with this form of militancy gathering momentum at the end of the year when WSPU members carried out a nation-wide 'pillar-box campaign'. Believing (rightly, as it turned out) that the government, whatever their promises, had no intention of allowing women's suffrage amendments to their Franchise Bill, militancy was escalated. Pillar boxes were termed 'government property' by *The Suffragette*, the paper launched that autumn by the WSPU, after Emmeline and Frederick Pethick-Lawrence, who owned *Votes for Women*, had been dismissed from the leadership. Under the headline, 'Why Letters are Burnt', the front page of *The Suffragette* (13 December 1912) explained, 'They want to make the electors and the Government so uncomfortable that in order to put an end to the nuisance, they will give women the vote. Women will never get the vote except by creating an intolerable situation for all the selfish and apathetic people who stand in their way.'[4]

Among those adopting the 'pillar-box campaign' was May Billinghurst (see Object 56), who was arrested as, from her 'Velociman', she poured a tar-like substance into a Blackheath post box on 17 December 1912, and Ella Stevenson (see Object 67), arrested on 22 February 1913 after she had placed a packet containing two tubes of phosphorous in the post box attached to the main post office in Richmond, Surrey. It is likely she was given the tubes by Edwy Clayton, an analytical chemist, husband of the secretary of the Richmond and Kew WSPU. He was later charged with conspiracy to commit damage by supplying bomb-making information and equipment. No nation was exempt from pillar box attack. In March 1913, for instance, Brunswick-black varnish was poured into pillar boxes in Dublin; in May oil and soot were poured into a St Andrews, Fife, pillar box; and in June Mrs Margaret Mackworth (later Lady Rhondda) was imprisoned after placing an explosive device in a Newport, Monmouthshire, post box. The latter incident had an afterlife, commemorated in 'Rhondda Rips It Up', the Welsh National Opera's 2018 romp through Lady Rhondda's life.

This, then, is the background to the production of Object 61. For, in the period 1912–14, the conjunction of 'pillar-boxes' and 'suffragettes' had swiftly taken hold of the popular imagination, a motif played out in numerous cartoons, on comic postcards, reaching its apogee, perhaps, in this moneybox. While, in the twenty-first century, Object 61 is eminently collectable, so too, if in a more minor way, are items of mail damaged in the WSPU pillar-box campaign.

Object 62

Anti-suffrage flyer, 1912

Object 62 is a flyer advertising a demonstration held by the National League for Opposing Woman Suffrage in the Royal Albert Hall on the evening of 28 February 1912. (Lesley Mees Collection.)

The National League for Opposing Woman Suffrage (NLOWS) had been formed in December 1910, an amalgamation of the Women's National Anti-Suffrage League and the Men's League for Opposing Woman Suffrage.[1] Its existence was testament to the fact that anti-suffragists recognized it was essential to form a consolidated opposition to the suffrage campaign. The NLOWS committee comprised seven men and seven women, but its presidents were always men, the first being Lord Cromer, succeeded in March 1912 by Lord Curzon. Lady Jersey, one of many aristocratic members, was deputy president. The 28 February 1912 meeting was convened to oppose the Second Conciliation Bill (see Object 58), which had been reintroduced and was due to have its Second Reading in the House of Commons on 22 March (although it was delayed until 28 March).

The flyer is printed in black and pink on white paper, black, pink and white being the colours adopted by the NLOWS, with an image of the society's badge hanging from the ribbon running across the top. The side garlands, linking photographs of the speakers, display repeats of a rose, thistle and shamrock motif, signifying the society's patriotism. Lord Cromer, former consul-general of Egypt, chaired the meeting and Lord Loreburn, the Lord Chancellor, moved the resolution 'that the extension of the Parliamentary franchise to women would be hostile to their own welfare and the welfare of the State, and that a change so momentous and so incalculable in its effects both socially and politically ought not to be entertained except upon a clear and deliberately expressed demand by the electorate'. This was seconded by Lord Curzon, former viceroy of India. That the NLOWS was distinctly Imperial-minded is evidenced in the leaflets the society produced. Leaflet number 32 answers 'Should Women Have Votes Because They Pay Taxes?' by concluding, 'The fact that women pay taxes is not sufficient reason for transferring the political sovereignty of the Empire from men to women.' Leaflet 52, headed 'Why the nation is opposed to the grant of the Parliamentary Vote to Women', gives among its reasons, 'Because any proposal to give votes to women would result in swamping the male voter and making women the real rulers of the Empire.'

While the 28 February speeches indicate the complacent mindset of those actively opposed to women's suffrage, they are doubtless also a good indication of the way the subject was viewed by the masses, who, uninterested in the subject, saw no need for any change to the existing system. Lewis Harcourt, Secretary of State for the Colonies, declared, to cheers, that there was 'nothing to suggest there was any widespread demand for votes for women' and that 'suffragists were gravely misled if they mistook the noise of a few for the demand of the many'. Another of the speakers, F.E. Smith, high-earning barrister and Conservative MP, remarked that 'he never heard at any meeting in any constituency at the last election the question of female suffrage mentioned by one candidate or the other, or even remotely referred to. (Cheers)'.

A leading woman member of the NLOWS, wealthy and philanthropic Violet Markham, recalled 'that four years ago in a small hall in Kensington it was her privilege to speak at the first anti-suffrage meeting held in London. [She] took a stand on the great principle that men and women were different with talents that were complementary, not identical, and that therefore they ought to have a different share in the management of the State'. She commented, 'Man was and man would continue to remain the business spirit of the world, and the work of Imperial Parliament was in the main work of a nature which lay outside woman's practical experience and with which man was best fitted to deal.' Markham believed women should confine themselves to working in local government for the good of their communities and implied that those campaigning for the parliamentary vote were ambitious for themselves, wanting to take part in 'the ugly scramble for place and power, for the loaves and fishes of preferment and office'.[2] The resolution was carried by a large majority.

On 28 March 1912 the Conciliation Bill was defeated on its Second Reading by fourteen votes. Apart from a parliamentary reaction to the increasing militancy of the Women's Social and Political Union (see Objects 61 and 63), a deciding factor was that Irish MPs had voted against it, worried that further discussion might delay a Home Rule bill. As this was the first time since 1884 that a women's suffrage bill had failed to pass its Second Reading, the NLOWS was, naturally, jubilant. However, the effect of the defeat was to cause the National Union of Women's Suffrage Societies to embark on an entirely new strategy (see Object 71).

Object 63

German photographic postcard of a window smashed by suffragettes, March 1912

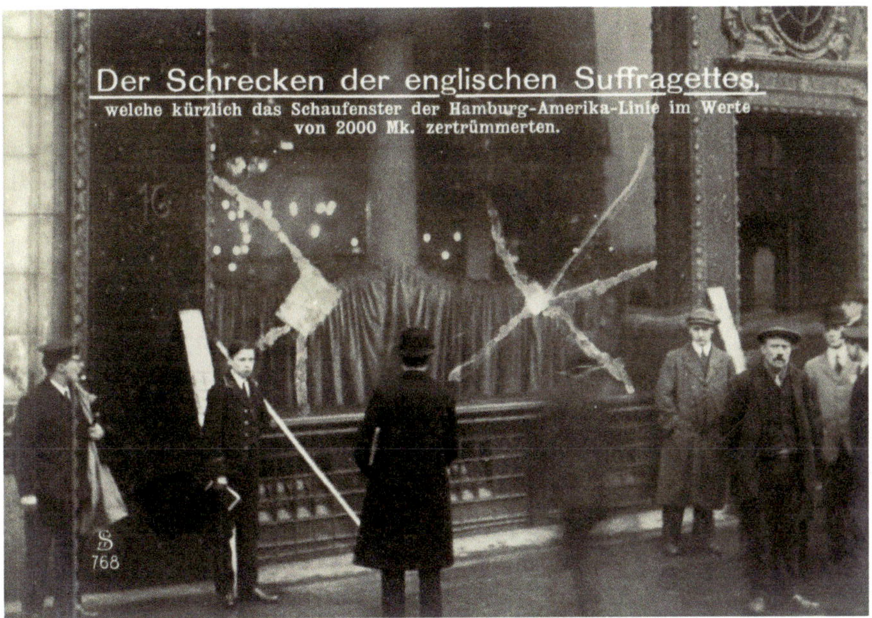

Object 63 is a German postcard published by Paul Hoffman & Co., Berlin. It is captioned, 'The terror of the English suffragettes, who recently smashed the shop window of the Hamburg-America Line worth 2000 marks'. (Lesley Mees Collection.)

On Friday 1 March 1912, two days after the National League for Opposing Women's Suffrage held their meeting in the Royal Albert Hall (see Object 62), 150 members of the Women's Social and Political Union (WSPU) broke the windows of shops and offices in the West End of London. Addressing a 16 February meeting to welcome prisoners released in the aftermath of the November 1911 window-smashing demonstration (see Object 60), Mrs Pankhurst had declared 'the argument of the broken pane of glass is the most valuable in modern politics'.[1] The reasoning behind the 'argument' was that if women damaged property they would be arrested, whereas if they tried to walk through Parliament Square to present petitions to Parliament they would be assaulted by the police and onlookers. The WSPU leaders also recognized that few things were more newsworthy than a phalanx of women attacking property, being arrested, tried and imprisoned.

While the National Union of Women's Suffrage Societies (NUWSS) still hoped to shepherd the Second Conciliation Bill through its Second Reading, fixed for 22 March (later moved to 28 March), the WSPU had lost all faith in the government and were determined to renew their militant campaign. For this they advertised a protest to take place in Parliament Square on 4 March but, in advance, secretly launched the 1 March demonstration, catching the police unawares.[2] Women were armed with hammers and instructions for their use and timing, coordinating the window smashing. Beginning *c*.5.30 pm, the main areas targeted were the Strand, Cockspur Street, Haymarket and Piccadilly. Object 62 shows the broken window of the Hamburg-America shipping office at 16 Cockspur Street, off Trafalgar Square. The large plate-glass windows that lined that street, in calmer times the route of suffrage processions, had proved an attractive target, with those of no. 26 and of the Grand Trunk Railway at 17–19 also attacked.

The photograph was probably taken the day after the raid, before it had been possible for glaziers to replace the window of what was the largest German shipping company. The photographer has captured the attention of passers-by as he set up his camera and the resulting image, clearly selected because of its German subject, was issued by a Berlin postcard firm, Paul Hoffman & Co. Although some news agency photographs showing similar window damage exist, there is, rather surprisingly, little evidence that they were issued as postcards by British publishers and, although the demonstration received full coverage in newspapers throughout the UK, most reports were unaccompanied by photographs. The government would have wanted as little publicity as possible given to the WSPU and individual firms may not have wished to deter customers by advertising damage to their property.

When captioning Object 63, the author was incorrect in thinking that the 'terror' had been created by 'English Suffragettes', for the woman responsible for breaking the window in the photograph, and that of the Grand Trunk Railway next door, was Margaret (Maggie) Macfarlane, a young Scotswoman, a trained nurse, secretary of the Dundee WSPU. She was one of 124 women arrested and appeared the next day at Bow Street court (see Object 37). It was reported that 'the court was crowded with men, very few women being admitted' (see Object 54).[3] Macfarlane had been detained by a Captain Bax, who reported to a policeman, 'I saw this woman with a hammer in her hand (she has a hammer in her muff now), I saw her break both the windows. When the hammer was taken, she said "I have broken the window as a protest against the Government."'[4] The damage to the Hamburg-America window amounted to £104 and to the Grand Trunk Railway window, £40. Macfarlane was sentenced to four months in Holloway, served her whole sentence, went on hunger strike, was forcibly fed and finally released on 29 June (see Object 66).

A further window-smashing demonstration took place on 4 March with some women supplied with stones from the WSPU's ammunition station at the Gardenia Restaurant, Covent Garden. As a result of these demonstrations, over 270 premises were attacked, creating £6,600 worth of damage. Over 220 arrests were made, suffragettes, including the composer Ethel Smyth (see Object 55), packed Holloway, Aylesbury and Birmingham prisons, Mrs Pankhurst and the Pethick-Lawrences, were taken to court on a charge of conspiracy to commit damage, and insurers were presented with numerous claims for recompense.[5] Frederick Pethick-Lawrence was sentenced to nine months' imprisonment, deemed culpable even though he had not participated. Most importantly, costs for the trial and for replacing the damaged windows were awarded against him. He refused to pay and was made bankrupt. In Pentonville prison he went on hunger strike and was forcibly fed before being released in June. He and Emmeline, who had also been imprisoned, went abroad to recuperate and discovered on their return they had been ousted from the WSPU. Although they did not agree with the increasingly militant tactics, the most likely reason for their dismissal was that they were considered a liability by the Pankhursts, their wealth a means by which the government would claw back damages, weakening the WSPU.

Object 64

'Elusive Christabel', optic toy, 1912

Object 64 is 'Elusive Christabel', an optic toy made by the Flashograph Co., 9 Tottenham St, London W. 150 mm x 90 mm. (Lesley Mees Collection.)

An advertisement in a 1911 issue of *Kinematograph Weekly* explained that 'the Flashograph is a picture card, the view or wording on which mysteriously changes' and, sure enough, by gently moving the cardboard 'handle', one moment Christabel is there and the next moment she has gone.[1] The Flashograph Co. had been registered in 1911, in time for the coronation of George V, the firm then issuing a Flashograph of the King that dissolved into a portrait of the Queen. 'Elusive Christabel' is the Flashograph Co.'s only other known product and must date from March/April 1912, at the time when the newspapers were packed with reports querying the whereabouts of Christabel Pankhurst, 'elusive' being the adjective most commonly used to describe her at that time. For, in the aftermath of the window-smashing demonstrations of 1 and 4 March (see Object 63), on 5 March the police had charged Frederick and Emmeline Pethick-Lawrence with conspiracy to commit damage under the terms of the Malicious Damage to Property Act 1861. Emmeline Pankhurst, already imprisoned, guilty of breaking windows in Downing Street, was also charged with conspiracy but the police had been unable to locate Christabel and had issued a warrant for her arrest.

The press revelled in the story. Describing Clement's Inn, where she was thought to have been living, the *Daily Mirror* noted, 'Solid, rotund constables guarded each entrance, and each person was subjected to close scrutiny before the iron gates would open a little way for him to enter.' The paper had been informed

that Christabel Pankhurst had returned there, unseen by the watching police early yesterday morning. 'I am told', said our informant, 'that she is in the building disguised in the costume of a maid-servant, and that it is her intention to endeavour to avoid arrest until the great suffragette demonstration at the London Opera House tonight, at which she wishes to be present'.[2]

The police did indeed search the Opera House, in Kingsway, but failed to find Christabel.

On 15 March 1912 the *Police Gazette* carried a 'Wanted' notice, 'For conspiracy, procuring, aiding and abetting persons to commit offences under Section 51 of the Malicious Damage to Property Act 1861 Christabel Pankhurst age about 30, height 5ft 6", colouring fresh, hair dark brown, eyes dark, usually dresses neatly. Warrant issued. Information to be forwarded to the Metropolitan Police Office New Scotland Yard.' The notice was accompanied by a full-face photograph of Christabel that dated from *c*.1908 and, ironically, had been issued as a postcard by the WSPU. This, too, is the image of Christabel, printed in purple and green, that appears on the Flashograph, while behind, the police, with outstretched hands, search for her, the accompanying verse declaring, 'They seek her here, They seek her there,/ Detectives Prowling Everywhere./ Their Heads with Big Importance Swell.' With one deft movement, the second picture appears, showing two policemen colliding, with the caption 'SHE'S GONE! ELUSIVE CHRISTABEL'. The Flashograph was the brainchild of E.T. Heron, in 1908 mayor of St Pancras, a successful and enterprising printer with premises in Tottenham Street, off Tottenham Court Road, London. A pioneering film enthusiast he had, in 1889, founded the *Optical Magic Lantern Journal* which by 1912 had become the *Kinematograph Weekly*, Britain's first cinema trade paper. Neither he or his wife appears to have had links with any suffrage society, so it is likely that, as with many other creators of novelties, he merely saw the campaign and its diverting incidents as a source of entertainment and profit.

Christabel did, indeed, prove elusive, evading the police and escaping from Clement's Inn in a cab to seek sanctuary in the Kensington nursing home run by nurses Catherine Pine and Gertrude Townend. From there, in the early hours of 6 March, dressed in a nurse's uniform, she made her way with Nurse Pine to a nearby flat, home of a supporter, and later in the day, now dressed in a nondescript fashion, took the boat train from Victoria to Paris. On arrival, she sent a telegram, to be forwarded to Clement's Inn, explaining she would 'control our paper and our business from Paris'.[3] Proving correct in thinking that, as a political offender, the French would refuse to extradite her, Christabel remained in Paris until the outbreak of war in August 1914. She lived first at 9 rue Roy, a nondescript, narrow street off the Boulevard Haussmann, before moving in the autumn of 1913 to a rather more central address, first at 11 Avenue de la Grande Armeé and then at no. 8. It was from here, in comfort, she conducted the last frenetic months of the WSPU campaign.

Object 65

'Topical Chessmen (Suffragettes v. The Law)'

Object 65 'Topical Chessmen (Suffragettes v. The Law)'. The pieces fit into a cardboard box (125 x 245 x 85 mm) printed with details of the maker, The Incorporated Soldiers and Sailors Help Society, 122 Brompton Road, London S.W. (Lesley Mees Collection.)

Object 65 was made in the workshop of the Incorporated Soldiers and Sailors Help Society, which had been set up after the Boer War to provide employment for disabled ex-servicemen. This chess set is so unusual that it is not clear if others were produced or whether this may have been a prototype, never put into production. The thirty-two figures, carved from wood and then painted, replace traditional chess pieces with their equivalent representations on the opposing sides of 'Suffragettes' and 'The Law'. Prison guards and society women replace knights, the rooks are burning buildings and prison cells, and the pawns are, on one side, policemen and, on the other, be-sashed suffragettes, lining up to do battle. There is no evidence to suggest that this workshop produced chess sets derived from any other 'Topical' subjects. Thus, dating from 1913–14, the existence of Object 65 is yet another example of the way in which the tropes of the suffragette campaign captured the popular imagination.

In fact, this chess set was making material a metaphor that had already been suggested in 1910 when Elsie Howey, a Women's Social and Political Union (WSPU) activist, at a meeting in Penzance 'likened [the WSPU's] persistent tactics to a game of chess: "We make a move, the Government make a move, and then we have to go one better"'.[1] This well describes the escalation, on the part of the WSPU, of physical activism and, from the government, legal retaliation that shaped the militant suffrage campaign from March 1912 until the outbreak of war in August 1914.

The immediate effect of the WSPU window-smashing campaign of early March 1912 (see Object 63) was that a charge of conspiracy to commit damage under the Malicious Injury to Property Act 1861 was laid against Emmeline and Christabel Pankhurst and Frederick and Emmeline Pethick-Lawrence. The police were unable to locate Christabel (see Object 64) but the others were held responsible for inciting members of the WSPU to damage property in London on 1 and 4 March. The trial was held at the Old Bailey in May, allowing the defendants ample opportunity to vent their political grievances before they were found guilty and sentenced to nine months' imprisonment, with the full costs of the prosecution awarded against Frederick Pethick-Lawrence and Mrs Pankhurst. This was the first of a number of legal attempts to drain the WSPU of funds. However, anticipating this move, on 1 March the WSPU had transferred £7,000 from its bank account, the money to be held by one of its wealthier members.

During the following couple of years, the Home Office was alert to any possibility that would allow them to instigate further prosecutions against any of the WSPU leaders; relevant phrases in their speeches were underlined and the prospects of prosecution carefully weighed. Mrs Pankhurst, in particular, did not flinch from giving the government direct cause for possible action. At a speech in the Royal Albert Hall on 17 October 1912 she declared, 'I incite this meeting to rebellion.'[2] The Home Office did not act then but did put pressure on hall managers not to let them to the WSPU; the last time the WSPU was able to hold a meeting in the Albert Hall was on 10 April 1913. Two days later the Metropolitan Police proscribed the WSPU from holding meetings in public parks.

It is clear from reports that as early as October 1906 the police were able to recognize leading members of the WSPU, singling out from the crowd demonstrating in the Lobby of the House of Commons, 'Mrs Pankhurst, Despard, [Pethick] Lawrence, Montefiore and [Cobden] Sanderson' (see Object 21). Subsequently the police had been forced to spend increasing amounts of time and resources on keeping WSPU activists under surveillance; by autumn 1913 the Metropolitan Police had employed a police motor cyclist whose sole job was to cover the movements of militant suffragettes who used cars. However, it was soon necessary to buy a faster motorcycle to keep up with the wily suffragettes.[3]

The chess game between the suffragettes and the law took a dramatic turn when in April 1913 the government passed the Prisoner's (Temporary Discharge for Ill-Health) Bill, popularly known as the 'Cat and Mouse Act' (see Object 67). Although prisoners released under the terms of this Act were required to return to prison once they had recovered from their hunger strike, many did not. These were then escaped prisoners, 'on the run', with little else left to lose. The result was, as illustrated by the prison cells and burning buildings of 'Topical Chessmen', an increasingly dangerous sequence of imprisonments and retaliatory arson and bombing, that was only brought to a halt by the outbreak of the First World War.

Object 66

A cloth embroidered with the signatures of suffragette prisoners, 1912

Object 66 A cloth, embroidered with the signatures of Women's Social and Political Union (WSPU) prisoners in Holloway Gaol, 1912. (TWL.2012.24, The Women's Library collection, London School of Economics and Political Science.)

Object 66 is a piece of fraying linen, embroidered in purple and green padded satin stitch with the signatures of seventy-eight members of the WSPU, imprisoned in Holloway Gaol in 1912. Most of the women had taken part in 'The Protest', as the window-smashing demonstrations of March 1912 were known, but at least one, Emily Wilding Davison, had been in Holloway on another charge since late 1911 (see Object 61). Although most of the names are not unfamiliar to those researching the suffrage movement, there is still scope for further investigation into identities.

Among the signatures is that of Margaret Macfarlane, who had broken the window of the Hamburg-America Line in Cockspur Street (see Object 63) and, in Holloway, signed at least two more embroidered works. One, known as the 'Suffragette Handkerchief', the work of Mary Hilliard, a nurse, bears sixty-six signatures and two sets of initials and the other, designed and worked by Janie Terrero, of Pinner, has twenty names of those who took part in two hunger strikes.[1] The idea of embroidering signatures was by no means novel nor peculiar to suffragettes; for instance, from the late 1880s Mrs Alec Tweedie, prolific journalist and travel writer, had asked her dinner guests to sign a 'tablecloth', and then embroidered over their names as a souvenir of the occasion.[2] It might seem bizarre to do so in prison, but pieces such as Object 66 are material proof of the way in which undergoing a common hardship only served to unite those who believed in the Cause.

From October 1905, when Christabel Pankhurst and Annie Kenney were the first to be imprisoned, until the outbreak of war in August 1914 brought the militant campaign to a close, over 1,000 women served prison sentences in pursuit of enfranchisement.[3] During that time neither their sentencing nor their treatment once in prison was ever consistent, the Home Office reacting in whatever manner was most expedient at the time. By the Prison Act of 1898, prisoners could be allocated to one of three divisions. The first division was for those who had committed contempt of court or sedition; they were not required to work, were allowed books, were able to wear their own clothes and to buy in food. Between the second and third divisions there was little difference in substance, a perception of 'class' being the main determinant; all such prisoners were required to wear prison clothes and were kept in solitary confinement for twenty-three hours out of twenty-four, with thirty minutes' exercise and thirty minutes' chapel. The 'hard labour' attached to some sentences was not unduly onerous.

In the early days of militancy, the government was not unwilling to allow suffrage prisoners first division status, but as their numbers increased this tolerance was forfeited. In October 1908 Mrs Pankhurst's claim to first division treatment as a political offender was denied. From July 1909 when Marion Wallace-Dunlop, sentenced to the second division, warned the governor that unless placed in the first division, she would undertake a hunger strike, this, for a time, became the way that many WSPU prisoners regained their freedom (see Object 67). Taking a pragmatic view of the situation, in March 1910 the new home secretary, Winston Churchill, introduced Rule 243A to deal with suffrage prisoners. This bestowed privileges, such as fortnightly visits and letters, the wearing of the prisoners' own clothes, exercise twice a day 'in association', first division food and books, but did not give first division status.

After the March 1912 'Protest', women sentenced to imprisonment in the second and third division were treated under Rule 243A, but a larger number had been sentenced to additional 'hard labour', to which Rule 243A did not apply. However, after many prisoners went on a hunger strike between 13 and 19 April, the home secretary reversed this decision so that Rule 243A was extended to all suffrage prisoners. Among the April hunger strikers signing Object 66 were Louie Hatfield, Mary Aldham and Frances Parker. In May other signatories went on hunger strike in an attempt to acquire first division status. Many were forcibly fed and some, although not Maggie Macfarlane, were released before the end of their sentence.

Unlike other 'signature' pieces similarly embroidered in prison by suffragettes, there is no evidence to tell us who mustered the signatures and wielded the needle to create Object 66. Although we can deduce it was made before 17 April 1912, as some of the signatories had been released by that date, it is not known whether there was ever an intention for it to be neatened and, perhaps, mounted and framed. Long held in the Women's Library collection, now at LSE, its provenance remains a mystery.[4]

Object 67

Forcible feeding: A 'comic' postcard

Object 67 is a 'comic' postcard depicting the forcible feeding of a suffragette, published by the 'National Series'. (Lesley Mees Collection.)

This 'comic' postcard dates from no later than 1910 when a copy was sent by a friend to a young policeman to mark his twenty-first birthday, with the message, 'I expect you would like to be this 'Slop' but wait 'till you're off duty'. 'Slop' was current slang for 'police', the recipient being PC Armstrong, then living in the police section house at 182 Long Lane, Southwark, London.[1] The publisher was a Glasgow printing company, Millar and Lang, who, in their 'National Series', produced other cards depicting suffragettes in ways inherently derogatory and, therefore, considered comic. Indeed, the firm clearly appreciated the humour of forcible feeding; Object 67 is #994 in their catalogue, while #993 has the same caption, but with the woman held down on the floor by the uniformed man, while the doctor pours soup into her mouth through a large funnel. As with other novelty manifestations, these cards were not specifically 'anti-suffrage' but merely evidence of a comprehensive national misogyny.

Forcible feeding had become a feature of the militant suffrage campaign the previous year, used in late September 1909 for the first time on five Women's Social and Political Union (WSPU) prisoners in Winson Green prison, Birmingham. The Home Office had considered it necessary because, since Marion Wallace-Dunlop had, in July, been the first to go on hunger strike, WSPU prisoners were using self-starvation as a tactic to secure an early release, with the authorities initially reluctant to introduce 'artificial feeding'. *Votes for Women* was quick to print 'Opinions of Medical Experts' explaining that

> this process constitutes an operation, and as such cannot lawfully be performed on any sane person without his consent. It consists in the insertion of an india rubber tube with a hard end down the throat of the patient. It is sometimes placed up through the nostrils, at other times it is inserted through the mouth. The chief risks are severe injury to the mouth by the gag, which must be used in such cases to force the mouth open, a serious tendency to break the teeth and injure the mouth.[2]

A week later a Memorial was sent to the prime minister, signed by numerous doctors, to 'urgently protest against the treatment by artificial feeding of the Suffragist prisoners now in Birmingham Gaol'.[3]

From September 1909 until the outbreak of war in 1914, forcible feeding was the retaliatory measure employed by the Home Office on hunger-striking suffragettes. Its application, however, was no more consistent than in any other facet of the handling of WSPU prisoners. For instance, in October 1909 Lady Constance Lytton was released after a short hunger strike without being forcibly fed, although in January 1910, when disguised as working-class 'Jane Warton', she was subjected to the 'treatment' in Walton Gaol, Liverpool, without any prior medical examination. At the same time, for the January 1910 general election the WSPU issued a coloured poster, created by Alfred Pearse, the *Votes for Women* weekly cartoonist. Showing a woman being forcibly fed by two doctors, while four wardresses held her down, the caption ran, 'The Modern Inquisition. Treatment of Political Prisoners under a Liberal Government. Electors Put a Stop to this Torture'. Was the artist who produced Object 67, sent with titillating comment to PC Armstrong, mocking this powerful image?

Throughout 1912 the increasing militancy of WSPU protesters, with the consequent imprisonments, hunger strikes and mass forcible feeding, forced the Cabinet to address the situation. The result was the passing in April 1913 of the Prisoners' (Temporary Discharge for Ill-Health) Bill, popularly known as the 'Cat and Mouse' Act. By this the home secretary was given the power to set a hunger-striking suffrage prisoner free temporarily to recover her health, without remission of her sentence, thereby avoiding the necessity of forcible feeding. One of the first prisoners to be released under this Act was Ella Stevenson (see Object 61), who while fiercely resisting forcible feeding in Holloway, had a front tooth knocked out and her nostrils severely damaged. She was required to return to prison on 12 May, but did not, re-arrested only in August. After the passing of the 'Cat and Mouse' Act the pages of the *Police Gazette* were packed with details of released suffrage prisoners now 'on the run'.

While 'comic' suffrage cards invariably present suffragettes as grotesques, even depicting them undergoing fantasy torture (see Object 50), those, such as Object 67 that refer specifically to forcible feeding, a very real practice, do seem particularly abhorrent. Yet there was a market for this 'humour', obligingly fulfilled by postcard artists and publishers. P.C. Armstrong must have liked the postcard. Presumably he kept it, for it is still in existence, in good condition, well into the second decade of the twenty-first century.

Object 68

A ceramic figurine of a suffragette

Object 68 is a ceramic figurine of a suffragette trampling a policeman. 260 x 240 mm. (Lesley Mees Collection.)

A harridan in green hat and purple dress waves her umbrella while trampling a policeman. She wears a 'Votes for Women' placard around her neck; his face is contorted. The design was registered in the UK on 26 August 1909, described as 'Suffragette standing on a prostrate policeman'; an impressed mark shows the figurine was made in Austria. Here we see the roles displayed in Object 67 reversed, yet Object 68 is no more designed to evoke sympathy for the suffragette than was the postcard.

Popular humour was invariably derived from depicting suffragettes as transgressive and the combination of their association with policemen was as potent source of amusement in clay as on postcards. Another piece, made in Thuringia, Germany, by the firm of Schafer & Vater, which specialized in producing quirky figurines, has a very tall policeman, hands over his ears, escorting a rotund little girl, who is waving an 'I want a vote' banner. 'Votes for Women' is repeated, inscribed on the front of the base. What could be more amusing than the contrast between the mighty policeman, in whom rests all the authority of the State and who can easily stop his ears against the shouts of the hapless suffragette, reduced to a childish flag-waving figure lacking any agency? The same firm capitalized on the market for suffrage-related figurines, also producing the figure of a screaming suffragette brandishing an 'I want a vote' flag, with 'Give me a vote and see what ill [*sic*] do' inscribed on the base. Cats, popular with both postcard publishers and manufacturers of ceramics, were anthropomorphized as suffragettes; Schafer & Vater produced a black cat standing on a plinth, inscribed 'I want my vote'. The same firm combined a cat with a bulldog in a piece declaring, 'Who says Votes for Women' and, in another, three geese stand on a plinth declaiming, 'We want our Votes!' Both were apparently intended as match holders, while another, perhaps from the same firm, certainly marked 'Germany', is a half bust of a suffragette as an 'Old Maid', attired in green and purple, the holes in the top of her head and the inscription 'A match for any man' making her purpose clear.

A month before the design of Object 68 was listed, Leslie Harradine, a ceramic modeller, registered two suffrage-related ceramic inkwells, to be produced by Doulton. One is in the shape of an angry baby with 'Votes for Women' inscribed on its blue/green bib. Its head tips back to reveal the ink. A companion piece is modelled as an angry old woman with folded arms, in blues, with her green apron inscribed 'Votes for Women'. She is hinged at the waist. It would seem these were the only suffrage-related ceramic figures to be produced for the artistic end of the trade. However, the idea of 'Votes for Women' had been enthusiastically adopted by firms producing miniature china items for the lowlier 'Bazaar Trade'. These souvenir pieces carried the coats of arms of the holiday resorts in which they were sold and were collectively known as 'crested china'. Thus, for instance, the Arcadian China Co. of Stoke on Trent produced a two-sided bust, one side a harridan, carrying a vestigial umbrella, with a coat of arms across her chest and 'Votes for Women' emblazoned across her hat. The other side shows a gentle-faced beauty with, across her chest, the message, 'This one shall have a Vote'. Victoria China made similar pieces. One is a handbell, with on one side a harridan with 'Votes for Women' written across her cap and below that 'I can talk/Ring the bell/And be forcibly fed as well'. 'Ring the bell' was an allusion to the well-publicized antics of a suffragette, Dorothy Moloney, who constantly rang a bell to interrupt Winston Churchill's meetings when he was contesting the Dundee by-election in May 1908. The other side has a gentle smiling face with ringlets and across her bust 'The lady shall have a vote'. The message the holiday maker took home with the china was clear: only the good deserve a vote.

Although these smaller crested pieces survive in quantity, the larger figurines, most of which were made in smaller numbers and imported, are now very scarce. With no known reference to their presence on a mantelpiece or shelf or in a cabinet, whether in fact or fiction, we can only imagine how pieces such as Object 68 were regarded by their original owners.

Object 69

Report book kept by an organizer for the New Constitutional Society for Women's Suffrage

Object 69 is the report book of an organizer for the New Constitutional Society for Women's Suffrage (NCS). (TWL 2NCS, The Women's Library collection, London School of Economics and Political Science.)

In the spring of 1912, at a time when increasing numbers of Women's Social and Political Union (WSPU) members were incarcerated (see Objects 63, 64 and 66), other suffrage societies were continuing to campaign in a non-militant manner. While the National Union of Women's Suffrage Societies (NUWSS) was the largest such organization, it was by no means the only one; in January 1910, former members of the London Society for Women's Suffrage had broken away to form the New Constitutional Society for Women's Suffrage (NCS). Unable to support militancy, yet considering the NUWSS insufficiently effective, they adopted what they termed an 'anti-government' policy, resolving to work against government (Liberal) candidates at elections. The NCS was, therefore, carrying out the election policy of the WSPU, but eschewing the WSPU's other weapon, militancy.

The headquarters of the NCS was in Knightsbridge, London, a distinctly 'shopping' area, consonant with the upper-middle-class inclinations of its founders. From March 1911 the organizer tasked with drumming-up support for the NCS in various areas of southern England was Kate Frye, the daughter of a former Liberal MP. His business had failed, and Kate now needed to support herself and, fortuitously, was friendly with the founders of the NCS, who asked her to take part in their campaign. Although she received no training, she had a long-standing interest in politics and suffrage and, having for a time been an (unsuccessful) touring actress, was well-prepared for the itinerant aspect of her new employment. Her salary of £2 a week was the rate paid to their organizers by other suffrage societies.

From April 1912 Kate's position with the NCS was put on a more permanent footing and she began to keep a Report Book, presumably scrutinized at intervals by a member of the NCS committee. The Report Book opens with notes of a stay in Dereham, Norfolk, which Kate had visited previously, although it is never explained why the NCS thought this small, albeit thriving, market town should be one of the main centres of the NCS propaganda efforts. The Report Book details Kate's canvassing for members. It was a slow business. On her first day, 29 April, in four-and-a-half hours of going door-to-door she made only one new member, on the second day, two more. On the third day she records calling on a 'Mrs Olly', her diary entry revealing she 'was just in time to save her retiring owing to the Militants', the WSPU's increasing militancy causing constant difficulty to constitutional campaigners such as Kate. At the end of the week she travelled to Fakenham, recording in the Report Book the type of information necessary to an organizer: that half day there was Wednesday, the name and address of a printer (essential for the printing of handbills and posters) and details of the public halls, their capacity and the days they were available for hire.

On 9 May the Report Book reveals that 'it was decided to form into a branch to be called the Mid Norfolk Branch of the New Constitutional Society for Women's Suffrage. It was decided to start a Library for Suffrage Books'. For headquarters, to this very welcome news she added in the Report Book details of the new secretary, treasurer and number of members, while in her diary she confessed to being very nervous before the members' meeting, but, when the decision had been taken to form the branch, was able to declare, 'It went off splendidly.' A few days later, the death of the sitting MP for Northwest Norfolk meant a by-election was imminent and by 16 May Kate had moved to Fakenham to campaign for the NCS, alongside fellow workers from both the NUWSS and the WSPU, her diary revealing she found the latter friendlier than the former.

Although WSPU organizers, who, between 1903 and 1914, numbered over 150, were required to send headquarters a weekly diary, of these there is now scant trace.[1] Similarly, although the reports of the numerous NUWSS organizers were itemized each week in *The Common Cause*, little original material survives.[2] However, with her eye on posterity, Kate Frye preserved her Report Book so that, from 1912 to 1914, the brief daily entries give us an unrivalled, dispassionate view of what it was like to attempt to interest the inhabitants of small towns and villages in the cause of women's suffrage. The diary she kept during this period colours the picture, detailing the triumphs and tragedies of organizing the NCS campaign in Essex villages, in Lowestoft, Folkestone, Hythe, Rye, Reading, Wantage and many small places in between.[3]

Object 70

A silver basket 'Sold for King's Taxes'

Object 70 A sterling silver basket, made by Henry Wilkinson, Sheffield, 1852, engraved 'Sold for King's Taxes 1912 Woman Suffrage, L.E. Turquand 1913'. (Author's Collection.)

On 14 May 1912, while Women's Social and Political Union (WSPU) prisoners were on hunger strike in Holloway (see Object 67) and Kate Frye was campaigning in Fakenham for the NCS (see Object 69), this silver basket was put up for sale at a Sydenham, south London, auction. It belonged to Miss Lizzie Emma Turquand, daughter of a nonconformist minister and the founder in 1910 of the Free Church League for Women's Suffrage (see Object 76). She was, first, the League's press secretary and then editor of its newspaper, *The Coming Day*. Also, for six years from 1907, she was a Croydon poor law guardian, had served as secretary of her local Liberal Association and was at one time the headmistress of a Croydon primary school. An early member of the WSPU she left it for the Women's Freedom League (WFL), and in due course also joined the Tax Resistance League (TRL).

The TRL had been formed in late 1909 to conduct a campaign of constitutional militancy by asking women to refuse to pay their taxes. Their slogan of 'No Vote No Tax' was, in essence, one that had been adopted on other continents and in other centuries, but in the context of the British women's suffrage campaign dated back to the 1870s, highlighting the anomaly of women being unable to vote and yet being subject to taxation. The TRL's banner, designed by Mary Sargant Florence and made by members of the Suffrage Atelier, bears the figure of John Hampden, popularly remembered as a seventeenth-century tax resister.[1]

Putting principle into practice, in May 1912 Turquand refused to pay House Duty Tax and, as a result, the silver cake basket was seized by a bailiff, in lieu of the 10s owed. It was reported that 'the silver basket [was] a household treasure, with tender memories to Miss Turquand it being her mother's'. Thus, the basket was auctioned in order to recoup the money she owed the tax authority. Capitalizing on the event, the TRL organized a poster and banner parade, at which lengthy speeches were delivered. The parade then continued to the Auction Rooms where Turquand, 'amidst renewed cheering', addressed the auctioneer and assembled company. The local paper gave ample coverage to the proceedings, including photographs of Turquand and of the secretary of the TRL, Mrs Kineton Parkes, together with an image of a TRL poster.[2]

The silver cake basket was sold to Mrs Beaumont Thomas, a Clapham member of the TRL, who must have returned it to Turquand because it was sold again in lieu of tax in May of the following year, on which occasion she again gave a consciousness-raising speech.[3] The basket was doubtless again returned to her and engraved for '1913' to add to the commemoration already applied for 1912. Many other auctions of TRL members' goods were held in the years immediately before the First World War, among them items of jewellery belonging to Princess Sophia Duleep Singh, one of the few women of colour known to have played a relatively prominent part in the suffrage campaign (see also Object 76). She was also among the most aristocratic – the daughter of Maharaja Duleep Singh, the last maharaja of the Sikh empire, and his German-born wife. Sophia was god-daughter to Queen Victoria, who had granted her a grace-and-favour residence at Hampton Court, Surrey. By 1910 Sophia was an active member of the WSPU, speaking regularly at meetings of the Richmond branch. A member of the TRL, in 1911 she had a diamond ring impounded against a fine for non-payment of licences for a male servant, a carriage and five dogs. In 1914 she was again fined for refusing to pay taxes; a pearl necklace and gold bangle were seized under distraint and auctioned at Twickenham Town Hall. While these items are now lost to history, Object 70 is unusual in having survived, with its history so clearly marked on it.

By its nature the TRL appealed mainly to middle-class women, particularly those working in the professions; it held its first conference in Alan's Tea Rooms (see Object 40). It was, however, open to members from all classes. For instance, in 1911 Emma Sproson, a working-class WFL member from Wolverhampton, refused to pay a dog licence, was imprisoned and went on hunger strike; the police shot her dog. Although as a society the TRL ended its campaign in August 1914, some members continued with the protest. The last tax resister, the author Evelyn Sharp, was in 1917 brought to bankruptcy by her continuing refusal to pay tax.

Object 71

The pendant/brooch presented to Millicent Fawcett by the National Union of Women's Suffrage Societies, 1913

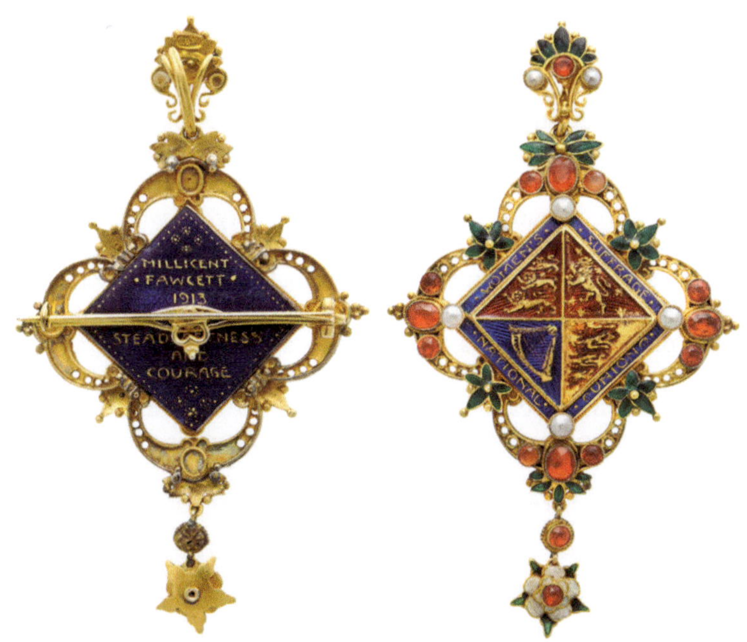

Object 71 is a gold and enamel pendant/brooch presented to Millicent Fawcett by the National Union of Women's Suffrage Societies (NUWSS), 27 February 1913. (The Millicent Fawcett brooch (L671) courtesy of Fawcett Society/London Museum.)

Both the design of Object 71 and the timing of its presentation are of great significance. On 10 February 1913 the NUWSS treasurer, Edith Palliser, wrote to the secretaries of all local societies, informing them of a decision taken to include in the imminent annual general meeting a demonstration 'in honour of Mrs Fawcett' and to present her with 'a little memento of the occasion ... a badge bearing the arms & colours of the National Union'.[1] To modern eyes, Object 71, worked in coloured enamels, pearls and fire opals, with fittings allowing it to be worn either as a pendant or a brooch, is demonstrably more a 'jewel' than a 'badge'. Indicating the nationwide reach of the NUWSS, the design displays a variation of the Royal Coat of Arms, in yellow, red and blue enamel, set in a lozenge, a heraldic shape traditionally associated with women. The Arms are slightly incorrect, probably a mistake by the designer, as the tinctures of the second (Scotland) and fourth (England) quarters are inverted. The border of the lozenge, set at each corner with a half pearl, carries the words 'National Union Women's Suffrage' in gold enamel, while the outermost border displays four ivy leaves, symbolic of faithfulness, enamelled in green. The latter, together with the red of the fire opals and the white of the pearls, comprise the NUWSS colours. Hanging from the main body of the jewel is a green and white enamel Tudor rose, set with a fire opal, a flower shape used by the NUWSS on other badges.[2] On the reverse, the lozenge is decorated with dark blue enamel, enamelled in yellow with the words, 'Millicent Fawcett 1913 Steadfastness and Courage'.

Research has revealed that the maker of the jewel was Florence Rimmington, an art jeweller who had recently been one of the exhibitors, alongside such suffrage artists as Mary Lowndes, at the arts and crafts exhibition mounted by the *Englishwoman* magazine.[3] Although no documentary evidence survives to indicate whether Rimmington was responsible for the design as well as the execution of the jewel, or the date on which she received the commission, the latter is likely to postdate 27 January 1913. This was the day on which the NUWSS was dealt a bitter blow when the speaker of the House of Commons made a surprise announcement, ruling that no women's suffrage amendment to the Franchise and Registration Bill, the electoral reform bill first mooted in November 1911 (see Object 60), was possible, for that would render it a new bill. Having pinned their hopes on Asquith's assurance that, if any women's suffrage amendment to this government bill were passed, it would be included, the NUWSS had now to face the prospect of a suffrage campaign prolonged into 1913 and beyond. Thus, as a first step, the decision was taken to strengthen morale by demonstrating loyalty to their leader, Mrs Fawcett.

The 27 January ruling was merely another hiatus in the campaign, new tactics having already been adopted by the NUWSS during 1912. For, after the defeat of the Second Reading of the Conciliation Bill in March 1912 (see Object 62), the NUWSS had looked for an alliance with the Labour party, which had passed a resolution to support women's suffrage. By the summer of 1912 the NUWSS had launched the Election Fighting Fund (EFF), chaired by Fawcett, to raise money to support Labour candidates at by-elections and thereby subject Liberals to greater opposition, a policy that proved unacceptable to some members. Local EFF committees were formed within the NUWSS federations and a new subsidiary, the Friends of Women's Suffrage, was launched, to attract working-class, Labour, women to the NUWSS.

Hopes were high at the beginning of 1913, with the NUWSS prepared to settle for any amendment that would establish the principle that 'sex should not disqualify, make all women potential voters and hold the door open for any future extensions'.[4] At the end of the month, with their hopes dashed by the speaker's ruling and having rejected the government's offer to make time for another private member's women's franchise bill, Fawcett commented, 'This present is a moment that puts the greatest strain upon the qualities of courage and steadfastness of our members.'[5] Shortly afterwards, when commissioning the 'badge', the committee decided it would carry a message of assurance to Mrs Fawcett that she could indeed 'rely on the "steadfastness & courage" of the Union'.[6]

In the ensuing years, Fawcett was often photographed wearing the pendant. She wore it at the 1925 Aubrey House garden party (see Object 88), and in 1928 when attending the Victory Breakfast to celebrate the passing of the Equal Franchise Act, and when sitting for her last portrait, commissioned by the NUWSS from the artist Lionel Ellis. The jewel was represented on Fawcett's memorial in Westminster Abbey but over the years was forgotten, until rediscovered by the Fawcett Society in 2016. In 2018 it featured in an Antiques Roadshow 'Pioneering Women Special' and, recreated in bronze, is worn on the lapel of Fawcett's statue (see Object 100). Since 2020 the Fawcett jewel has been on permanent loan to the London Museum.

Object 72

Photographic postcard of 'Suffragette Fire, Nevill Cricket Ground, Tunbridge Wells'

Object 72 is a photographic postcard of the cricket pavilion in Tunbridge Wells, set on fire by 'suffragettes' during the night of 10/11 April 1913. Photograph by Percy Lankester, Tunbridge Wells. (Lesley Mees Collection.)

On 20 February 1913, a week before Millicent Fawcett accepted Object 71 from the National Union of Women's Suffrage Societies (NUWSS), Mrs Pankhurst accepted responsibility for an attempt to destroy a house being built for Lloyd George in Surrey, declaring, 'We have blown up the Chancellor of the Exchequer's house.' She went on to say, 'For all that has been done in the past I accept responsibility. I have advised, I have incited, I have conspired, and the authorities need not look for the women who have done what they did, because I myself accept full responsibility for it.'[1] She was speaking at a Women's Social and Political Union (WSPU) meeting in Cardiff, attended by a large force of police. Her speech was transcribed by a *Western Mail* reporter and sent to the Home Office. For over a year the government had been waiting for this moment, hoping to gather sufficient evidence to instigate legal action against the WSPU leaders, for, as Objects 60, 61 and 63 reveal, attacks on property were escalating, becoming increasingly violent and spectacular.

The decision to prosecute Mrs Pankhurst was taken by the home secretary on 21 February and she stood trial, conducting her own defence, at the Old Bailey at the beginning of April, on a charge of inciting certain persons unknown to place explosives in the Surrey building. She was found guilty on 3 April, was sentenced to three years' penal servitude and immediately went on hunger strike. It was never deemed prudent to forcibly feed Mrs Pankhurst and on 12 April she was released from Holloway on a Special Licence to recover from her hunger strike. Faced with this intractable situation and with an increasing number of other hunger-striking suffragette prisoners, the government was forced to rush the Prisoners' (Temporary Discharge for Ill-Health) Bill through Parliament. Popularly known as the 'Cat and Mouse' Act, it became law on 25 April 1913 (see Object 67).

Meanwhile, under the headline, 'The Women's Revolution – A Reign of Terror – Fire and Bombs', the 11 April issue of *The Suffragette* carried a double-page spread describing the protests its members had already made against Mrs Pankhurst's imprisonment. These included the burning of the grandstand at Ayr racecourse, a bomb explosion at Oxted railway station and the shattering of the glass in thirteen pictures in Manchester Art Gallery. The following week *The Suffragette* carried details of further arson attacks attributed to the WSPU, highlighting the burning of 'the handsome cricket pavilion used by the Kent County Club in the Nevill cricket ground at Tunbridge Wells'.[2] Object 72 is a postcard produced from a photograph taken on 11 April by Percy Lankester, one of Tunbridge Wells' leading photographers, who, from several different angles, had recorded the ruined cricket pavilion. Although no-one was ever held responsible, the arson attack was ascribed to the action of militant suffragettes; a photograph of Mrs Pankhurst was left at the scene. It is notable that sites associated with men's sports were particularly prone to damage at this time. The Nevill Pavilion was one of the first casualties in this new stage in the long fight for 'votes for women'.

In the two years before the First World War brought the campaign to an end, besides numerous acts of arson, suffragettes set off street fire alarms, cut telephone wires, destroyed post, slashed paintings in art galleries, attacked exhibition cases at the British Museum and set bombs. These were planted beside canals, at waterworks, at a lighthouse, in trains and in churches, including St Paul's Cathedral and Westminster Abbey. Some of the perpetrators, such as Kitty Marion and Ethel Moorhead, left detailed testimony of their activities, while others were recorded in the 1970s discussing their militancy. For instance, Maude Kate Smith described how she was involved in a plot to blow up a Birmingham canal and Lillian Lenton was filmed by the BBC in 1955, proudly claiming that 'I was one of the first people to start burning buildings and I burned them at a rate of about two a week, when not in prison'.[3] While the WSPU always maintained that the intention was never to endanger life, it was probably a matter of luck that no member of the public was injured.

Although the economic consequences of WSPU militancy were felt by property owners and insurance companies, there is no evidence to show that the public was fearful of being caught up in an arson or bomb attack. Indeed, if the postcards issued by commercial publishers reflect popular opinion, the actions of the militants and their punishment were regarded as comic (see Objects 61 and 67). Meanwhile, photographers such as Mr Lankester saw a commercial opportunity in creating the souvenirs of suffragette militancy that now constitute an interesting sub-genre for the collector of suffragette postcards.

Object 73

A lily carried at Emily Wilding Davison's funeral, 14 June 1913

Object 73 is a lily carried by **Agnes Kelly** at the funeral of **Emily Wilding Davison, 14 June 1913.** (7EWD/M/28, The Women's Library collection, London School of Economics and Political Science.)

A couple of months after the burning of Tunbridge Wells cricket pavilion (see Object 72), Women's Social and Political Union (WSPU) militancy received worldwide publicity when an act of one of its members, Emily Wilding Davison (see Objects 61 and 66), resulted in her death.[1] With a history of increasingly violent activism, she had been sentenced to six months' imprisonment in late 1911 for setting fire to a pillar box and during her time in Holloway had suffered injuries after twice throwing herself over the landing railings. Although there is no evidence she was involved in acts of arson carried out by suffragettes in the first six months of 1913, she did keep company with arsonists for, on the evening of 3 June, she attended the WSPU's summer fund-raising fair with Kitty Marion, who had recently set fire to at least three houses.[2] It was on the following day, Wednesday 4 June, 'Derby Day', that Davison took the train to Epsom Racecourse, stepped out onto the course and collided with the horses running in the main event, the Derby Stakes.

In 1913 the Derby, the most prestigious flat horse race, was a national institution, akin to a national holiday, attracting huge crowds to Epsom. Davison joined the hordes on a train from Victoria Station, after visiting the WSPU Kingsway office to pick up two WSPU flags. It has been suggested she was trying to attach some such item to the bridle of the King's horse when she suffered the injuries from which on 8 June she died. Although she divulged her intention to no-one, she did position herself, whether on purpose or not, opposite a newsreel camera at Tattenham Corner, with the result that over a century later we can watch the moment of impact.[3]

The main witness at the inquest, a policeman standing nearby when Davison went under the guard rail, gave evidence of the items found in her possession at Epsom Cottage Hospital. Among them were two long WSPU flags, folded up and pinned to the inside back of her jacket, and a return half railway ticket from Epsom to Victoria. However, the flags were not unfurled and on Derby Day railway excursion tickets to Epsom were invariably sold as 'Returns', making it impossible to say with certainty whether Davison expected to make use of it. The jury returned a verdict of 'Misadventure', the coroner dismissing the idea that Davison had aimed 'specially for the King's horse, [suggesting] her intention was merely to disturb or upset the race'.[4]

After Davison's death, the WSPU lost no time in announcing that the funeral of this first martyr to the Cause was to be made 'the occasion [of] a public demonstration in London', with the actual burial taking place in Northumberland, her home county.[5] The procession on Saturday 14 June was a marvel of organization, executed at speed under the greatest difficulty. With Christabel Pankhurst in Paris, Emmeline Pankhurst liable to arrest after overstaying her licence from Holloway, and Annie Kenney and the WSPU office staff on trial at the Old Bailey on charges of conspiracy, the onus fell on Grace Roe, Kenney's deputy, to arrange the event. With a warrant out for her arrest, she was forced to travel in disguise around London, but within four days of Davison's death had devised the complicated details of the 'Funeral Arrangements' that appeared in the issue of *The Suffragette*, published on the day preceding the procession.[6] The route took the coffin through central London, from Victoria Station to St George's Church, Bloomsbury, for a memorial service, and then on to King's Cross station to be carried north for interment.

Flowers in vast quantity were a dominating feature of the procession, piled on motor cars and carriages and carried singly by those participating. Roe had devised a strict colour combination, with some processionists, dressed in white, carrying a Madonna lily, others in purple, carrying a red peony, and yet others in black, carrying a purple iris. Laurel wreaths also featured. Every woman was required to bring her own flower but, even so, looking at the photographs and newsreel taken on the day, one cannot help but consider the amount of work that had been required so quickly of a florist.[7] Robert Green Ltd, of Crawford Street, Marylebone, subsequently advertised they had supplied the flowers and laurel wreaths, adding they were 'London's cheapest florist', which may explain the commission.[8]

Of all those flowers, the only known survivor is Object 73, the lily, symbol of virtue and purity, carried, probably in Section D of the procession, by Dublin-born Agnes Kelly, who for some years had been a speaker for the WSPU. She and her sister, Kathleen, a university graduate, with whom she lived in Pimlico, were also members of the English committee of the Irish League for Women's Suffrage (see Object 45). Other items of Agnes Kelly's suffrage memorabilia are held by the London Museum, probably donated to the Suffragette Fellowship collection (see Object 96), while the lily forms part of the Emily Wilding Davison archive at the Women's Library collection at LSE.

Object 74

National Union of Women's Suffrage Societies Pilgrimage haversack, 1913

Object 74 is a haversack sold by the National Union of Women's Suffrage Societies (NU-WSS) to members taking part in its Pilgrimage, June/July 1913. (TWL.2012.28, The Women's Library collection, London School of Economics and Political Science.)

In April 1913, a week after *The Suffragette* ran the headline *The Women's Revolution – A Reign of Terror – Fire and Bombs* and the Tunbridge Wells cricket pavilion was burned down (see Object 72), a suggestion was made to the NUWSS that, to differentiate themselves from the militants' campaign of destruction, they should stage a 'Woman's Suffrage Pilgrimage'.[1] The idea was not original for, a few months earlier, six suffragists had undertaken a 'Woman's March' from Edinburgh to London. However, although resonating with spirituality, this had been on too small a scale to make a mark. The NUWSS plan was much bolder; hundreds of members would walk from all parts of the country, along dedicated routes, to converge on London for a rally in Hyde Park on 26 July.

Under the headline 'The Pilgrimage of Grace', the idea was first announced in *The Common Cause* on 9 May, four days after the latest women's suffrage private member's bill had failed to pass its Second Reading in the House of Commons, vindicating Millicent Fawcett's view, expressed in January, that enfranchisement was unlikely to be achieved by such a method under the present government.[2] Now, three months later, the NUWSS was energized by the prospect of the Pilgrimage, believing it would 'impress the world as an object lesson in women's power of self-denial, earnestness, and enthusiasm'. The inclusion of an afternoon service at St Paul's Cathedral on Sunday 27 July as a final event underlined the spiritual nature of the endeavour.[3]

Working through its seventeen federations, the NUWSS executed the plan with exemplary speed. Restricted to England, four main routes were designated, the Great North Road, Watling Street, the Bath Road and the Portsmouth Road, into which lesser tributaries would feed. Pilgrims were urged to dress only in white, grey, black or navy. This 'uniform' was a concept close to the heart of the Pilgrimage's instigator, Mrs Katherine Harley, chairman of the (West) Midland Federation, sister of Charlotte Despard and the widow of an army officer. Hats, in the 'uniform' colours, were to be simple and for pinning to them the NUWSS would, for 3d, supply a red, white and green raffia 'cockleshell', the traditional symbol of pilgrimage. Among other items of Pilgrimage merchandise, the NUWSS produced a haversack, of which Object 74 is an example. It was to be worn crosswise across the body so that the red, white and green strap resembled a sash. Although, when originally described in *Common Cause* each bag was to be identified with the name of the route travelled, it seems this elaboration was dropped and a swag of red cotton substituted, for neither Object 74, nor any of the haversacks shown in photographs worn by pilgrims, carry any lettering. Ready-made by members of the London Society for Women's Suffrage, haversacks cost 2s 3d, but, for 1s 6d, the materials only could be bought, to be made up at home. Promoted as a means of raising awareness of the NUWSS brand, the haversacks were dutifully worn by many pilgrims. However, run up quickly, with, as we see from Object 74, imperfect machining, and, as photographs show, the strap a little short for the taller or fuller figure, they were unlikely to have proved very useful, incapable of holding many of the items necessary for the days or weeks spent away from home. Yet the pilgrims had to make do with only one other piece of luggage.

The pilgrims furthest from London set out from Carlisle on the Watling Street route and from Newcastle on the Great North Road on 18 June, at a time when the public was still bemused by the eccentric death of Emily Wilding Davison and bedazzled by images of her funeral procession. Other contingents stepped out on dates arranged to get them safely to London by 26 July, the latest being those from Brighton who left on the twenty-first. The pilgrims, some travelling with horse-drawn caravans or bicycles, enjoyed numerous adventures along the way, newspaper reports, their diaries and letters describing both generous hospitality and threats of assault from village roughs. Object 74 belonged to Miss Amelia Scott, a Tunbridge Wells poor law guardian, who participated in a section of the Kentish route, speaking at a Pilgrimage meeting in Southborough on 11 July.

The final rally in Hyde Park, attended by over 50,000 and addressed from nineteen platforms by seventy-eight speakers, received nationwide coverage. The Pilgrimage had helped to distance the NUWSS from the militants and engendered the camaraderie that its instigators had sought. Asquith received an NUWSS deputation, listened politely as he was told the Pilgrimage had engaged with thousands of working-class women, said he had been impressed by its organization, but, as to their hope of achieving enfranchisement, promised the NUWSS nothing specific. In early 1914, as a by-product of the Pilgrimage, the NUWSS formed the Active Service League, enrolling middle-class women specifically to encourage working-class women to join the Friends of Women's Suffrage scheme (see Objects 32 and 71). As this often involved 'open-air work', the NUWSS once again offered a branded haversack among its ASL merchandise.

Object 75

A still from the film
The Hunger Strike, 1913

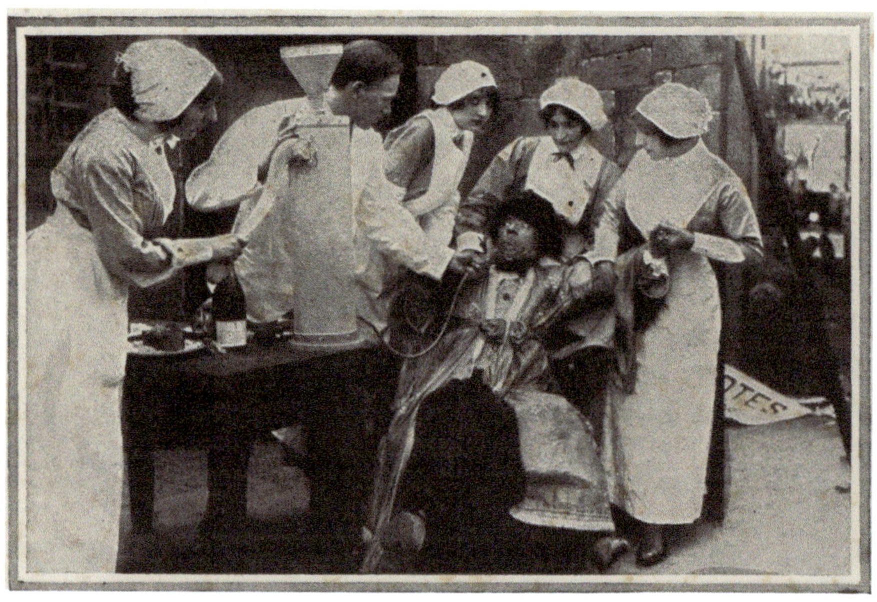

Object 75 is a still from the 1913 film, *The Hunger Strike*. (Lesley Mees Collection.)

On 11 June 1913, as the Women's Social and Political Union (WSPU) was hurriedly planning Emily Wilding Davison's funeral procession (see Object 73) and the National Union of Women's Suffrage Societies (NUWSS) was about to embark on its Pilgrimage (see Object 74), *The Sketch* announced the imminent release of *The Hunger Strike*, a film starring Edmund Payne, a variety hall favourite, in which 'it is expected that the forcible-feeding scene, especially, will cause a great deal of amusement'.[1] Object 75, a still from that scene, shows the suffragette, Payne in disguise, about to be forcibly fed before it is realized he is a man and is, instead, fortified with champagne. This film did, indeed, prove popular, shown throughout the UK from its release in the summer of 1913 until late-1916, just one of many 'suffragette' feature films produced after 1908 by the burgeoning British film industry. Mainly comedies, they drew on the same tropes as commercial postcard publishers, capitalizing on the humour axiomatic in placing women in situations that differed from those traditionally expected. For instance, one of the earliest, *If Women Were Policemen*, directed in May 1908 by Percy Stow for the Croydon-based Clarendon Film Company, showed what happened when militant suffragettes took over the police force. The combination of women and policemen was irresistible. Stow also directed one of the few surviving feature films, *Milling the Militants*, made in 1913.[2]

Film companies were quick to exploit every new twist in the suffrage narrative. On 14 March 1912, an advertisement appeared for *The Elusive Miss Pinkhurst*, a film by the Warwick Trading Company in which trick photography was used to show a cabinet minister attempting to catch a suffragette; it was only eight days since Christabel had fled to France.[3] By April 1913, as the militant campaign increased in intensity, bombs were playing their part in films such as *The Child of a Suffragette*, in which a young girl trails her suffragette mother and extinguishes her bomb.

Although most of these short films were gently mocking, there were also a few that took the suffrage campaign seriously. In 1911, Barker's Motion Photography filmed *True Womanhood*, based on a play by Inez Bensusan who, with Decima Moore, a fellow member of the Actresses' Franchise League, also appeared in the film. In 1913 an American company, the Unique Film Co., made *What 80 Million Women Want*, a feature film fifty-five minutes long, in which Emmeline Pankhurst, then in the United States on a lecture tour, featured as herself, and, together with Harriot Stanton Blatch, the leader of the more militant wing of the American suffrage movement, plotted to expose a corrupt politician.

By 1914 there were *c.*4,500 cinemas in Britain, their programmes constructed around feature films, such as *The Hunger Strike*, preceded by newsreels each shown for three or four days, with the reels circulating around the country for several weeks. In 1907 the founder of the Warwick Trading Company, Charles Urban, who, as well as *The Elusive Miss Pinkhurst*, filmed a number of suffrage newsreels, wrote of the importance of cinematograph film in the study of history, noting that 'affairs of state, royal movements, naval and military demonstrations are all depicted as they are actually seen by the accurate and truthful eye of the camera, and the day has arrived when motion pictures of current events should be treasured as vital documents among the historical archives of our museums'.[4] Unfortunately, Charles Urban's plea was not heeded and only a handful of the actuality films recording moments from both the militant and the constitutional campaign have survived. Among those preserved by the British Film Institute and available to view online are short newsreels recording both processions and protests, allowing us a glimpse of the moving, breathing protagonists. At Westminster we see the reality of the mobbing of WSPU members on 'Black Friday', 18 November 1910, and, on 27 January 1913, suffragists parading with placards calling, fruitlessly, on MPs to honour a commitment to amend the Franchise and Registration Bill (see Object 71). One of the longest newsreels gives us an intimate view of the WSPU's 18 June 1910 London procession, making it possible to spot a familiar face and admire the banners, some of which are still extant. There is no doubt that the WSPU were more successful in attracting film cameras to their events than were the NUWSS; even with the Pathé camera present at the Pilgrimage rally in Hyde Park, 1913 (see Object 74), it was the male audience, clamouring for attention, that it captured rather than the NUWSS pilgrims.

As applied to the suffrage movement, Charles Urban was correct in recognizing news films as documents vital to the study of history and, although he did not give the same status to feature films, we can see that they, too, however feebly comic, illuminate the mores of the time. Indeed, on occasion fact came close to fiction, for, as Kitty Marion commented of the antics involved when, with a companion, she burned down the grandstand at Hurst Park racecourse in June 1913 as a tribute to Emily Wilding Davison, 'We both regretted that there was no movie camera to immortalise the comedy of it.'[5]

Object 76

Group photograph of delegates to the Church League for Women's Suffrage General Council Meeting, 2 July 1913

Object 76 is a group photograph of women and (male) clergy, delegates attending the General Council Meeting of the Church League for Women's Suffrage (CLWS), held at Brighton on 2 July 1913. The photographer was Muriel Darton, who advertised regularly in the *CLWS Monthly Paper*. (TWL.2004.250, The Women's Library collection, London School of Economics and Political Science.)

The July date appointed for the 1913 meeting of the General Council of the CLWS coincided with the National Union of Women's Suffrage Society (NUWSS) Pilgrimage (see Object 74) and the immediate aftermath of Emily Wilding Davison's death (see Object 73), events that both served to intensify the spiritual aspect of the suffrage campaign and to escalate WSPU militancy, while around the country the comic film, *The Hunger Strike*, was packing cinemas (see Object

75). It was a febrile summer. At the Council meeting, the CLWS, which had been founded in 1909 with a remit to carry out a 'Devotional and Educational' campaign, acknowledged the situation by resolving 'that being a religious League, the spiritual and religious side of our work should be well emphasized, especially at this time of crisis'. Reporting this, the August issue of the *CLWS Monthly Paper* also covered the welcome and help given by CLWS branches to NUWSS pilgrims as they passed through the country. By the end of the year the CLWS had 103 branches and over 5,000 members, many of whom also belonged to other suffrage societies, particularly the NUWSS or Women's Freedom League (WFL). Apart from allowing us to view a group of the leading members of the CLWS, Object 76 proves that at this time membership of the militant Women's Social and Political Union (WSPU) was no bar to that of the CLWS. For, sitting on the grass, fourth from the right, is Norah Smyth, who occasionally acted as chauffeur to Emmeline Pankhurst and was to work with Sylvia Pankhurst's East London Federation of Suffragettes (see Object 81). Moreover, although we have so little evidence of the involvement in the suffrage campaign of women of colour, Object 76 reveals the presence of two women hitherto previously unremarked. For sitting on Smyth's right is Dr Susila Bonnerjee, secretary of the Ealing branch of the CLWS, and at the end of the row is a woman provisionally identified as her sister, Dr Nalini Blair.[1] They were daughters of the founder of the Indian National Congress and had been educated at Newnham College, Cambridge, and the London School of Medicine for Women.

The CLWS stressed that, while allowing individual members freedom to protest in whatever way they chose, as an organization it 'dissociates itself from the distinctive methods, violent or otherwise, of all Suffrage Societies founded on a political rather than a religious basis'.[2] The CLWS was particularly keen to distance itself from the Suffragist Churchwomen's Protest Committee, a group that in 1912 broke away to boycott the churches of anti-suffrage clergy, a campaign that, by 1914, escalated into the interruption of church services with calls for 'Votes for Women'.

While the CLWS had been the first of the religious suffrage societies, others followed, usually initiated by women already active in the suffrage movement.[3] In 1910 the Free Church League for Women's Suffrage (FCLWS) was formed by Miss L.E. Turquand, a member of the Tax Resistance League (see Object 70); in 1911 the Catholic Women's Suffrage Society (CWSS) by two members of the WSPU (see Object 45); and in 1912 the Friends' [Quaker] League and the Scottish Churches' League, both by members of the NUWSS, and the Jewish Women's Suffrage League, the first Jewish society in the world to campaign for women's enfranchisement (see Object 45). Each society had its own badge, colours and banners and the CLWS, FCLWS and CWSS (after 1915) published their own newspapers.

As with the CLWS, rather than attempting a general campaign, the concern of these religious societies was to convert their co-religionists to the suffrage cause and to widen opportunities for women within their faiths. Although executive committees tended to be dominated by women, men were involved in the societies as advisors and members, except in the case of the CWSS, which kept its affairs out of the hands of clergy, while acknowledging support from those sympathetic to the cause. The principal methods of persuasion were pamphlets and prayer, the latter both organized, through regular 'intercessions', and private. These societies were collaborative, forming the United Religious League for Women's Suffrage to hold public meetings and, in July 1913, sending to the home secretary a joint letter of protest against forcible feeding.[4]

On the outbreak of war in August 1914 the Jewish League suspended its activities, but the other societies were still in existence in 1917, endorsing a call to the government to introduce the Representation of the People Bill recommended by the Speaker's Conference.[5] Of the religious societies, two continued campaigning after the passing of the Representation of the People Act in 1918. In 1919 the CLWS changed its name to the League of the Church Militant and continued to campaign for an equal franchise and for women's ordination, while in 1923 the CWSS became the St Joan Social and Political Alliance and, now an international organization, continues to campaign.

Object 77

The Suffrage Annual and Women's Who's Who, 1913

Object 77 is the *Suffrage Annual and Women's Who's Who,* published by Stanley Paul, 1913. (Author's collection.)

Throughout 1913, as suffrage activity, militant and constitutional, increased in volume and intensity, police, press and public desirous of further information were able to consult a new publication, *The Suffrage Annual and Women's Who's Who.* Over a century later, invariably much thumbed, it is still one of the most useful research tools available to suffrage historians.[1]

The book, 405 pages in length, is divided into six sections, of which the first and last are perhaps now the most useful. The first lists thirty-six suffrage societies in Great Britain and eight in Ireland, detailing their histories and tactics and listing names and addresses of branches and personnel. The final section, containing biographies of 692 women and 69 men currently involved in the suffrage campaign, is particularly interesting and intriguing. Of the women, 233 were members of the National Union of Women's Suffrage Societies (NUWSS) and 164 of the Women's Social and Political Union (WSPU). An article, published in 1988, revealed that about 80 per cent of those listed held official positions in the forty-four local and national UK suffrage societies, while many of the others were prominent WSPU militants. Furthermore, virtually all the women were of upper- or middle-class origin, with only three identified as working-class.[2] Now that, four decades later, we know so much more about the individual suffrage campaigners from all classes, it is worthwhile investigating something of the background of Object 77 itself.

The Suffrage Annual was published on 5 February 1913 by Stanley Paul, 31 Essex Street, Strand, a small independent publisher. The firm does not appear to have had any suffrage bias, publishing in 1911 *Suffragette Sally*, a popular pro-militant novel by Gertrude Colmore, and in 1912 Harold Owen's anti-suffrage diatribe, *Woman Adrift: The Menace of Suffragism*. Thus, it is likely the decision to publish Object 77 was commercial; 'suffrage' in any form was good for sales. At the same time as publishing *The Suffrage Annual*, Stanley Paul announced the launch of a 'Votes for Women Series' of novels.[3]

Although we know the publisher, it is more difficult to discover who was the prime mover behind the *Suffrage Annual* project. On the title page the editor is given as 'A.J.R.', a resolutely anonymous set of initials, while those compiling the book went under the name of the 'Vectis Publishing Society', operating from 29 New Bridge Street, London E.C. Of 'Vectis' nothing substantial can be discovered, the handful of surviving documents only including one name, 'Miss M.T. Hogg'. She is likely to be Minnie Trower Hogg, a journalist who, from 1910, worked on the *Standard*, a London evening paper, becoming its woman's editor, 1916–48. In October 1911 the *Standard* instituted a 'Woman's Platform' page, carrying detailed information on the suffrage movement, both pro and anti, and it is here that an advance notice of the *Suffrage Annual* appears.[4] Indeed, it is rather too full a notice as various of the promised features did not appear in the published edition.

It is apparent from the tone and content of the extant correspondence that neither 'Vectis' nor Minnie Hogg was actively involved in the suffrage movement. This exchange of letters concerned the entry for the London Society for Women's Suffrage, supplied by Philippa Strachey a mere two weeks before publication. Also included in the *Suffrage Annual* is Strachey's biographical entry; on 19 January Minnie Hogg had sent her a number of 'Vectis' forms, asking 'would you be so kind as to fill in particulars if you will allow your biography to appear, and perhaps there would be others in the office who would do the same'.[5] Here is proof of what was suspected; the biographical entries are, in fact, autobiographical and inclusion was to some degree self-selective.

Apart from Stanley Paul and 'Vectis', yet another organization was involved in the production of Object 77; 'Selfridge and Co: The Modern Woman's Club-Store' put its stamp on the purple cover and ran advertisements along the foot of every page, presumably underwriting some of the expense of production. Selfridge's department store had opened in Oxford Street in 1909, was renowned for the slickness of its advertising and known to be supportive of the suffragettes. It had escaped the WSPU window-smashing campaigns of 1911 and 1912 but in February 1913 the publication of Object 77 did not protect it from £160 of damage inflicted by Sarah Benett, treasurer of the Women's Freedom League (WFL), who was subsequently sentenced to six months' imprisonment.

On publication of Object 77, reviewers noted the absence of some well-known names, although, as we now appreciate, these women may have chosen not to be included, while the *Standard* reviewer was amused at the amount of detail offered by others. Emily Wilding Davison's lengthy entry, listing her numerous imprisonments, was reprinted in full by several newspapers in the aftermath of her Derby demonstration (see Object 73).[6] Copies of *The Suffrage Annual* were taken when police raided Lincoln's Inn House on 30 April 1913, but it is not known to what purpose they were put.[7] Although both title and editorial foreword suggested a new edition would appear in 1914, that of 1913 is the only version published of Object 77.

Object 78

Mrs Pankhurst's shoe

Object 78 is a single black kid leather court shoe with a small Louis heel, decorated with a black satin rosette and black beadwork on the vamp. It once belonged to Emmeline Pankhurst. (© London Museum.)

The story attached to this shoe is that it was lost by Mrs Pankhurst in a scuffle with the police. This may be apocryphal, but it is not unlikely. For, from 3 April 1913, when found guilty of incitement to cause damage and sentenced to three years' penal servitude (see Object 72), until the Women's Social and Political Union (WSPU) campaign ended in August 1914, Pankhurst's life followed a pattern of hunger strike (or hunger-and-thirst strike), subsequent release from prison under the 'Cat and Mouse' Act, a short or prolonged period 'on the run', ending in a forcible rearrest. In this period, she was rearrested on nine occasions, during any one of which a shoe might have been lost. On 23 June 1914 the government calculated that, in fourteen months, Pankhurst had spent only sixteen days of her sentence in prison. While 'on the run' she contrived to visit Christabel in Paris and undertake a speaking tour in the United States.

Pankhurst's seventh rearrest took place on 21 May 1914 outside Buckingham Palace, leading a deputation to petition the King. Determined to bypass government ministers, she had seen that when Irishmen had appealed to the King, backed up by a call to arms, a conference had been convened to discuss their grievances. However, women's militancy did not have the same effect; the WSPU deputation brought no intervention from the Palace but was instead met by ranks of police. In her diary an onlooker, Kate Frye (see Object 69), wrote,

I went to Buckingham Palace to see the Women's deputation – led by Mrs Pankhurst which went to try and see the King. It was simply awful – oh! those poor pathetic women – dresses half torn off – hair down, hats off, covered with mud and paint and some dragged along looking in the greatest agony. But the wonderful courage of it all. It is the most wicked and futile persecution because they know we have got to have "Votes" – and to think they have got us to this state – some women thinking it necessary and right to do the most awful burnings etc in order to bring the question forward. Oh what a pass to come to in a so-called civilized country. Mrs Pankhurst herself was arrested at the gates of the Palace.[1]

On this occasion several photographs were taken from different angles of Mrs Pankhurst under arrest, carried by Chief Inspector Rolfe of A Division. They represent her apotheosis as a leader of the suffragette movement, much reproduced, both then and now. Rolfe has his arms wrapped around her midriff, her head, topped by a neat little feathered hat, is thrown back, her eyes are closed. Although under normal circumstances skirts were then sufficiently long as to hide shoes, in this position Pankhurst's is rucked up so that her tiny feet (size 3½) are clearly shown, dangling off the ground. Although the design is not exactly that of Object 78, her court shoes have the same small Louis heel, a fashionable shape. Mrs Pankhurst was not prepared to don button boots in the summer to battle with the police. Sylvia Pankhurst notes that for her mother the French style of dress was the 'best in the world', commenting, 'What pretty clothes she wore, and how well she knew how to wear them, so that they seemed wholly artless in their grace.'[2] Even when on trial she did so in style, the *Daily Mirror* remarking in April 1912, 'Women dressed in an untidy or eccentric way have frequently been hailed as "suffragettes", but Mrs Pankhurst, when released [from Bow Street Court] yesterday, was fashionably dressed in a tailor-made costume, a long musquash stole edged with three rows of chinchilla, and carrying a large musquash muff.'[3] As Lydia Becker had recognized in the nineteenth century (see Object 2), the appearance of women who campaigned for the vote was always to be given serious consideration.

The day after Pankhurst's Buckingham Palace arrest, six paintings were slashed in national collections. After hunger striking, she was released on licence but failed to return to Holloway and was rearrested on 8 July. That night a bomb was placed at Robert Burns' cottage in Alloway. Pankhurst's disruptive behaviour added another week to her sentence, but after hunger striking, she was released on 11 July, to be rearrested on the sixteenth. The following day the portrait of Thomas Carlyle, ironically a hero to Pankhurst, was slashed in the National Portrait Gallery. She was released on 18 July, having completed her tenth hunger strike, and managed to slip over to France. It was there, at St Malo, that she learned that war had been declared.

Mrs Pankhurst's shoe is by way of a relic, part of the collection amassed by the Suffragette Fellowship and later presented to the London Museum (see Object 96). Perhaps surprisingly, there are very few extant objects associated with Emmeline Pankhurst, her peripatetic life not conducive to the retention of material goods.

Object 79

Irish Citizen leaflet, 15 August 1914

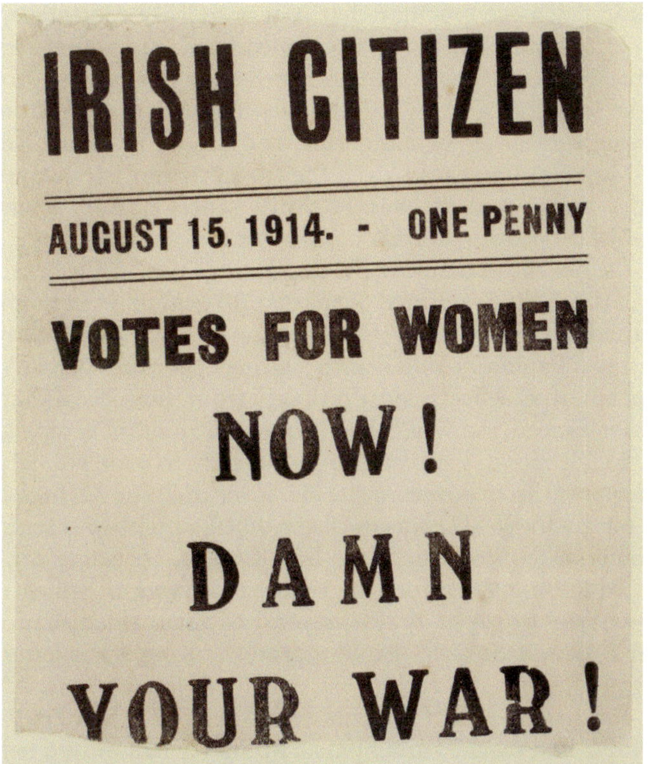

Object 79 is a small leaflet (23 x 15 cm) stating the *Irish Citizen*'s attitude to the war declared between the United Kingdom and Germany on 4 August 1914. (Courtesy of the National Library of Ireland.)

Founded in Dublin in 1912 with financial help from the Pethick-Lawrences, the *Irish Citizen* supported women's suffrage, feminism and the rights of women workers.[1] Its first editors were Francis Sheehy-Skeffington and James Cousins, husbands of the founders of the nationalist Irish Women's Franchise League (IWFL), Hanna Sheehy-Skeffington and Margaret Cousins (see Objects 8 and 45). The latter explained the IWFL's task as one of seeing that women's suffrage was incorporated in the Home Rule Bill for which Ireland was fighting.

The conflict between nationalism and suffragism haunted the Irish suffrage campaign but was merely one of the points of difference responsible for producing Ireland's plethora of suffrage societies.[2] These reflected the range of opinions that could be held on the issues of the day, for instance, on the suffrage campaign (militant/constitutional), Irish politics (nationalist/ unionist), national politics (Conservative/Unionist/Liberal/Labour) and, after 4 August 1914, war (militant/pacifist). The IWFL's pacifist position is crystallized in Object 79, a leaflet in which 'YOUR' encompasses both 'men' and 'the British' and 'damns' both. It was first issued to street sellers as an advertising placard for the 17 August issue of the *Irish Citizen*, or for 'those who are not selling [to] display in their windows or on their gate-post'. But the poster's 'succinct and vigorous expression' was so popular that it was quickly reprinted, both in its original form and as Object 79, 'a small leaflet, with gummed back, to facilitate its being stuck up on hoardings, etc.'[3] In the 17 August issue Hanna Sheehy-Skeffington implored Irish women not to be seduced from the suffrage cause by calls to help the war effort. Although the Government of Ireland Act, allowing a measure of home rule, had passed its Third Reading in the House of Commons on 25 May 1914 and was given the Royal Assent in September, implementation was suspended for the duration of the war. For Irish suffrage campaigners there was now no immediate hope of legislation from an Irish parliament.

The war did have the benefit of defusing the impending crisis in Ulster where, since 1913, the Ulster Volunteer Force (UVF) had recruited over 100,000 men to resist home rule. In retaliation, nationalist Ireland raised the Irish Volunteers, mustering 75,000 men by May 1914. In articles in *The Suffragette* Christabel Pankhurst had drawn legitimacy for the Women's Social and Political Union (WSPU) campaign of violence against property from the success that threats by the UVF were achieving in Ulster. Indeed, the WSPU had brought its militant campaign there intending to force Sir Edward Carson, leader of the Ulster Unionist party, to state publicly that women would be enfranchised under any Ulster government. He never did. On 31 July 1914 one of the last militant acts carried out by the WSPU was in Ulster, when a bomb was set in Lisburn Cathedral by Lilian Metge, a sometime contributor to the *Irish Citizen*. The same day saw the publication of the last issue of *The Suffragette* before the outbreak of war, in which it was reported that on 23 and 24 July women from the WSPU, several of them titled, had been arrested while attempting to deliver a letter from Mrs Pankhurst to the King. That letter compared the case of Irish representatives, unionist and nationalist, equally described as Irish 'militants', who had been received by the King, with that of the women of the WSPU, who had not.

But by now the WSPU had reached an impasse. Militancy had moved neither Parliament nor the King, both Emmeline and Christabel Pankhurst were out of the country and the WSPU's remaining leaders were either in hiding or in prison, where staff had perfected a forcible feeding technique that did not lead to release under the 'Cat and Mouse' Act. On 22 May, the day after the deputation to the King, the police had raided the WSPU office at Lincoln's Inn House and seized its contents. Every office subsequently occupied by the WSPU received the same treatment. The Home Office was intent on stifling the WSPU's access to funds. By 27 July all mail thought to contain *The Suffragette* was to be opened and detained and the names and addresses of those to whom the paper was sent were to be recorded; by 1 August the decision had been taken to institute civil proceedings against all subscribers to the WSPU as a means of paying for the repair of property damaged by activists. There is no way of knowing whether the WSPU would have survived this concentrated attack if war had not intervened.

In Britain the outbreak of war on 4 August did not elicit from the suffrage societies headlines as melodramatic as that displayed by Object 79. But it did result in a total change of policy for both the militant and the constitutional wings of the suffrage movement, with most societies suspending direct campaigning in favour of activities that reflected their individual philosophies.

Object 80

A Flyer for 'The Right to Serve' March, 1915

Object 80 is a flyer for 'The Right to Serve' March organized by the Women's Social and Political Union (WSPU), 17 July 1915. (From the Collection of Dr Kenneth Florey. Photograph by Emilia van Beugen.)

On 12 August 1914, Emmeline Pankhurst sent a letter to members of the WSPU informing them that the militant suffrage campaign had been suspended for the duration of the war. Emmeline and Christabel Pankhurst took the patriotic line, stating there was nothing to be gained by opposing the government at a time of national crisis. At the beginning of August twelve WSPU members were in prison, nine of them being forcibly fed, one having endured this treatment for as long as thirteen weeks. But as a result of the declaration of war a Home Office official, in a minute dated 9 August, suggested the immediate remission of all convicted suffragette prisoners, writing, 'I think the announcement could be worded in such a way as to put them on their honour not to abuse the Royal clemency and I personally should have no fear of their committing further outrages.'[1] Thus, on 10 August all WSPU prisoners were granted an amnesty, allowing the Pankhursts to end the militant campaign. On 3 September mother and daughter, now safe from arrest, returned to England from France.

In London on 8 September Christabel gave a speech, declaring, 'It is the women who prevent the collapse of the nation while men are fighting the enemy' and that once the war was over, with England victorious, women would insist upon 'being brought into equal partnership as enfranchised citizens of the country'.[2] In October she sailed to the United States, where, with the approval of the British government, she urged America to support the Allies by entering the war. When she returned, it was not to England but to Paris, from where she edited *The Suffragette*. Publication of the paper, suspended after the issue of 7 August 1914, only resumed on 16 April 1915, now making little mention of 'the vote'. On 8 October 1915 it was reborn as *Britannia*, taking an increasingly anti-German and anti-pacifist stance. Not all members were happy with the Pankhursts' decisions and two groups broke away to form the Suffragettes of the WSPU and the Independent WSPU. Their members rejected the Pankhursts' patriotic feminism, reviving the suffrage campaign by lobbying MPs and picketing Parliament, while eschewing active militancy.[3]

Object 80, a flyer for the 'Right to Serve March' of 17 July 1915, is a manifestation of the WSPU's commitment to the war effort, revealing a new close cooperation with a former adversary, Lloyd George, recently appointed as minister of munitions. After a year of war, the belief held by Emmeline and Christabel Pankhurst that much more should be done to co-opt women into the workforce coincided with the need to increase the production of munitions. The King, who had a year earlier refused to receive her letter (see Object 79), suggested that Mrs Pankhurst could prove useful.[4] With the Munitions of War Bill under discussion, pragmatism prevailed; Lloyd George gave Emmeline £3,000 with which to organize a procession to demonstrate women's willingness to engage in war work, especially in munition factories.[5] Open to all women, of all classes, the WSPU intended the procession to impress 'the Government and the men of the country generally with women's devotion to country and determination to render national service'.[6] It is to be noted that, printed in green on flimsy white war-economy paper, the flyer omits the purple that would have identified the event directly with the WSPU. It does, however, include a quote from a speech given in London on 1 July by Mrs Pankhurst and an exhortation to read *The Suffragette*, 'the best patriotic war paper'.

The weather was not kind to 'The Right to Serve March' and the organization less skilled than for the glorious pre-war suffrage processions. As a participant, Kate Frye (see Object 69), wrote in her diary,

It turned out a wicked day and rained till 4 o'clock. Just before 3.30 we discovered we must arrange ourselves – so a few people did one thing – a few another. Banners and bannerettes were hastily pulled out of carts and we were off. I went up and down giving directions and making us as trim as possible. We were a motley crew, but we had some fine banner bearers and the greater number of us looked very neat in rainproof coats. Mr Lloyd George received a deputation of women concerning Munitions. I saw him watching the whole thing from a balcony as we went along. At intervals tables with ladies taking signatures of women ready to do munition work. It was very inspiring and invigorating.[7]

'The Right to Serve March' played a part in ensuring nearly a million women were employed in munition factories by the end of the war.

Lloyd George also used the Pankhursts and their followers to help combat dissension in industry, to prevent strikes and minimize the influence of trade unions and left-wing activists. In June 1917 he sent Emmeline Pankhurst to Russia to encourage Russian women to lobby to keep their country in the war. She left as revolution broke out, her mission a failure.

Object 81

East London Federation of the Suffragettes: First Annual Report

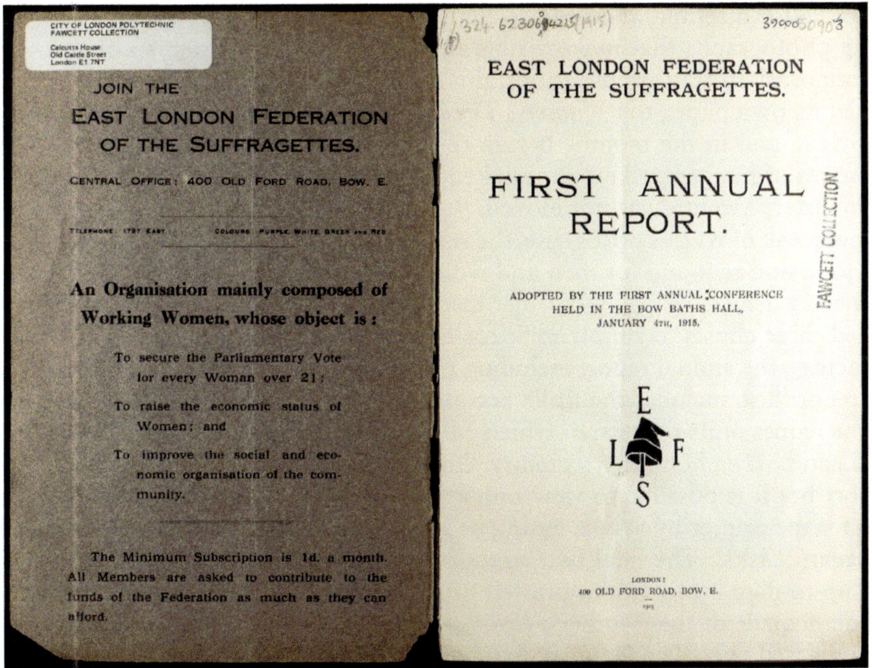

Object 81 is the First Annual Report of the East London Federation of the Suffragettes, published in early 1915. (324.62306094215 EAS, The Women's Library collection, London School of Economics and Political Science.)

The East London Federation of the Women's Social and Political Union, through which Sylvia Pankhurst had been conducting her own suffrage campaign in the East End of London since the summer of 1912, became a distinct organization on 27 January 1914 when Emmeline and Christabel Pankhurst set it adrift from the Women's Social and Political Union (WSPU). Disagreeing with the autocratic control exercised over the WSPU by her mother and sister and with the increasingly destructive militancy that was becoming WSPU policy, Sylvia renamed her organization the East London Federation of Suffragettes (ELFS), believing it was only by rousing the masses that pressure could be brought to bear on Parliament. After the outbreak of war Sylvia, a socialist and pacifist, was shocked by the extremist pro-war stand taken by her mother and sister and continued to campaign for the vote while working to alleviate the sufferings the new situation caused to women and children.

This first annual report gave legitimacy to the ELFS, setting out its history over eighteen of its thirty pages. The title page shows the society's emblem, the red cap of liberty, a symbol of the French Revolution, surrounded by the initials ELFS. On the front cover the cap is indeed printed in red. The details inside the front cover include the address of the ELFS, 400 Old Ford Road, Bow, to which it had moved on 5 May 1914, and the society's objects: to secure the parliamentary vote for women over 21; to raise the economic status of women; and to improve the social and economic organization of the community. Here set out are the ELFS' colours, the 'purple, white and green' of the WSPU, with the addition of socialist 'red'. The house in Old Ford Road, now demolished, is commemorated (2025) by a plaque and by a mural of Sylvia, painted on the side wall of the adjacent building. Behind the house was a large hall, put to good use by the ELFS for meetings and welfare clinics.

Including photographs that make visible the working-class women so often overlooked in other contemporary suffrage publications, this short history tells how in March 1914 the ELFS had launched its own paper, the *Women's Dreadnought*, 'the working woman's suffrage paper' edited by Sylvia, and in the months before the war held rallies in the East End, while Sylvia endured a series of hunger strikes, undertaken in public. The intention was to put pressure on the prime minister; Asquith was not moved.

On the outbreak of war, as prices rose, the report details how the ELFS campaigned to control the cost of food and rent and for men and women put out of work by the war to be employed on government schemes. Helped by former members of the Kensington and Chelsea WSPU, the ELFS opened three clinics to supply milk for babies, two cost-price restaurants, a day nursery and a toy factory, the annual report including photographs of some of the products made in the latter. The report also includes the ELFS accounts covering the period August 1914 to January 1915 and the names of its officers, of which Mrs Evelina Haverfield was the honorary treasurer (see item 82) and Sylvia honorary secretary. Object 81 is, of course, the final version of this first annual report but it is possible to view online the galley proofs of that for the following year, marked up for the printer by Sylvia, letting us glimpse the attention to detail she applied to just one of her many tasks.[1] The final two pages of the report, the inside and outside of the back cover, give up-to-date information, printed after the main text was written. Here for the first time mention is made of the 'Mother's Arms', the centre for mothers and babies that the ELFS opened in a disused pub, 'The Gunmakers' Arms', at 438 Old Ford Road.

The annual report records that since the outbreak of war the ELFS had continued to hold suffrage meetings and had taken deputations to Westminster to lobby MPs both on their concerns for war relief and for the enfranchisement of women. However, Object 81 is a record of just one moment in the life of the ELFS. For, in March 1916 it was renamed the Workers' Suffrage Federation (WSF), with the *Women's Dreadnought* later becoming the *Workers' Dreadnought*, and, although continuing to lobby for suffrage, widened its remit to call for the enfranchisement of all men and women over twenty-one, that is, for adult suffrage. In 1916 Sylvia was unsuccessful in persuading the other suffrage societies to join the WSF in calling for adult suffrage; in March 1917 Lloyd George, now prime minister, refused to allow the WSF, as adult suffragists, to be included in the women's suffrage deputation he had agreed to meet. Sylvia Pankhurst termed the age restriction imposed on women voters by the 1918 Representation of the People Act as 'absurd' (see Object 83) and renamed the WSF the Workers' Socialist Federation.

Object 82

Photographs of ambulances of the Scottish Women's Hospitals for Foreign Service, 1915–17

Object 82 comprises two photographs held in a collection of images kept by Vera Holme, a former member of the Women's Social and Political Union (WSPU), who served as a driver with the transport section of the Scottish Women's Hospitals (SWH) in Serbia, Romania and Russia, 1915–17. (7VJH/5/3/32 and 33, The Women's Library collection, London School of Economics and Political Science.)

After the outbreak of war on 4 August 1914 the National Union of Women's Suffrage Societies (NUWSS) suspended direct political campaigning, redirecting its organizing capacity into relief work, both at home and overseas. A rather dramatic split occurred in April 1915 when the decision not to support the Women's Peace Congress at The Hague, organized by the International Woman Suffrage Alliance, led to the resignation of all NUWSS officers, except the president (Mrs Fawcett), the treasurer (Mrs Auerbach) and ten members of the executive committee. However, although the rift was personally painful, there was no attempt to oust Fawcett from the presidency, and she retained popular support within the organization.

Of the NUWSS war relief initiatives perhaps the most remarkable was the Scottish Women's Hospitals for Foreign Service (SWH), founded by Dr Elsie Inglis, secretary of the Federation of Scottish Societies (NUWSS) whose service as a doctor was decisively declined by the War Office. Instead, by 3 October, with the backing of the entire NUWSS, she offered a fully equipped hospital unit staffed by women to an ally, either France or Serbia. The SWH doctors, nurses and orderlies, many of whom were members of the NUWSS or the Women's Social and Political Union (WSPU), served throughout the war in France, Serbia, Russia, Salonica, Malta and Macedonia. The work was arduous and dangerous; thousands of men were treated, fifteen SWH women died. The SWH headquarters were in Edinburgh, with committees also in Glasgow and in London, where the chairman was Edith Palliser, secretary of the NUWSS, 1913–15. Totally financed by private donations, from both Britain and abroad, by 1919 the SWH had raised £449,000 to support its work.[1]

The first Scottish Women's Hospital was established at Calais in November 1914 and in December a second was opened at Royaumont Abbey in France. At the same time a hospital unit was sent to Serbia, joined some months later by Vera Holme, former chauffeur to Emmeline Pankhurst (see Object 33), now serving as an SWH ambulance driver. An active suffragette, she had been briefly imprisoned for stone throwing in November 1911 as had been her companion and lover, the Hon. Evelina Haverfield, now the administrator of this Serbian SWH Unit.[2] The first tour lasted eight months and in August 1916 both women set out again, this time for Russia in a unit led by Dr Inglis, with Haverfield in charge of a transport column and Holme again a driver/mechanic. Transport columns, comprising ambulances, trucks, cars and, perhaps, an x-ray van, provided essential support to the SWH medical units. Holme's collection of photographs was informal in that she did not keep it in an album. Now archived, the images have been sorted thematically and those relating to the First World War include many images of SWH members in Serbia. However, it cannot be assumed that all the images relate directly to Holme's own experience as some were sent to her by friends. The origin of others is less clear, such as the snapshots of the impressive fleet of ambulances that comprise Object 82, which carry no annotations. The only clue as to their provenance is 'Scottish Women's Hospital No 2' painted on the side of the ambulances but evidence has not yet been found to link a hospital of that designation with Holme. It is always necessary to interrogate an object for itself, separate from what may be an artificial context.

As for the home front, in the first month of the war the NUWSS stated that 'our political work has taken the form of social service. It is none the less political because it is social'.[3] The first initiative undertaken by their country-wide network of 602 societies was to adopt a relief scheme to help refugees arriving from Belgium, now under attack from Germany. The London Society for Women's Suffrage then quickly opened the Women's Service Bureau to place women in employment, releasing men for war service.[4] One of its initiatives was to set up a school to train women as oxyacetylene welders to manufacture aircraft. This was run by Mary Lowndes (see Object 30), whose work as a stained-glass artist had made her well-acquainted with welding. Like the ELFS (see Object 81), the London Society opened a workroom, the Bee Toymakers, to give employment to dressmakers put out of work by the war. Its most successful line was in the 'Bimbo' toy, designed by Mary Constance Lloyd, an artist who had returned to England from her life in Paris to help the war effort. Thus, the NUWSS kept their banner flying by, among many local community efforts, designing soft toys, producing aircraft parts and supplying hospital orderlies, nurses, ambulance drivers and doctors to Britain's allies.

Object 83

'The Suffrage Oak', Kelvingrove Park, Glasgow

Object 83 is a Hungarian oak (*quercus frainetto*) planted on 20 April 1918 in Kelvingrove Park, Glasgow, to commemorate the passing into law on 6 February of the Representation of the People Act, by which some women were granted the parliamentary vote. (Glasgow Women's Library.)

Although most suffrage societies suspended direct political campaigning after the outbreak of war, none lost sight of their goal, 'votes for women on the same terms as it is given to men'. Some women achieved the vote with the passing of the Representation of the People Act, 1918, but they had yet to achieve an equal franchise.

The Scottish commemoration of this partial enfranchisement was organized jointly by the Glasgow Society for Women's Suffrage, which was a member of the National Union of Women's Suffrage Societies (NUWSS), the Scottish Women's Suffrage Union, the Women's Freedom League (WFL), the Conservative and Unionist Franchise Association and the United Suffragists (US). The latter group had been formed in February 1914 by women and men who had become disillusioned with WSPU militancy.[1] At the outbreak of war, the Pethick-Lawrences gave their paper, *Votes for Women*, to the United Suffragists, which continued to combine a suffrage propaganda campaign with philanthropic work. Similarly, during the war the WFL was quick to direct its energies into welfare work, to which its campaign for the vote had always been targeted. It swiftly inaugurated the Women's Police Volunteers, arguing that, with police officers drafted into the trenches, it was now necessary to form a women's police force, for which it had already been campaigning.

Women offered themselves in great numbers for war service, for instance, as nurses (around 34,000 joined the Voluntary Aid Detachments) and as workers in the munition factories (see Object 80). By 1917 the War Office had admitted the need for women's services, allowing for the formation of the Women's Army Auxiliary Corps (WAAC), the Women's Royal Naval Service (WRNS) and the Women's Royal Air Force (WRAF). On the Home Front, with the men off to the war, women took over their jobs becoming, for instance, bus conductors, postwomen, window cleaners, factory and agricultural workers. Thus, in just two or three years the position of women had dramatically altered.

However, although after 1914 individual women saw a very great change in their social and economic circumstances, nothing changed politically until the government realized it had to deal with a new problem concerning 'votes for men'. For many men had lost their right to the vote because, away fighting for their country, they no longer met the residential requirements, while others had been too young to qualify as voters before the war. Once the government made it known it did not feel able to deny these men the prospect of a vote, in June 1916 a suffrage conference organized by the constitutional suffrage societies decided that if the government intended to extend the male franchise, a constitutional campaign for female suffrage must be resumed. Members of the NUWSS lobbied MPs, by letter and in person, until in October Parliament set up an all-party committee chaired by the Speaker to discuss possible changes to the electoral register.

In January 1917 the Speaker's Conference reported it had decided, not unanimously but by a majority, that some women should be granted a measure of enfranchisement. The proposal was that a woman on the Local Government Register, or the wife of a man on the register, should be entitled to a parliamentary vote. However, the conference was not prepared to grant the vote to women on exactly the same terms as men, that is, at the age of twenty-one, and suggested that women should be thirty or thirty-five. In March 1917 Lloyd George, who had recently succeeded Asquith as prime minister, received a deputation, led by Mrs Fawcett, that included representatives of twenty-four women's suffrage societies and ten other women's organizations. Knowing that politics is the art of the possible, Fawcett emphasized to Lloyd George that, if the women's suffrage clause in any proposed bill were to have government backing, 'we greatly preferred an imperfect Bill which could pass to the most perfect measure in the world which could not'.[2] Lloyd George assured the deputation of his sympathy with their demands. Although experience had taught suffragists to be wary of such a claim, a couple of months later they were able to take strength from a good omen when Parliament voted to remove the grille that caged women in the Ladies' Gallery (see Object 36). Then, when the Women's Suffrage Clause was debated in the Commons, it became clear that, for the very first time, such a measure did indeed have government support. Despite hostile speeches in the House of Lords, the bill was safely passed, allowing 8.5 million women who were over thirty years old and met a small property qualification to vote in parliamentary elections.

As well as organizing the planting of the Suffrage Oak to mark the historic moment, from 6 February 1919 until 1966 the Glasgow Society for Equal Citizenship held an annual Commemoration Dinner. These were recorded each year in a scrapbook, and, with the Suffrage Oak, which over one hundred years later is still standing, battered by gales but unbowed, are a visible commemoration of this stage in women's enfranchisement.[3]

Object 84

Mrs Despard's election card, 1918

Object 84 is a card advertising Mrs Charlotte Despard's candidature at the 1918 general election. (From the Collection of Dr Kenneth Florey. Photograph by Emilia van Beugen.)

As early as 20 April 1918, during the ceremonials accompanying the planting of the Glasgow Suffrage Oak (see Object 83), Eunice Murray, president of the Women's Freedom League (WFL) in Scotland, declared she would stand as a parliamentary candidate for the Glasgow constituency of Bridgeton at the next general election and on 23 May the *Daily Record and Mail* reported details of her manifesto. However, it was not until 21 November, with the passing of the Parliament (Qualification of Women) Act, that women did acquire the right to stand for election as members of Parliament. Curiously, the short bill, passing rapidly through all stages of the parliamentary process with little opposition, granted the right to all women over the age of twenty-one, although no woman of that age was able to vote. It had taken over fifty years of arduous campaigning to achieve the parliamentary vote, yet within a few months the walls of the Westminster stronghold had been further breached without a fight.

With a general election called for 14 December, there was little time for women to organize election campaigns, but in the event seventeen women took to the hustings. Eunice Murray was the only woman candidate in Scotland, two women stood in Ireland and one in Wales, with the remaining thirteen contesting English seats. Mrs Charlotte Despard, president of the WFL, was selected by the Labour party to stand in North Battersea, a new constituency in the area in which she had lived since 1890, renowned for her social work as 'the Mother of Battersea'. John Archer, who in 1913 had been the first person of colour to be elected a mayor in London, was her election agent, and her registration agent was a printer, Charles Mason, whose name appears on Object 84. The wording on Object 84, stressing Despard's status as 'The Children's Friend' and 'The People's Champion', echoes that used on Object 13, issued in 1885 when a woman, Helen Taylor, last stood for a south London constituency. However, standing against a Liberal candidate who was backed by a 'coupon' of Coalition endorsement, Despard had little hope of success, polling 5,634 votes against her rival's 11,231. She was never again a parliamentary candidate, subsequently devoting her remarkable energies to the cause of Irish freedom and Irish socialism.

Although most other of the women standing for British constituencies were affiliated to one of the three main parties, Liberal, Conservative/Unionist or Labour, Christabel Pankhurst alone stood as a candidate for the Women's Party. This organization was a relaunching of the Women's Social and Political Union (WSPU) by Emmeline and Christabel Pankhurst, effected in 1917 with a programme based on 'equality of rights and responsibilities in the social and political life of the nation'. During 1917 and 1918 the Women's Party, with the backing of Lloyd George, campaigned in the industrial heartlands, particularly in south Wales, advocating industrial peace and warning against the dangers of Bolshevism. As a reward, for the general election Christabel, standing at Smethwick, was given a coveted Coalition 'coupon', the only woman candidate to receive one. Her manifesto was not particularly feminist and, although in a speech reported in the final edition of *Britannia*, she appeared confident of success, she was defeated, polling 8,614 votes to the Labour candidate's 9,389.[1] She never repeated the experience, eventually moving to the United States and devoting herself to Second Adventism.

The only successful woman candidate in the 1918 general election was Mme Constance Markievicz (née Gore-Booth), who stood as a Sinn Féin candidate in the St Patrick's constituency in Dublin. However, with other elected members of Sinn Féin, she refused to take her seat at Westminster, becoming instead a member of the first Dáil, the parliament of the new Irish Republic. She was an artist, a member of a landed Anglo-Irish family, whose sister, Eva, worked with the radical suffragists in Manchester (see Object 20). Markievicz campaigned for Irish independence, took part in the Easter Rising in 1916 and when she stood for Parliament in 1918 was in Holloway, sentenced for taking part in anti-conscription activity. She was still in prison when the first Dáil met, but once released, served as minister of labour from 1919 to January 1922, becoming the first Irish woman to be a member of the Cabinet.

In 1932, a few years after her death, Markievicz was commemorated by a portrait bust placed on St Stephen's Green, Dublin. This was the work of the sculptor responsible for the nearby seat memorializing Anna and Thomas Haslam (see Object 8), and although the bust was subsequently damaged, it was replaced by another. In one glance these two objects together encapsulate the seed and the fruit of the suffrage campaign. In Battersea, although she never achieved election, Despard is commemorated by a street in her name and two plaques, one on the site of her former Nine Elms home and another at 177 Lavender Hill, headquarters of Battersea Labour party, a property bought with funds she donated.

Object 85

Lady Astor's parliamentary outfit

Object 85 is a display that contains the outfit worn in Parliament by Lady Astor, the first woman to be elected an MP. (The Box, Plymouth; photograph © House of Commons.)

Although the 1918 general election brought no woman MP into Parliament, it was not long before one was to sit on the green benches. For on 1 December 1919, at 3.25 pm, Nancy Astor entered the House of Commons as the newly elected Unionist (Conservative) member of the

Sutton Division of Plymouth. Her husband had been the Plymouth MP since 1910 and had held the new Sutton seat since the 1918 general election, but his recent elevation to the House of Lords on the death of his father had caused a by-election, at which his wife held the seat. When Lady Astor was elected, the youngest of her six children was a year old.

It was a doubly notable occasion in that for the first time women reporters were allowed in the press gallery to witness the crowded scene on the floor of the House, where, the *Daily Mirror* commented, the new MP 'might have been Portia from her appearance'.[1] The syndicated newspaper reports of the scene made no mention of the quirks of the situation, such as the fact that the first woman MP was American-born, had played no part in the suffrage campaign on either side of the Atlantic and that one of her campaigners was the daughter of Lord Curzon, the pre-war leader of the National League for Opposing Woman Suffrage. They did, however, take careful note of the costume she wore on the day, the *Daily Mirror* describing the 'graceful, fair-headed woman in a small black velvet toque ornamented with jet, a simple black coat and skirt and white crepe de Chine blouse and turnover collar'. This is the outfit seen in Object 85, as displayed in the exhibition 'Voice and Vote: Women's Place in Parliament', staged in 2018 in Westminster Hall as part of the centenary celebrations to commemorate the passing of the Representation of the People Act.[2]

Recognizing the importance of presentation, Astor chose her costume wisely, eschewing frivolity, but dressing with style, perfecting a parliamentary uniform. On its report of that first outing, under the main headline 'First Woman MP Takes Her Seat', the *Daily Mirror* did what it could to spice up the event with comment on her attire but could only produce as a subheading: 'Kept Her Hat On'. This alluded to a debate raging in the press, for at that time it was considered as improper for a woman to appear hatless in public as it was for a man to wear a hat indoors. Thus, sitting in the House of Commons, MPs, hitherto male, were hatless unless raising a point of order when a division was called, in which case they were required, by ancient tradition, to don a top hat. *The Times* pondered this question of etiquette; Astor solved it by retaining her hat, although by 1925 Ellen Wilkinson, a less traditionally minded MP, chose to address the Speaker hatless, attracting some criticism.[3] However, in 1929 the Speaker ruled definitively that women were not required to wear hats.

Featured at the back of Object 85, above Astor's outfit, is a reproduction of a section of the painting by Charles Henry Sims commissioned by Lord Astor to commemorate the introduction of the first woman MP, in which his wife stands between her sponsors, Lloyd George and Arthur Balfour. The painting was initially given to Parliament in July 1924 and hung in a prominent position on the staircase leading to the committee rooms. However, there was an immediate outcry, within a week it had been slightly defaced and six months later it was removed.[4] Opposition had crystallized around the notion that Parliament should not hang pictures of the living; it is unlikely that misogyny was entirely absent.

Holding her Plymouth seat until her retirement in 1945, Astor campaigned assiduously for temperance, a range of women's causes, children's education and welfare.[5] She maintained her parliamentary uniform over the years, choosing to wear the Object 85 outfit in studio photographs taken in the couple of years after her election and in 1924 in a group photograph with other women MPs.[6] The simple tailored suit she wore in her final parliamentary year, in outline similar to that displayed in Object 85, albeit in a style updated to 1945, is held in the London Museum.[7] The choice of attire for Astor's statue, erected in Plymouth in 2019, was carefully considered, the result an outfit such as she wore in the mid to later 1930s, with a nod to that displayed in Object 85.

Object 86

Helena Normanton's KC jabot

Object 86 is a lace jabot, from the robes worn by Helena Normanton, one the first two women barristers in England and Wales to be appointed King's Counsel, 1949. (7HLN/G/0486, The Women's Library collection, London School of Economics and Political Science.)

On 23 December 1919, just three weeks after Lady Astor took her seat as the first woman MP, Parliament passed the Sex Disqualification (Removal) Act, by which women were permitted for the first time to become lawyers and civil servants. The following day, Christmas Eve 1919, Helena Normanton was the first woman to be admitted to an Inn of Court, the Middle Temple. She had applied previously, but been refused entrance, for until then both arms of the legal profession had been closed to women, prevented by the Law Society from becoming solicitors and by the Inns of Court from becoming barristers. For instance, in 1904, while reading for a law degree in Manchester, Christabel Pankhurst had been rebuffed when she applied for admission to Lincoln's Inn. But with the new Act decreeing that 'a person shall not be disqualified by sex or marriage from the exercise of any public function, or from being appointed to or holding any civil or judicial post, or from entering or assuming or carrying on any civil profession or vocation', women were now able to enter professions such as law and accountancy and could hold public positions as magistrates and jurors.[1] However, the Act was a government measure replacing a more ambitious Labour party private member's Women's Emancipation Bill that, besides including a clause allowing women to hold judicial and civil appointments, had also called for an equal franchise and for women to be allowed to sit and vote in the House of Lords. The government was not ready to back those two last clauses.

That Helena Normanton was able so swiftly to take advantage of the new Act was not fortuitous. She had long been working towards the goal of becoming a lawyer for, brought up in an impoverished single-parent family, she had recognized from an early age how disadvantaged women were when confronted with the legal system. With the profession then closed to her, she became a teacher, achieving a first-class University of London history degree as well as various other diplomas. As her 'Census Resisted' badge was among Normanton's papers donated to the Women's Library collection, LSE (see Object 45), she was probably already a member of the Women's Freedom League (WFL) by 1911 and by 1913 was lecturing for the WFL on subjects such as 'English Reform Bills' and 'The History of the Poor Law', writing in *The Vote* on 'The Legal Position of Women in the British Isles' and speaking at meetings in both England and Scotland. As a lecturer, first, at Glasgow University and later for university extension courses, during the First World War she continued to speak and write regularly on behalf of the WFL, interested in the peace movement as well as women's enfranchisement.

On 17 November 1922 Normanton became the second woman in England to be called to the Bar.[2] Now married, she suffered no restriction on practising as a barrister, although the drafting of the Act did not prove sufficiently robust to prevent the civil service and the teaching profession from imposing on women a requirement to resign on marriage, that is, a marriage bar. In December 1922 Carrie Morrison became the first woman in England and Wales to qualify as a solicitor.

Although women lawyers could now join women doctors as members of a recognized profession, the ability to practise as a barrister or solicitor in no way guaranteed success. In fact, of the early cohort of women barristers only Normanton and Monica Geikie Cobb (whose father delivered the address at Emmeline Pankhurst's funeral in 1928, see Object 93) remained at the Bar and it was only in 1949, with twenty-seven years' call, that Normanton was appointed King's Counsel. It was for the ceremony endorsing this appointment that Normanton acquired Object 86.

Object 87

A Minerva Club plate

Object 87 is a china plate made for the Minerva Club by Pountney & Co. (2 WFL/0/01, The Women's Library collection, London School of Economics and Political Science.)

This plate is a rare survivor of china commissioned for the Women Freedom League's (WFL) Minerva Club from Pountney & Co., a Bristol pottery with a factory at Fishponds. Decorated in the WFL colours of green, white and gold, it features the Club's Head of Minerva motif and the legends 'Women's Freedom League' and 'Minerva Club'. As Roman goddess of wisdom, justice, law and (strategic) warfare, Minerva had been adopted by the WFL in 1909 when they named the publisher of *The Vote* the 'Minerva Publishing Company'.

Object 87 is unlikely to date from earlier than March 1920 when the WFL opened the Minerva Club in a tall, late-eighteenth-century house at 56 Hunter Street, Bloomsbury, London, on the west side of Brunswick Square in a stretch of street that already included several ladies' hostels. From *c.*1930 the address was usually rendered as 28a Brunswick Square, but both addresses refer to the same premises.[1] In June 1916 Helena Normanton (see Object 86) had been a participant at the ceremonial opening of the WFL's Minerva Café at 144 High Holborn, the League's headquarters. This café, offering vegetarian luncheons and teas and providing a room for lectures, had proved popular not only with suffrage sympathizers but with all manner of radical men and women, and the idea of a residential club along the same lines would have seemed a natural progression.

The Minerva Club's purpose was 'to supply a common meeting ground for men and women interested in progressive thought and social reform [and] to stimulate that thought by debates and discussions. Here, however, will be no merely high-brow gatherings – the lighter side of life will be cultivated also'.[2] The Club's daily facilities, which, besides the dining room, included a smoking room and a library with newspapers, were open to both men and women, although the residential quarters were reserved for women. Dr Elizabeth Knight, the WFL treasurer, who put much of her sizeable inherited fortune towards the work of the League, funded the Club's very long lease.

The Minerva Club became a rallying point in the campaigns for the extension of the franchise to women under thirty years old, for equal pay and for the entrance of women to the House of Lords, attracting members from all branches of the erstwhile militant suffrage campaign. In 1926 the first reunion dinner organized by the newly formed Suffragette Fellowship (see Object 96) was held at the Club, as were meetings of the WFL national executive and, over the years, numerous events celebrating Mrs Despard. Its dining room preserved the WFL's close connection to vegetarianism, advertisements painstakingly detailing that the vegetarian meals served were cooked separately from meat dishes.

However, after Dr Knight's sudden death in a road accident in 1933, with no specific mention made of the Club in her will, its finances became increasingly precarious, the surroundings, 'furnished somewhat heavily in the Victorian style',[3] shabby and the food indifferent, although that did not dissuade E.M. Forster from breakfasting there when living close by.[4] From *c.*1924 the Club was run by Marian Reeves, an experienced book keeper, who had joined the WFL in 1909, by 1912 was secretary of the Kensington branch, and by 1950 was the organization's president. In the years after the Second World War the Minerva Club was still the site of feminist meetings until Reeves' death in 1961 led to the demise of both the Club and the WFL. Reeves was in Ireland when she died, having attended an IWSA congress, and her last act, very fittingly, had been to lay flowers on Mrs Despard's grave in Glasnevin cemetery.

By 1961 Britain was changing, the time of ladies' residential clubs such as the Minerva was passing, the building itself soon to be swept away by the development that became the Brunswick Centre. The Minerva was the last in a long line of clubs founded by suffrage campaigners stretching back to the opening of the Ladies' Institute by Bessie Parkes and Barbara Bodichon in 1860 and including in the nineteenth and the early years of the twentieth centuries, the Pioneer, the Somerville and the Suffrage Club.[5] While aware of the reality that, over the years, for many women, particularly young teachers, nurses, social workers and typists, the Club was merely a cheap, safe place to stay, Object 87 also speaks of forty years of companionable meals taken, as its founders intended, by those with shared ideals.

Object 88

Photograph of a garden party at Aubrey House, Kensington, 1925

Object 88 **is a photograph taken on Thursday 23 July 1925 at a garden party to honour Dame Millicent Fawcett.** (TWL.2009.02.018, The Women's Library collection, London School of Economics and Political Science.)

Millicent Fawcett had retired as president of the National Union of Women's Suffrage Societies (NUWSS) in March 1919 when that organization became the National Union of Societies for Equal Citizenship (NUSEC). The change of name indicated the broadening of its interests, the equal franchise now not being its only goal. Four years later, with NUSEC as the sponsor of the event, this scene captures another pivotal moment in the long history of the women's suffrage movement. Although quite correctly catalogued as a photograph showing Fawcett speaking at Aubrey House, Camden Hill, Kensington, on 23 July 1925, the image carries a subtext known to her contemporaries but now veiled.

The idea for such an event had been mooted in the *Woman's Leader*, successor to *The Common Cause*, in early January 1925 as a response to the news that Fawcett had been made a Dame Grand Cross of the Order of the British Empire (GBE) in the New Year's Honours List. That ceremony was held on 12 February, but, with two of Fawcett's sisters seriously ill, the date for the NUSEC party was only fixed in mid-June after their deaths. The chosen venue could not have been more suitable, made available courtesy of the Misses Alexander, whose father had bought the property in the 1870s from the Liberal MP, P.A. Taylor. As Fawcett mentioned in her speech on that July afternoon, it was at a gathering in the house behind her that, sixty years earlier, on 1 April 1865, she had first met her future husband and where, two years later, as a member of its first executive committee she had attended the first formal meeting of the London National Society for Women's Suffrage. Moreover, it was in Aubrey House, courtesy of Taylor's wife, Clementia, that in the preceding year, 1866, the signatures to the first suffrage petition were collated (see Object 1).

Close inspection of the photograph reveals that Fawcett is wearing the pendant presented to her by the NUWSS in 1913 (see Object 71) and behind her on the platform are three banners dating from the pre-war campaign, those of the Edinburgh and London societies and of the NUWSS. The table is wrapped in cloth that is surely in the NUWSS/NUSEC colours of red, white and green and beside it sits Eleanor Rathbone, president of NUSEC. All seems entirely harmonious and yet under the surface runs an ideological rift.

The immediate point of contention was the support by Rathbone for the principle of 'Family Endowment' (that is, 'Family Allowance', to be paid to the mother of a family). Believing this idea would undermine parental responsibility, in the 30 January issue of the *Woman's Leader* Fawcett had written a critical article, to which Rathbone had responded the following week. Matters had come to a head in March at a debate at the NUSEC annual conference, at which Rathbone's proposition in favour of Family Endowment took 111 votes against Fawcett's 42. The debate had been preceded by Rathbone's presidential address on 'The Old and New Feminism', which promoted women-centred policies and protective legislation ('New Feminism'), in opposition to Fawcett's long-held egalitarianism that sought for equality with men, politically and economically, now categorized as the 'Old Feminism'. As a result, in a letter of 28 March, Fawcett resigned as chairman of the board of directors of the *Woman's Leader* and from NUSEC, writing, 'I dissent from the policy, adopted at the recent Council meeting of NUSEC, usually called Family Endowment' unable to 'be in any degree responsible for a paper which is now bound to advocate an economic change of great importance of which I entirely disapprove'.[1]

However, bitterness was avoided by all parties and Fawcett continued to contribute to the *Woman's Leader* and to compile *What the Vote Has Done*, pamphlets published by NUSEC describing 'the changes in the law favourable to women, which have been made in the United Kingdom since the passing of the Representation of the People Act in February, 1918'.[2] Among the new laws she details in her final two pamphlets are the Infanticide Act, 1922, the Criminal Law Amendment Act, 1922, the Matrimonial Causes Act (England and Wales), 1923, the Guardianship of Infants Act, 1925 and the Adoption of Children Act, 1926, while also including sections on subjects of interest still under discussion, such as the position of women in the civil service, women police and the nationality of married women.[3]

As they gazed towards the platform on that July afternoon, Fawcett's audience would have been aware of the very real divergence of policy that separated the two women they saw before them. It is salutary to realize that an image as apparently bland as Object 88 marks a division in the women's movement. Images cannot be taken at face value; it is always necessary to be aware of the context.

Object 89

A poster advertising *Time and Tide*

Object 89 is an undated poster advertising the journal *Time and Tide*. (AntikBar Vintage Posters.)

Among those listening to Dame Millicent Fawcett at the Aubrey House garden party on 23 July 1925 (see Object 88) was Lady Rhondda, described by the *Westminster Gazette* as 'a feminist of the more modern variety'.[1] A former member of the Women's Social and Political Union (WSPU) and now a very successful businesswoman, having inherited her title and commercial enterprises from her father, she had launched *Time and Tide* five years earlier, in May 1920, as a weekly political and literary review.[2] Of its kind it was unusual in having an all-female board of directors, while commissioning both men and women as contributors and addressing both male and female readers. However, while commercial success dictated the necessity of appealing to as wide an audience as possible, there was no disguising its feminist mandate or the suffrage backstories of its most prominent supporters, such as Elizabeth Robins, Cicely Hamilton and Helen Archdale. The journal's masthead, incorporating the vignette of Big Ben and the Thames, played on the idea of 'time' and 'tide', directing the viewer's thoughts to Westminster and the recent arrival there of women, while its sans serif typeface boasted of modernity, distancing it from the 'look', as well as the content, of the established suffrage weeklies. Of these, *The Vote* continued as 'the organ of the Women's Freedom League', while *The Common Cause* had been reborn in February 1920 as the *Woman's Leader*, ostensibly no longer the organ of the National Union of Societies for Equal Citizenship (NUSEC), while continuing to propound that organization's news and views and retaining the same design and typeface.

In terms of the 'Old Feminism' and the 'New Feminism' (see Object 88), rather confusingly Rhondda, although characterized in the press as 'modern', was a proponent of the 'Old Feminism', as was Winifred Holtby, one of the leading contributors to *Time and Tide*, who declared 'while the inequality exists- I have to be a feminist and an Old Feminist with the motto Equality First'.[3] To that end, in February 1921 Rhondda had founded a new campaigning organization, the Six Point Group, the initial programme for which had been outlined in *Time and Tide*.[4] The Six Points had by 1926 evolved into six general points necessary for the achievement of women's equality: political, occupational, moral, social, economic and legal. Campaigning constitutionally, although with many former Women's Social and Political Union activists, such as Winifred Mayo, Dorothy Evans, Helen Archdale and Charlotte Marsh, among its members, and with Emmeline Pethick-Lawrence as a vice-president, the Six Point Group worked through its parliamentary committee to lobby MPs, publishing lists of those who opposed women's causes as well as those of supporters.

By January 1926 the Six Point Group had laid plans to launch a new campaign to demand the equal franchise, the centrepiece of which was to be an Equal Political Rights Demonstration on 3 July, with numerous women's organizations marching from the Embankment to Hyde Park, taking over that space a fortnight after the rally held there by the Peace Pilgrimage (see Object 90). Masterminded by the Equal Political Rights Demonstration Committee, chaired by Rhondda, it had the backing of Lady Astor MP, Ellen Wilkinson MP, Mrs Despard, Mrs Flora Drummond and Mrs Pankhurst, who had recently returned to Britain and on 3 March had been feted at a Six Point Group dinner. On the day, the procession attracted women from all sections of the women's movement, with the presence of Millicent Fawcett noted as well as that of Mrs Pankhurst, though it must be admitted that, as ever, it was the latter who captured the headlines. Kate Frye, sometime organizer for the New Constitutional Society for Women's Suffrage (see Object 69), was there, a spectator rather than a participant, and particularly recorded in her diary that she 'Heard Mrs Pankhurst and she was quite delightful'.[5]

With the Equal Political Rights Demonstration deemed a success, its committee transformed itself into the Equal Political Rights Campaign Committee (EPRCC), coordinating twenty-two societies as it continued to press for the equal franchise. However, although both 'Old Feminists' and 'New Feminists' had united in the 3 July procession, NUSEC was not affiliated to the EPRCC, conducting its own campaign.

Object 89 is undated, but a study of its content reveals it was issued no earlier than June 1929 when *Time and Tide* adopted the slogan 'The review with independent views'. Besides demonstrating by way of its colouring and design the journal's stylish modernity, the information displayed also tells us that Rhondda was its editor (she had taken over that position in 1926), the price was now 6d (it had risen from 4d in October 1928) and that G.B. Shaw was a star contributor. In November 1929, an article highlighting Shaw's attendance at an event to mark *Time and Tide*'s move to Bloomsbury was accompanied by an illustration by David Wilson, the artist responsible for the 'Haunted House' image associated over twenty years earlier with the first issues of *Votes for Women* (see Object 27).

Object 90

'Pilgrimage of Peace' banner, 1926

Object 90 A banner, yellow cotton sateen ground with black cotton sateen borders, appliquéd black cotton sateen lettering 'LAW NOT WAR'. (TWL.1998.48, The Women's Library collection, London School of Economics and Political Science.)

In January 1926, women's organizations were planning two major demonstrations, with Hyde Park chosen to host the culmination of both. For one, demanding Equal Rights, see Object 89, while the other, calling for nations to disarm and settle disputes not by war but by conciliation, law or arbitration, was to take place a fortnight earlier, on 19 June, at the end of a country-wide 'Peace Pilgrimage'. In the inter-war period internationalism was an important aspect of feminism. Organized by the Women's International League for Peace and Freedom (WILPF) and modelled closely on the 1913 NUWSS Pilgrimage (see Object 74), the intention was for women to walk from all parts of Britain to London, along set routes, to highlight their concern for the prevention of future wars.

Among the twenty-eight participating organizations were societies rooted in the suffrage movement, such as the National Union of Societies for Equal Citizenship (NUSEC formerly the National Union of Women's Suffrage Societies, NUWSS), the Women's Freedom League (WFL), the St Joan's Social and Political Alliance (formerly the Catholic Women's Suffrage Society, see Object 45) and the League of the Church Militant (formerly the Church League for Women's Suffrage, see Object 76). One of the principal organizers was Kathleen Courtney who in 1915 had resigned her position as honorary secretary of the NUWSS, protesting its decision not to back the proposed Women's Peace Congress at the Hague (see Object 82). After the First World War she became a member of the NUSEC executive committee as well as president of the British section of the WILPF. Courtney had previously worked in the Friends' Relief Mission in Vienna with Dr Hilda Clark who in 1926 acted as secretary to the Peace Pilgrimage. Clark was a member of the family of Quaker shoemakers of Street, Somerset, daughter of Helen Bright Clark, a signatory to the 1866 petition (see Object 1), and niece to Jacob Bright (see Object 3). Her sister, Alice, and brother, Roger, had in 1912 been the founders of the Friends' League for Women's Suffrage.

On 27 April 1926 at a meeting in Trowbridge, Wiltshire, Clark gave details of the arrangements for the Pilgrimage to pass through the district. She explained that the point of the Pilgrimage was 'to impress the rising generation with the horrors of war and create such a public opinion against it as to make it impossible'. She described how 'the general colour [of the Pilgrimage] was blue, but there would also be group colours. For this district the colours would be green and blue' and asked her audience to 'show their sympathy by wearing a tabard, armlet or badge'.[1] The Peace Pilgrimage committee had followed the example of their 1913 predecessors and, to raise money and create a 'look', had devised these three items of merchandise, each blue, printed with a white dove of peace.

While the slogan 'Law Not War' was that promoted by the Peace Pilgrimage, the black and yellow material with which Object 90 is constructed is anomalous with the 1926 colour scheme but does link this banner directly with the suffrage movement. For, the reverse of 'Law Not War' shows signs of the original appliquéd lettering spelling out 'Men's League for Women's Suffrage' (MLWS), the colours of which were yellow and black. Also stitched to the reverse is an ownership label for 'A. [Alice] Clark, Millfield, Street, Somerset'. The positioning suggests that it was added in 1926 and that Alice was responsible for the re-creation. We have no way of knowing how the MLWS banner came into her possession, but, in addition to the male members of the Clark family likely to have been involved with the MLWS, in 1924 a close friend, Laurence Housman, formerly a leading member of that society and a renowned banner designer, had settled in Street.

Describing the Peace Pilgrimage as it passed through Street on 3 June 1926, a reporter particularly mentions the banners carried, among which were 'Blessed are the peacemakers' (white and green); 'Arbitration our hope at home and abroad' (blue with green border and white lettering), 'Law Not War' (black, yellow and green).[2] As we have seen, a month earlier Hilda Clark had mentioned that green would be, with blue, the colour for the local group and the banner makers had attempted some approximation to that directive. It may be that what now appears to be a black border to the 'Law Not War' banner was once a darkish green. Thanks to the detail given in that newspaper report, the three banners, all held in the Women's Library collection, can be firmly linked to the Clark family and to Street.[3]

Despite the General Strike of 4–12 May disrupting the plans of those journeying from the farthest points, the organizers persevered with the scheme, attracting a crowd of 7,000–8,000 to the final rally on 19 June. Among the eighty speakers was Dame Millicent Fawcett, now seventy-nine years old, who a couple of weeks earlier had returned from Paris, where she had attended the Congress of the International Women's Suffrage Alliance, and who was to be back in Hyde Park on 3 July, walking in the Equal Rights procession.

Object 91

Postcard of members of the National Union of Societies for Equal Citizenship photographed at Westminster, 2 July 1928

Object 91 is a photographic postcard, issued by the National Union of Societies for Equal Citizenship (NUSEC) to mark the passing of the Representation of the People (Equal Franchise) Act, 1928. (TWL.2002.328, The Women's Library collection, London School of Economics and Political Science.)

Although the passing of the Representation of the People (Equal Franchise) Act on 2 July 1928 was mentioned as a short item in most newspapers, the news went unillustrated; no Fleet Street photographer was sent to Westminster to cover the story. Thus, other than a photograph of the Act itself, Object 91 is one of only two images available in our media age to represent the culmination of the sixty-two-year-long 'Votes for Women' campaign. Both images were commissioned by NUSEC, no other society having had the foresight to record the presence of their members in Parliament on the day the Act was passed, thereby rendering them less visible to posterity.

Buoyed up by the success of the 1926 Equal Rights Procession (see Object 89) and then dashed when no mention of equal franchise was made in the King's speech at the opening of Parliament in February 1927, pressure continued to be exerted by all sections of the campaign. In early March, when delegates were in London for the annual Council, NUSEC organized a mass lobby of MPs. Campaigners recognized that a government-backed equal franchise bill was required, private members' bills having failed. While not allocating the women's cause priority over what it considered more pressing matters, the Conservative government was by now favourable and on 8 March the prime minister, Stanley Baldwin, felt able to receive a women's franchise deputation, the first since 1918. Organized by the Equal Political Rights Campaign Committee (EPRCC), it was introduced by Lady Astor MP and supported by fifty-six women's societies. That evening the delegates gathered in the Minerva Club (see Object 87) to discuss the event with other representatives of the societies composing the EPRCC. Plans were laid for a vigorous campaign to encompass both public meetings and the lobbying of MPs. For their part, NUSEC sent a circular to all MPs reminding them of the government's pledges on the subject of equal franchise.

All were rewarded when, on 13 April, in reply to a question from Frederick Pethick- Lawrence, a Labour MP since 1923, Baldwin announced that an equal franchise bill, giving women over twenty-one the right to vote on the same terms as men, would be introduced during the next session. Homage to John Stuart Mill was invoked on 20 May with a wreath-laying ceremony at his statue, NUSEC again evidencing a flair for publicity by publishing a photographic postcard of the scene (see Object 6). Once the campaigning season began in the autumn, meetings were held around the country and, on 7 February 1928, the women were rewarded by hearing a bill 'to amend the law relating to the parliamentary and local government franchise' proposed in the King's Speech. That morning a group of NUSEC Young Suffragists arrived in Downing Street with a nationwide petition from women under thirty for the bill to be put first on the statute book, while another group, which included a niece of Mrs Pankhurst, tried to deliver a letter to the King. These demonstrations, hinting at past militancy, excited the newspapers, although not sufficiently as to call out photographers.

On 29 March 1928 the Franchise Bill passed its Second Reading, 387 to 10, and on 7 May its Third Reading, this time with no dissent. On 2 July it was carried easily in the House of Lords and then received the Royal Assent, increasing the electorate by 5 million. Recorded in every London and provincial newspaper, although not in the *Woman's Leader*, was the fact that Dame Millicent Fawcett had missed witnessing the event by a minute or so, the timing of the procedure having been moved forward from 6.30 pm to 6 pm. Fawcett was able to watch the remainder of the House of Lords' ceremony from Black Rod's box before, with fellow NUSEC members representing both the 'New' and the 'Old Feminism' (see Object 88), lining up for the photographer at the entrance. A second photograph was then taken, of Fawcett, with her daughter, Philippa, and sister, Agnes Garrett, sitting in Ray Strachey's open-top car, with Strachey at the wheel. It is likely that Strachey was about to drive her passengers along the Embankment to Savoy Hill, where, from the 2LO radio station, Fawcett gave a short address to the nation, marking the historic occasion.[1] While that recording, a testament to modernity, has not survived, Object 91 and its companion, issued as postcards by NUSEC to memorialize the event, remains, placing Fawcett, a tiny indomitable figure, at the centre of the achievement.

Object 92

A pamphlet, *The Need for Women Members of Parliament*, 1921

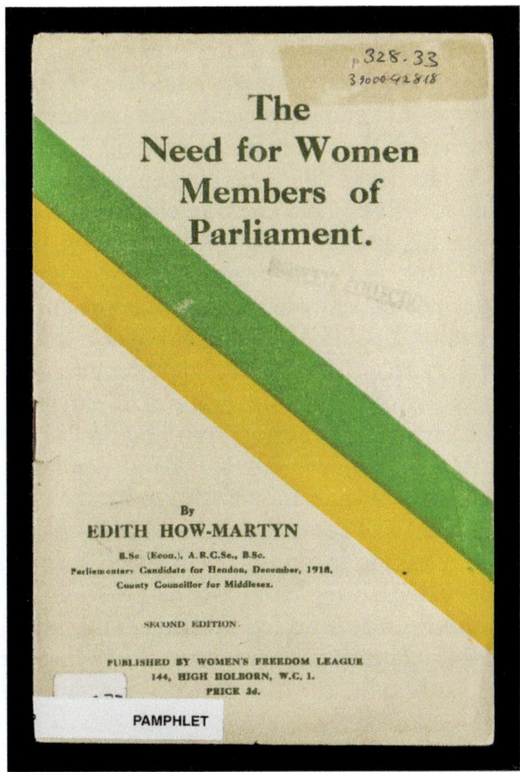

Object 92 is the 2nd edition of *The Need for Women Members of Parliament*, a pamphlet by Edith How-Martyn, published by the Women's Freedom League (WFL), **1921**, price 3d. (328.33 HOW, The Women's Library collection, London School of Economics and Political Science.)

Running parallel with the campaign to equalize the women's franchise was that to return women as members of Parliament. For that purpose, this eight-page pamphlet had first been published, price 2d, in September 1919, before any woman had taken her seat in the House of Commons. The author, Mrs Edith How-Martyn, had been head of the WFL's political department, had stood as a candidate in the 1918 general election, in 1919 was the first woman member of the Middlesex County Council and, eventually, its first woman chairman. The main difference between the text of the two editions is the foreword added by How-Martyn to the second edition, rejoicing in the election of Lady Astor, at the time of publication the lone woman member amidst 706 men.

Having been campaigning since 1906, How-Martyn was an experienced public speaker and 'the need for women MPs' was the subject of many talks she gave in the early 1920s. Extrapolating from her County Council experience, she illustrated how much easier it was to get things done from within a legislature and in the pamphlet stressed 'that powerful as the possession of a vote may be, the actual representation within the House by women is immeasurably more so and the chief aim of feminists for the next few years should be to increase the number of women Members of Parliament'. She considered a propaganda campaign necessary to acclimatize the public to the idea of women MPs, likening this to the 'votes for women' campaign, but without the militancy. In this vein, she encouraged women candidates to fight by-elections, for, even if they were unlikely to win, they would gain experience and create useful propaganda.

During the 1920s all branches of the woman's movement encouraged women to stand for Parliament; Lady Astor held At Homes at which women could meet MPs, the National Union of Societies for Equal Citizenship (NUSEC) held election classes addressed by political strategists, and, besides publishing Object 92, in *The Vote* the WFL ran a long series of articles, many written by former suffrage activists, under the headings, 'When I am MP', or 'If I were MP'.

In the pamphlet How-Martyn discussed whether it was better for women to stand as party or independent candidates. Backed by a political party, a candidate would obviously attract greater resources, and so it was necessary to ensure that as many women as possible were included on the local party committees selecting candidates. However, despite mentioning the disadvantages of standing as an independent, How-Martyn thought it good for women to do so and for other women to help make it possible. She had been one of five independent candidates in 1918, but in the following decade only Ray Strachey, Eleanor Rathbone and Mary Richardson repeated the experience, and it was only at the 1929 general election that Rathbone, on her second attempt, was successful, and then only by taking second place in a two-seat constituency. Perhaps How-Martyn might have revised her advice if the pamphlet had been updated in later years.

There was no shortage of opportunity for electioneering in this period. At the general elections in 1918, 1922, 1923 and 1924, respectively, seventeen, thirty-three, thirty-four and forty-one women stood as candidates, although, of 196 by-elections, only seventeen were contested by women. In that time twelve women were elected, with eleven taking their seats, Countess Markievicz having excluded herself. Of these, not only were the first three party candidates, but all were married to men who had previously contested the seats. Standing at a by-election, in 1919 Astor, a Conservative, succeeded her husband at Plymouth Sutton (see Object 85), in 1921 Mrs Margaret Wintringham, a Liberal, succeeded her dead husband at Louth and in 1923, as a Conservative, Mrs Mabel Philipson won Berwick-on-Tweed, her husband's election at the 1922 general election having been declared void. Excluding Markievicz, it was not until the 1923 general election that women without a familial link to the parliamentary seat were elected. Three, Margaret Bondfield, Dorothy Jewson and Susan Lawrence, had strong Labour party backing, the fourth, Lady Terrington, was a Liberal and the fifth, the Duchess of Atholl,

Scotland's first woman MP, was a Unionist. However, at the 1924 general election, Atholl was the only one of these newcomers to retain her seat, although Labour did gain one new woman MP, Ellen Wilkinson, who, before the war, had been a paid organizer for the National Union of Women's Suffrage Societies. At by-elections Bondfield and Lawrence were returned in 1926, joined in 1927 by a Conservative, Lady Iveagh, and in 1928 by a Liberal, Mrs Hilda Runciman, niece to Louisa and Flora Stevenson who had been at the vanguard of the nineteenth-century suffrage campaign in Scotland. Thus, on 2 July 1928, when the Equal Franchise Act was passed, there were eight women MPs sitting on the green benches of the House of Commons, four Conservative/Unionist, three Labour and one Liberal.

Object 93

Mrs Pankhurst's grave

Object 93 is Mrs Emmeline Pankhurst's grave in Brompton Cemetery. (©sim canetty-clarke.)

On Monday 18 June 1928, as the Representation of the People (Equal Franchise) Bill was passing through Parliament, Emmeline Pankhurst was laid in her grave in Brompton Cemetery, west London. Aged sixty-nine, she had died of septicaemia four days earlier, on 14 June, at a nursing home in Wimpole Street where she had been taken from her small, rented flat above a shop in Wapping High Street. For the previous couple of months she had been living in this working-class area of east London for which, in February 1927, she had been adopted, 'unanimously, and amid scenes of great enthusiasm', as the Conservative parliamentary candidate for Whitechapel and St George's.[1] It had been thought that the Labour MP, who was in indifferent health, might retire, causing a by-election, but he recovered and it was in preparation for the next general election, due in 1929, that Pankhurst was nursing the seat.

Soon after her selection, she contributed the twenty-third article in *The Vote* series 'When I am MP', in which she claimed for women 'equality in every sphere' and opposed all forms of protective legislation for women.[2] In that respect she was, like Millicent Fawcett, a proponent of the 'Old Feminism'. However, in other newspaper interviews she was more candid, remarking, 'I do not think the franchise is the burning question it once was. If our revolutionary friends get the upper hand, there will be no votes for men or women.'[3]

Listening to Pankhurst's address to the annual conference of Women's Unionist Organizations in May 1927, Helen Archdale described her 'voice, every syllable, [ringing] out as of old in passionate intensity', but the speech itself as 'purely Conservative in note', denouncing Russia and praising the Empire, with no mention of the condition of women.[4]

As Edith How-Martyn had commented in her pamphlet (see Object 92), even with party backing, women candidates were not offered safe seats. Pankhurst, entirely aware that Whitechapel was unwinnable for the Conservatives, was less than happy with the support she received from headquarters and yet spoke for the party not only at meetings in London, but around the country. Lacking any regular source of income, she had been assured of private financial backing if she stood in Whitechapel, where she was aided in her campaigning by former suffragettes, who approached old comrades asking them to help with canvassing and fund-raising.[5]

On 18 June Pankhurst's funeral service was held in St John's, Smith Square, a church in which, in March 1914, there had been an explosion attributed to suffragette activity. Afterwards her coffin was taken to Brompton Cemetery for burial. Among the hundreds attending both ceremonies was Kate Parry Frye (see Object 69), who in her diary described the day.

> To St John's Church Smith Square. Had no ticket but being very early before 10 – I was let in up in the Gallery of the Church and sat over the Chancel and in front of Mrs Pankhurst's Coffin. The flowers were marvellous – most beautiful. A wonderful service but very sad. A bus to Brompton Cemetery an enormous crowd there. Followed the Coffin and saw the end.[6]

Newspaper reports described how, at the cemetery, women wearing their 'old faded colours, their ribbons, banners and hat trimming of white, green and mauve'[7] 'pushed and jostled to get near the graveside. They surged completely round the spot, and the police had difficulty in keeping them back'.[8]

With Pankhurst's estate amounting only to £86, to ensure she would not be forgotten Kitty Marshall opened a fund for a 'Mrs Pankhurst Memorial', with Lady Rhondda as its treasurer. To that end, Pankhurst's portrait was commissioned from Georgina Brackenbury (a former suffragette) and given to the National Portrait Gallery and a full-length statue of her by A.G. Walker was placed in Victoria Tower Gardens, adjacent to the Houses of Parliament, unveiled in 1930 by the former Prime Minister, Stanley Baldwin. The headstone for Pankhurst's grave was dedicated on the second anniversary of her death, 14 June 1930. The work of Julian Phelps Allan (born Eva Dorothy Allan), it is of red sandstone, in the form of a Celtic cross. The shaft carries, in low relief, a somewhat enigmatic haloed figure with a hand raised in blessing, while the head of the cross depicts two angels, with the hand of God reaching down from the heavens. The inscription is simple: 'In Loving Memory of/ Emmeline/ Pankhurst wife/ of R.M. Pankhurst LLD/ At Rest/ June 14 1928.' Clearly by choice, there is no mention of her children, or her life's work for women.

Pankhurst's grave, Grade II* on the National Heritage List, is easily found on the left-hand of Brompton Cemetery's Central Avenue, close to the imposing North Lodge (Old Brompton Road) entrance. It is invariably marked by floral tributes in colours approximating purple, white and green. By way of contrast, Millicent Fawcett, who died on 5 August 1929, chose to be cremated and, although she is now well-memorialized (see Object 100), her ashes have no known resting place.

Object 94

A pamphlet, *Women and the General Election*, 1929

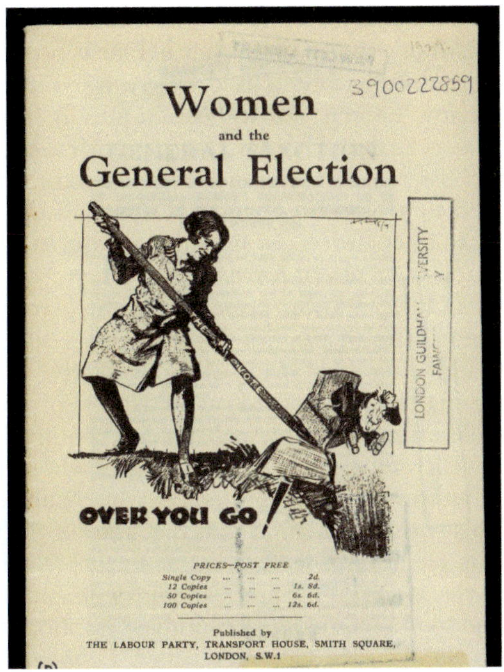

Object 94 is a thirty-five-page pamphlet, *Women and the General Election*, a report prepared by the Standing Joint Committee of Industrial Women's Organizations to be presented to the National Conference of Labour Women, **1929.** (324.24107 LAB, The Women's Library collection, London School of Economics and Political Science.)

At the general election of 30 May 1929, Millicent Fawcett voted for the last time, a couple of months before her death. One of the longest serving of the suffrage campaigners, she cast her vote, aged eighty-one, alongside women who were voting for the first time. Among these were the 'Flappers', young women of twenty-one or over, who gave the event its nickname, the 'Flapper Election'. The new electoral register, published in January, now included women on the same terms as men, with property qualifications abolished. The result was, as the authors of Object 94 point out, that *c.*14 million women were eligible to vote, outnumbering *c.*11 million men. Of the 5 million women enfranchised by the 1928 Act, about half were women over the age of thirty, living-in as domestic servants, nurses etc., or married women whose husbands were not on the local government register. The pamphlet identified the 'flapper' vote only with young women between the ages of twenty-one and twenty-five, of which it was calculated there were about 1.5 million.

Although 'flapper' carried with it a dismissively pejorative connotation, identifying young women with hedonistic carelessness, we can see from the cover illustration of the pamphlet that the Labour party viewed her rather differently. She has, admittedly, fashionably bobbed hair, but her costume is workmanlike, hinting at a factory overall rather than flapper frivolity. Moreover, with her lance, labelled 'The Vote', she is exercising her new power, unseating the capitalist Conservative. The trope of the lance had been used by pre-war suffrage artists to illustrate the potential power of the vote, now Labour was indicating how it should be used by the newly enfranchised. The illustrator was Arthur Thomas Hagg, a professional artist and Labour party stalwart, who, after being registered as a conscientious objector when called up during the First World War and assigned to a Non-Combatant Corps, had then spent his war in prison, court-martialled for refusing to obey orders. Despite this unequivocal stance, he clearly had no objection to depicting a metaphorical use of force.

The report that constitutes Object 94 was presented at the National Conference of Labour Women that opened at Buxton, Derbyshire, on 23 April. At a time of industrial unrest and increasing unemployment, and after five years of Conservative government, the pamphlet devotes many pages to attacking the Tory record on all aspects of policy as it affected women. The authors by no means underestimate their female readers' political understanding and desire for detail. The report was well received by the conference, whose president condemned the 'money spent by the rich on gluttony and extravagance' while 'our people are housed in slums and many are homeless'.[1] This was the situation that the lance of the vote could rectify.

In an election noted for its plethora of leaflets it was unsurprising that many were directed to women, the majority of the electorate. Three leading women MPs, one from each party, even made records, addressed to voters, for the Columbia Graphophone Company (see Object 39). In addition, each party published a woman's paper, *Labour Woman*, founded in 1911, being the most long-established, with the Conservatives' *Home and Politics* dating from 1921 and the *Liberal Women's News* from 1925. In the run-up to the election all parties held afternoon meetings especially for women, with Labour introducing mass canvassing and open-air meetings, in the style of suffrage campaigning of old.

Despite setting out its agenda for women, it is notable that Object 94 makes no mention of encouraging their candidature. That campaign was left to the erstwhile suffrage societies, with both *The Vote* and *The Woman's Leader* asking for money and volunteers to canvass for women candidates, of all parties. The National Union of Societies for Equal Citizenship (NUSEC) also issued leaflets such as *To Men and Women Voters – Send Back Another Woman*, *A Manifesto to the New Voter – Why Should You Vote?* and *What Women Voters Want*, with the Women's

Freedom League (WFL) issuing 200,000 leaflets for the use of women candidates. On 17 May *The Vote* published the names, with their party and constituency, of the seventy-two women candidates then thought to be standing.[2]

Although not with an outright majority, Labour had the most seats in the new Parliament, making Ramsay MacDonald prime minister. Of the fourteen women elected, three were Conservative, one Liberal, one Independent and nine Labour. One of the latter, Margaret Bondfield now became the first woman to sit in the Cabinet, as minister of labour, remarking in her autobiography that she considered her appointment as 'part of the great revolution in the position of women'.[3]

Object 95

Library, Women's Service House, Westminster, London

Object 95 is a photograph of the library in Women's Service House, Marsham Street, Westminster, London, _c._1927. (In Strachey, _Women's Suffrage and Women's Service_, 324.62306041.STR, The Women's Library collection, London School of Economics and Political Science.)

On 14 May 1924 the London Society for Women's Service (LSWS, formerly the London Society for Women's Suffrage) moved into Women's Service House at 35-37 Marsham Street, Westminster, a building that had formerly been a pub, the Fleece Inn.[1] The society had changed its name in 1919, the better to reflect its new purpose of obtaining economic equality for women now that (partial) suffrage had been obtained. To that end, one of its main services was to run an Information and Advisory Bureau, to which women might apply for help in tackling the job market. After an opening ceremony marked by speeches from Millicent Fawcett, president of LSWS, Mrs Wintringham MP and Ray Strachey, *The Woman's Leader* wrote of the society and its premises,

> the entire scheme has all the attraction of newness – from its statement of aims and objects, to the artistic decoration and furnishings and the liquid linoleums with which the floor of the lounge hall is covered. Women's Service House possesses what promises to develop in time into a very valuable collection of books of reference dealing with all branches of woman's work and of women's movements. It has a Silent Room for reading and writing and study.[2]

It also had a restaurant, with the added attraction of being so near the House of Commons as to be almost within sound of the Division Bell.

As money became available, more work was carried out to improve the original premises and on 24 April 1929, the day after the contents of Object 94 were presented to the Labour Women in Buxton, in Westminster Millicent Fawcett was laying the foundation stone of a new addition to Women's Service House.[3] Completed in 1931, this included, in the basement, a new restaurant and on the ground floor a lecture hall, with a proscenium arch and stage, together with a new, top-lit, library.

In 1927 Philippa Strachey, secretary of the society, now renamed the London and National Society for Women's Service (LNSWS) to reflect its nationwide appeal, mentioned that, apart from up-to-date holdings, its library also included 'a valuable historical collection on the women's movement'.[4] In 1931, with more space, this was augmented by two book collections previously in the care of the National Union of Societies for Equal Citizenship (NUSEC). These had been compiled, separately, in the earlier twentieth century by two suffrage supporters. By 1919 Lady (Jane Georgina) Wright, who had subscribed to suffrage societies since the late 1890s, had given to NUSEC her library of feminist books, now renamed the 'Edward Wright Library' in memory of her son. Her library was, perhaps, a riposte to her husband, Sir Almroth Wright, whose diatribe, *The Unexpurgated Case Against Woman Suffrage*, purported 'to show that the Women's Suffrage Movement has no real intellectual or moral sanction, and that there are very weighty reasons why the suffrage should not be conceded to women'.[5] By the time of its publication the couple, perhaps unsurprisingly, had been separated for some time. In April 1919 Lady Wright's collection was joined at NUSEC by that of Mrs Ruth Cavendish-Bentinck, containing a large collection of antiquarian books as well as contemporary studies. When under the care of NUSEC all but the valuable antiquarian books in the collections had been available for loan, sent out in 'book boxes', each containing as many as twenty books, to local societies and study circles. In 1922 the NUSEC Library produced a 'List of Books for Women Citizens', describing it as 'the first bibliography on subjects specially concerning the interests of women', which also served as a catalogue to the modern section of the Edward Wright and Cavendish-Bentinck Library.[6]

From 1926, until her retirement in 1967, the Women's Service House Library had the services of Vera Douie, a trained librarian. After the merger of the libraries in 1931, book boxes were no longer sent out, but members of the LNSWS had borrowing rights. Many books were acquired by donation, book plates often now indicating the donor. For instance, grateful for information she had received from the Library, Virginia Woolf in 1938 offered to supply any books, new or antiquarian that it required, an offer that was duly accepted.

Even in the late-1920s the bookcase shown in Object 95 would have held only a small section of the Women's Service House Library. Renamed the Fawcett Library in 1957 and then the Women's Library in 2002, since being photographed in Marsham Street it has had several other homes but is now safely berthed within the library of the London School of Economics. Apart from books and the archives of many institutions involved in all aspects of the women's movement worldwide, it holds the largest suffrage collection in the UK, comprising archives, printed material and objects from both the constitutional and the militant wings of the campaign. Open to researchers in person, but with large sections of its holdings now digitized, the library continues to be an invaluable research source.

Object 96

Sign for the Suffragette Fellowship's 'Women's Record House', Westminster, London

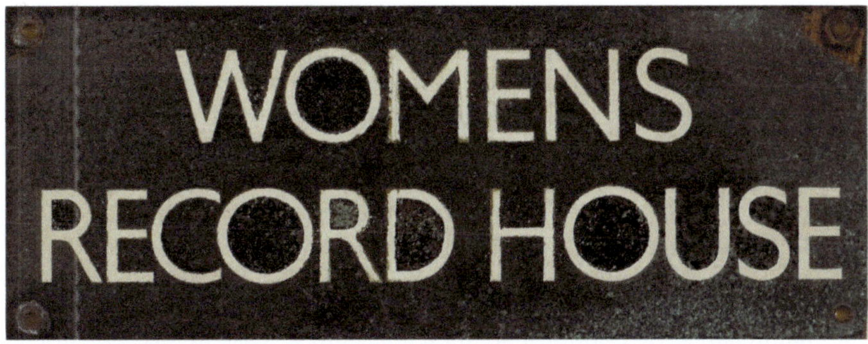

Object 96 is a metal sign once fixed to the Suffragette Fellowship's Women's Record House at 6 Great Smith Street, Westminster. (7EWD/M/01, The Women's Library collection, London School of Economics and Political Science.)

'Women's Record House' was the name given for a brief period in 1939/40 to the home of the collection of artefacts, manuscripts and printed material created by the Suffragette Fellowship to commemorate the militant suffrage campaign. At various stages the collection's home was also known as the 'Women's Record Room' or the 'Suffragette Museum'.

In 1926, while the former constitutional wing of the suffrage movement was creating an archive of its history and associated library in Women's Service House (see Object 95), former members of the Women's Social and Political Union (WSPU) and Women's Freedom League (WFL) founded the 'Suffragette Club' 'to perpetuate the memory of the pioneers and outstanding events connected with women's emancipation, and especially with the militant suffrage campaign, 1905–14, and thus keep alive the suffragette spirit'.[1]

The memory of the suffragette campaign was to be preserved in two ways. The first was by asking for short autobiographical or biographical articles from former WSPU and WFL members to create a 'Book of Suffragette Prisoners'. Although the project proved too unwieldy and a book never materialized, the biographical information sourced now forms an important part of the Suffragette Fellowship Collection held by the London Museum. However, by early 1932 the Fellowship had decided to assemble not merely written memories but a collection of artefacts relating to the militant campaign. Calls went out to suffragettes now scattered 'all over the world [for] books, cuttings, pictures, prison souvenirs, and personal mementoes', and the Women's Record Room was eventually opened in 1936 by Emmeline Pethick-Lawrence.[2] The choice of name suggests that at this time the purpose of the collection was to act as a record of women's experience, that it was a suffragette experience appears to have been understood.

Housed in a basement room at the Minerva Club (see Object 87), the collection attracted some interest, one newspaper describing it as 'one of the oddest museums in the world' and singling out for attention Emily Wilding Davison's race card from the 1913 Derby and the 'Shadow Over the House' poster (see Object 28).[3] Other reports highlighted relics of imprisonment and battles with the police.

The Suffragette Fellowship clearly hoped to give the collection a home both more prominent and more permanent and by early 1939 Rose Lamartine Yates, one-time leader of the Wimbledon WSPU and, from 1916, a founding member of the 'Suffragettes of the WSPU', had rented a house, 6 Great Smith Street, Westminster, the press relating that this site was chosen because it was between Mrs Pankhurst's statue and the church in which her memorial services were held, St John's, Smith Square. It was for these premises that Object 96 was commissioned. It is to be noted that not only was the new name, 'Women's Record House', reminiscent of 'Women's Service House', but the buildings containing the archives of the two wings of the suffrage movement were, briefly, only a short walk apart. However, a few months later, soon after the outbreak of war, Women's Record House was vacated, Object 96 was removed from its door and the collection packed away for safekeeping.[4]

After the war, on 6 February 1947, what was now called a 'Suffragette Museum' was re-opened in a room in the headquarters of the National Union of Women Teachers, 41 Cromwell Road, Kensington. Later in the year Nancy Astor, Cicely Hamilton, Emmeline Pethick-Lawrence and Rebecca West, among others, appealed for more 'mementoes of the movement [and] for funds for the maintenance of London's smallest museum – least in size but not we hope in importance'. They described how 'the mass demonstrations and great processions of women, which were such a feature of the movement, are illustrated in a collection of contemporary photographs; there are also portraits and personal relics of the women – militants, tax resisters, prisoners, hunger strikers, speakers – who carried on the agitation from 1905 to 1914'.[5] Not only did the Suffragette Fellowship hope their collection would have an educative effect, but at this time journalists and filmmakers were beginning to rediscover the suffragette movement and the archive proved useful to researchers.

By 1951 the running of the museum was proving too arduous for a group of elderly women, and the Suffragette Fellowship Collection was handed to the care of the London Museum. As the history of the suffrage movement has become increasingly popular, the collection has grown, attracting donations from descendants of suffragettes, with the Museum's permanent display of suffragette material augmented by special exhibitions in 1992 and 2018. In its new home in Smithfield, the Museum will continue to value the Suffragette Fellowship collection as one of its most important assets and, alongside a permanent presence in the galleries, it will increasingly feature in the Museum's developing online resources.

Object 97

Sylvia Pankhurst's typewriter

Object 97 is Sylvia Pankhurst's typewriter, donated to the Pankhurst Museum, Manchester (see Object 19), by her son, Dr Richard Pankhurst. (The Pankhurst Centre.)

Although the principal collections of objects relating to the constitutional and militant wings of the suffrage movement are now held in, respectively, the Women's Library collection at the London School of Economics (see Object 95) and in the London Museum (see Object 96), provincial museums, galleries and record offices throughout Britain are also repositories of a wide range of local suffrage material. Rather different in concept is the small Pankhurst Museum in Nelson Street, Manchester, which honours the space in which the Women's Social and Political Union (WSPU) was founded in October 1903 (see Object 19), recreating something of the ambience of the house when lived in by the Pankhurst family at the beginning of the twentieth century. Caught up in the suffrage campaign after leaving Manchester, Emmeline and her daughters retained few possessions from their early life and Sylvia's typewriter is one of only a couple of objects on display to have once been owned by a member of the family.

While nineteenth-century suffrage campaigners had no alternative but to write out laboriously by hand letters and all manner of copy for annual reports, advertisements, circulars, press reports, etc., the typewriter had come to the aid of twentieth-century activists, the well-worn keys and typebars of Sylvia's typewriter evidence of decades of energetic action. It is, however, always necessary to interrogate any legend surrounding an object and, thanks to detailed information now available online, it has been established that, carrying the serial number 4978645-114, Sylvia's typewriter, an Underwood 6, was manufactured between January and July 1939 and, although used in later campaigning, could not have been the one on which her son thought Sylvia might have written *The Suffragette Movement*, published in 1931.[1]

This latter book, with nothing to rival it for its wealth of detail, was for decades the main source of information on the militant suffrage movement. Part history and part autobiography, it is undeniably partisan, critical of Pankhurst's mother and of Christabel, although in 1935 Sylvia published a rather more empathetic biography of her mother, *The Life of Emmeline Pankhurst: The Suffragette Struggle for Woman's Citizenship*, which took its place alongside the autobiographies of Annie Kenney (*Memories of a Militant*, 1924), Evelyn Sharp (*Unfinished Adventure*, 1933), Lady Rhondda (*This Was My World*, 1933) and Emmeline Pethick-Lawrence (*My Part in a Changing World*, 1938) in shaping the public perception of the militant movement.

In the same period the history of the constitutional suffrage campaign was delineated by works published by Millicent Fawcett and Ray Strachey. Fawcett had covered the earlier stage of the campaign in *Women's Suffrage: A Short History of a Great Movement* (1912) and in 1920 completed her concise history by publishing *Victory – and After: Personal Reminiscences, 1911–1918*, which took the story up to the granting of partial enfranchisement. She followed *Victory* with her autobiography, *What I Remember* (1924). In 1928 Strachey published *The Cause*, in the main a history of the constitutional suffrage movement, and followed it with *Millicent Garrett Fawcett* (1931), an official biography as reticent as its subject. Published a few months after Pankhurst's *The Suffragette Movement*, reviewers did not fail to comment on the lack of excitement in Fawcett's life, while admiring the serenity with which she conducted her campaign. One reviewer, having considered both books, posed the question that has beset later historians, 'was Mrs Fawcett, with her knowledge of men and affairs, of procedure, and of the whole Parliamentary machine, helped or hindered in the last stage of her peaceful campaign by the methods of Mrs Pankhurst, who incited women to violence, and whose statue now stands in Westminster, to the amazement of many who recollect the past'.[2]

Former constitutional suffragists did not seek publishers and in the years after the Second World War it was the personalities and antics of the former suffragettes that continued to intrigue the public. By now not all accounts could be relied on to be strictly accurate; Mary Richardson, for instance, when writing her autobiography *Laugh a Defiance* (1953), knew that to maximise her royalties she had to produce newsworthy material that coincided with recognized suffragette tropes.[3] While members of the Suffragette Fellowship do not appear to have criticized the writings of their own, they did take outsiders, particularly male historians, to task. Although Roger Fulford had access to the London Museum's Suffragette Fellowship Collection when writing *Votes for Women* (1957), as, later, did David Mitchell (*The Fighting Pankhursts*, 1967 and *Queen Christabel*, 1977), their works were excoriated by surviving suffragettes. The latter did cooperate with Antonia Raeburn, who was able to draw extensively on interviews with surviving members of the Suffragette Fellowship when researching *The Militant Suffragettes* (1973), a popular, unreferenced narrative (see Object 47). However, from the late 1970s suffrage history experienced a renaissance when women historians, propelled by second wave feminism, began looking beyond the leaders and party politics to investigate more thoroughly the long campaign in all its diversity.

Object 98

The Suffragette Fellowship Memorial, Christchurch Gardens, Westminster, London

Object 98 is the Suffragette Fellowship Memorial, sited in Christchurch Gardens, Westminster, lying between Victoria Street and Caxton Hall. (7JCC/0/02/164, The Women's Library collection, London School of Economics and Political Science.)

While assiduously attempting to protect their history from the attention of male historians (see Object 97), members of the Suffragette Fellowship were at the same time keen to leave their own mark, in bronze rather than in print. This photograph was taken at the unveiling of Object 98 on 14 July 1970, the date being Emmeline Pankhurst's official birthday and one that the Fellowship had long held as a 'Day of Obligation'. Six feet (1.8 metres) in height, resting on a granite base, it takes the form of a bronze scroll and carries the wording, 'This tribute is erected by the Suffragette Fellowship to commemorate the courage and perseverance of all those men and women who in the long struggle for votes for women selflessly braved derision, opposition and ostracism, many enduring physical violence and suffering', adding, in smaller script, 'Nearby Caxton Hall was historically associated with Women's Suffrage meetings'.

Since erected in 1930, the nearby statue to Mrs Pankhurst (see Object 93) had been the locus of suffragette commemoration, the site of an annual July ceremony staged by the Suffragette Fellowship. In 1955, its members had waged war, successfully, with the Ministry of Works to ensure that the statue did not suffer from a planned redesign of Victoria Tower Gardens and in 1959 had added to it a plinth incorporating a bronze portrait roundel of Christabel Pankhurst and a replica of a Women's Social and Political Union (WSPU) 'Holloway' badge, its significance explained (see Object 41). Although the Women's Freedom League (WFL) had campaigned for over fifty years (see Object 87) and the WSPU for barely ten, there had been no move to give similar public prominence to Mrs Despard. So successful had been the propagandizing power of the WSPU that to the public 'suffragettes' meant only the Pankhursts and their followers. Constitutional suffragists were forgotten.

The idea of erecting a memorial in Christchurch Gardens to honour the rank and file of all militant suffrage societies had first been publicly aired in early 1965 at a Suffragette Fellowship meeting in Caxton Hall.[1] Approval had already been sought and received from Westminster Council and funding was to come from legacies left to the Fellowship by Edith How-Martyn and Ellen Crocker. As the former had been a leader of the WFL and the latter a cousin of Emmeline Pethick-Lawrence, it was fitting this new memorial would commemorate members of both pre-war militant suffrage societies. However, the cult of the prisoner was so deeply embodied in the Suffragette Fellowship's conception of what it was to be a suffragette that, although mention of the 'many' who had endured physical violence implied that there were others who had not, rather than simple membership badges it was the prison ('Holloway') brooches of the WFL and WSPU that were replicated on the scroll. However, with no explanation attached, by 1970 it was doubtful if any passing member of the public would have known what those images signified.

The sculptors chosen to design the memorial were Lorne McKean and her husband Edwin Russell, the latter having previously created a statue for a garden in nearby Westminster Abbey. Although Russell alone is often named as the sculptor of the Suffragette Memorial, Lorne McKean has commented,

> Edwin (my husband) and I worked on many of our sculptures together. Usually one of us took the leadership on a particular sculpture and in the case of the Suffragette memorial this was Edwin. I do recall that the actual idea that developed from just the idea of a shape more like a memorial gravestone to the S shaped scroll that you now see, developed organically between us.[2]

This statement suggests the scroll was merely a pleasing shape devised by the designers and not, as has sometimes been postulated, an 'S for Suffragette'.

The photograph shows, from the left, Lilian Lenton, treasurer of the Suffragette Fellowship, Dr Horace King MP, speaker of the House of Commons, Grace Roe, president of the Fellowship, and the lord mayor of Westminster. Both Lenton and Roe are wearing their hunger strike medals (see Object 41). Also present were Baroness Summerskill, who from 1938 to 1961 had been a Labour MP, Enid Goulden Bach, niece to Emmeline Pankhurst and, among other elderly suffragettes, Leonora Cohen, who, aged ninety-seven, had travelled unaccompanied from Colwyn Bay for the occasion. In 1984 Sybil Goulden Bach, now president of the Fellowship, leapt to the defence of the Memorial when there was a suggestion that the Diocesan Fund that owned Christchurch Gardens would sell it for redevelopment. Bought by Westminster Council, the area has been retained as an open space, the setting of the Memorial enhanced in 2020 by new landscaping.

Object 99

'New Dawn', a contemporary light sculpture celebrating the campaign for women's suffrage, sited at the entrance to St Stephen's Hall in the Houses of Parliament, 2016

Object 99 is a light sculpture celebrating all those who participated in the 'Votes for Women' campaign, commissioned in 2015 from artist Mary Branson by the Speaker's Advisory Committee on Works of Art. (© Emma Brown Photography.)

The ceremony marking the installation of Object 99 took place on 7 June 2016, the 150th anniversary of the day on which Emily Davies and Elizabeth Garrett presented John Stuart Mill with the first women's suffrage petition (see Object 1). The site chosen for 'New Dawn', a large arched compartment in St Stephen's Porch at the south end of Westminster Hall, is significant in that it marks the entrance to St Stephen's Hall, through which suffrage campaigners had to pass to lobby MPs and deliver petitions.

'New Dawn' draws on themes associated with the suffrage campaign, both in its political and social manifestations. The overall concept of the artwork alludes to the visual and rhetorical image of a 'new dawn' that enfranchisement would bring, a trope commonly used by suffrage artists on postcards and posters in the early twentieth century. The metal framework supporting the installation was based on the portcullis, symbol of Parliament, adapted by Sylvia Pankhurst in her design for the WSPU 'Holloway brooch' (see Object 41). The sculpture itself is composed of 168 glass scrolls, an idea suggested to the artist by the sight of the rolled acts of Parliament on the packed shelves of the Original Act Room. These glass scrolls incorporate the colours of a wide range of suffrage societies and, unlike the Suffragette Fellowship Memorial (see Object 98), establish 'New Dawn' as a tribute to all nineteenth- and twentieth-century campaigners, constitutional as well as militant, celebrating their ultimate success in effecting the entry of women into the parliamentary process. 'New Dawn' is dynamic, with the lighting of the coloured scrolls directly linked to the ebb and flow of the tide of the river Thames, as it runs past the Houses of Parliament, and perhaps fortuitously, to the interwar feminist journal *Time and Tide* (see Object 89). By linking the artwork to the outside world, the artist considered 'New Dawn' would reflect the continuing battle for equality in all areas of life.[1]

While 'New Dawn' marks the cultural apotheosis of Parliament's recognition of the efforts to gain the parliamentary vote for women, an earlier memorial to the suffrage campaign, a stained-glass window known as the 'Dearsley Bequest', was installed in St Stephen's Hall in 2002. Tracing the campaign from the formation of the National Union of Women's Suffrage Societies in 1897, it brought women's politics further into what had been a male-dominated space. The female invasion of the Hall, which is packed with statues of past parliamentarians and had been the scene of vigorous suffragette protests, was led in 1993 by Margaret Thatcher who unveiled a plaque commemorating a young suffragette who had chained herself to the statue of Viscount Falkland in 1909. On this occasion Thatcher was photographed alongside Sybil Goulden Bach, Emmeline Pankhurst's niece and last trustee of the Suffragette Fellowship.[2] Whatever their own political attachments, members of the Suffragette Fellowship had relished the fact that in 1979 Britain had acquired its first woman prime minister. Today Thatcher's statue stands in the Members' Lobby, opposite that of Churchill, onetime opponent of 'votes for women'.

The 150th anniversary of the presentation of the first suffrage petition was also marked in the summer of 2016 by an exhibition at the London School of Economics. Displaying material from the Women's Library collection, 'Endless Endeavours' linked the history of the constitutional suffrage campaign from 1866 to the work of today's Fawcett Society, a direct descendant of the first petition committee. One of the exhibits was a 1910 painting by Bertha Newcombe in which Garrett and Davies rather coyly display the petition to Mill.[3] When Newcombe entered the painting for the Royal Academy's 1910 Summer Exhibition, she wrote on the accompanying label not only her personal details but also, in its entirety, the description of the Westminster Hall event, as detailed by Helen Blackburn in her *Record of Women's Suffrage* (see Object 17). A related object, a black-and-white postcard reproduction of Newcombe's painting, carries a caption briefly explaining the scene and giving the name and address of the issuer, the 'Fawcett Society, 27 Wilfred Street, London S.W.' Although its provenance is unrecorded, it is likely the postcard was issued at the time of the centenary of the presentation of the petition, when the Fawcett Library mounted a small commemorative exhibition, opening on 7 June 1966.[4]

The increased importance attached to remembrance of the campaign for women's enfranchisement can be measured in the difference between one memorializing postcard produced in 1966 by a small campaigning organization, and, fifty years later, the commissioning by Parliament of 'New Dawn', a large, sophisticated artwork, installed in the heart of the Palace of Westminster.

Object 100

The statue of Millicent Garrett Fawcett in Parliament Square, London, erected 2018

Object 100 is the bronze statue of Millicent Garrett Fawcett by sculptor Gillian Wearing, sited in Parliament Square, London. Commissioned in 2017 by the Mayor of London through the government's National Centenary Fund, it was unveiled on 24 April 2018 to mark the centenary of the Representation of the People Act 1918 (see Object 83). (Agnes Crawford.)

It is entirely fitting that in the centenary year of 2018 Millicent Fawcett should have been the first woman to be represented in statue form in Parliament Square, in the heart of political London. She now stands, facing Parliament, in the company of seven prime ministers, an American president, two South African leaders and Mahatma Ghandi. As in 1930, when the former prime minister, Stanley Baldwin, unveiled the statue of Emmeline Pankhurst, across the road in Victoria Tower Gardens, so in 2018 the prime minister, Theresa May, took a leading part in the unveiling of Object 100, commenting, 'I would not be here today as prime minister, no female MPs would have taken their seats in parliament, none of us would have the rights and protections we now enjoy, were it not for Dame Millicent Garrett Fawcett.'[1]

Wearing portrays Fawcett at the age of fifty in 1897, at the time of the formation of the National Union of Women's Suffrage Societies (NUWSS), of which she was informally the leader (see Object 18). Anachronistically, she is wearing on the lapel of her realistically rendered tweed jacket, the brooch with which she was presented by the NUWSS in 1913 (see Object 71) and is holding a banner inscribed 'Courage calls to courage everywhere', a phrase taken from her 1920 publication *Victory – and After*. That was a comment, seven years after the event, on the action and subsequent death in 1913 of Emily Wilding Davison, at the time deplored by the NUWSS because 'however much it might have been done in good faith, it alienated otherwise sympathetic people'.[2] Although Fawcett was opposed to the action of the militants, even when only harming themselves, the comment was a belated concession to the role militancy had played in feminist consciousness raising. In the late twentieth century the phrase began to appear, deprived of its context, in published compilations of woman-centred inspiring words. By the early twenty-first century it was the first, and pithiest, produced by an online search for a Fawcett quotation and, as such, admirably fitted its proselytizing role in Wearing's concept for the statue.

Object 100 is given resonance over and above its figurative representation of Fawcett by the addition, wrapped around the plinth, of the photographic images and names of fifty-nine women and four men who were also active in the suffrage campaign. Reflecting its political, social, geographical and religious diversity, they include nineteenth-century pioneers such as Elizabeth Wolstenholme Elmy, Lydia Becker, Helen Blackburn and Anna Haslam, and, from the twentieth century, the militant Pankhursts, Minnie Baldock, Annie Kenney and Charlotte Despard, and constitutionalist Mary Lowndes, Annot Robinson, Ray Strachey and Ellen Wilkinson. The totality of Object 100 speaks to the breadth and depth of research undertaken in recent decades, revealing the suffrage campaign in all its complexity, the work not only of exceptional figures such as Fawcett and the Pankhursts, but of women – and men – from all stations in life, from all four nations and beyond.

Object 100 was not the only statue to be erected in the centenary year. Several communities had the foresight to mount campaigns to commemorate local suffrage heroines, with the result that statues were erected in 2018 to Emmeline Pankhurst in Manchester, Annie Kenney in Oldham, Alice Hawkins in Leicester and Emily Wilding Davison in Morpeth (with another in Epsom in 2020). In 2019, to mark the centenary of her entry to Parliament as the first woman MP, Lady Astor was cast in bronze in Plymouth and in 2022 Elizabeth Wolstenholme Elmy was similarly commemorated in Congleton.

Object 100 and other suffrage statues, together with plaques memorializing places in which campaigners lived or were active, are now an established part of the urban landscape. Their presence is a recognition of the value placed today on the women's campaign for political equality. But that value is not immutable. As demonstrated by members of the Women's Social and Political Union in St Stephen's Hall, statues were in 1909 a convenient medium for public protest (see Object 99) and have notoriously become more so in the twenty-first century.[3]

However, since 2018 Fawcett's statue has become a meeting place for organized protest regarding women's rights, while the message carried by it has taken on a life of its own, featuring on a wide range of objects, such as mugs, jewellery, fridge magnets, t-shirts and ribbons.[4]

Thus, through time and space the circle is complete. As Object 100, Fawcett stands in Parliament Square looking across at the spot barely 100 metres away where her sister Elizabeth Garrett, with Emily Davies, alighted from a cab in 1866, carried the first mass suffrage petition (see Object 1) into Westminster Hall and delivered it to John Stuart Mill MP who, two hours later, laid it before the House of Commons, setting in motion the long campaign that eventually enfranchised British women.

NOTES

Introduction

1   Malcolm Chase, 'The Popular Movement for Parliamentary Reform in Provincial Britain during the 1860s', *Parliamentary History*, vol. 36 (no.1), 2017, 14–30.

2   Serena Dyer, 'State of the Field: Material Culture', *History*, vol. 106 (no.370), 2021, 282–92. https://doi.org/10.1111/1468-229X.13104 (open access).

3   Jules David Prown, 'Mind in Matter: An Introduction to Material Culture Theory and Method', *Winterthur Portfolio*, vol. 17 (no.1), 1982, 1–19.

4   Lisa Tickner, *The Spectacle of Women: Imagery of the Suffrage Campaign 1907–14* (London: Chatto & Windus, 1987).

5   Lisa Tickner, 'Suffrage Campaigns: The Political Imagery of the British Women's Suffrage Movement', in Jane Beckett and Deborah Cherry (eds), *The Edwardian Era* (London: Phaidon Press and Barbican Art Gallery, 1987), 100–16, to accompany the exhibition.

6   Diane Atkinson, *Suffragettes in the Purple, White and Green. London 1906–14* (London: Museum of London, 1992).

7   The exhibitions were 'Cooks and Campaigners', 2002, 'Treasures of the Women's Library', 2012 and 'Endless Endeavours: From the 1866 Women's Suffrage Petition to the Fawcett Society', 2016.

8   Kenneth Florey, *Women's Suffrage Memorabilia: An Illustrated Historical Study* (Jefferson, NC: McFarland, 2013).

9   Christabel Pankhurst, *Unshackled* (London: Cresset Press, 1987), 63.

10   See Lot 13 Bonhams: Deeds Not Words: A Women's Suffrage Collection, 10–20 November 2025.

11   For a photograph of the 1930s Suffragette Fellowship display, see https://www.alamy.com/stock-photo-a-museum-in-south-kensington-london-which-holds-militant-equipment-83746468.html.

12   Sumita Mukherjee, *Indian Suffragettes: Female Identities and Transnational Networks* (Oxford: Oxford University Press, 2018), 27.

13   Elizabeth Crawford, 'Deeds and Words: Suffrage and the London Library', *Women's History Review*, vol. 32 (no.6), 2022, 879–86. https://doi.org/10.1080/09612025.2022.2150434.

Object 1. The printed pamphlet form of the 1866 women's suffrage petition

1   For the total number of petitions, see Mary Branson, *New Dawn* (London: Parliamentary Curator's Office, 2018), 6.

2   The only two other known copies of the printed petition, one of which belonged to Emily Davies, are both held by Girton College, Cambridge.

3   Elizabeth Wolstenholme Elmy collected 300 Manchester signatures, probably by a door-to-door canvass. *Votes for Women*, 8 March 1910, 12.

4   Garrett qualified as Britain's first woman doctor in 1865. For Mill quote, see *The Globe*, 8 June 1866, 4.

5   Davies to Taylor, 18 July 1866. LSE, Mill-Taylor Papers, vol. 13, 174–94.

6   3rd Earl Cathcart, landowner. A Penny Red stamp was the price of posting a standard letter in the UK, 1841–79.
7   Anon (Helen Taylor), 'The Ladies Petition', *Westminster Review*, January 1867.
8   For a list of the petition names, see UK Parliament website: Collecting the signatures for the 1866 petition.

Object 2. Lydia Becker's dress, 1889

1   Joanna M. Williams, *The Great Miss Becker* (Barnsley: Pen & Sword, 2022), 28.
2   Lydia Becker, 'Female Suffrage', *The Contemporary Review*, March 1867.
3   Becker spoke in favour of the corset at British Association for the Advancement of Science meetings, 1888 and 1889. See also her article 'On Stays and Dress Reform', *Sanitary Record*, October 1888, 149–51.
4   *The Glossop-dale Chronicle and North Derbyshire Reporter*, 27 July 1889, 6.
5   Princess Louise, daughter of Queen Victoria, married four days after Becker's brother wearing a dress with a Medici collar.
6   Madame Brownjohn's label is sewn onto the waistband of the skirt. Her atelier was at 46 Elizabeth Street, Belgravia.
7   Becker's dress is mentioned in 'Pageant of Dress: From Stuart Period to Victorian', *The Manchester Guardian*, 30 March 1932, 7.

Object 3. Cartoon of Lydia Becker and Jacob Bright, *ca.* 1868

1   Williams, *The Great Miss Becker*, 115–16.
2   The British Cartoon Archive holds fifty-two cartoons featuring Jacob Bright, of which sixteen include Becker. https://www.kent.ac.uk/library-it/special-collections/british-cartoon-archive.
3   They were J. Murray, 4 Blue Boars Court, Market Place and Rothwell, 64 Corporation Street, Manchester.
4   For the 1876 cartoon, see Jacob Bright cartoons at https://www.kent.ac.uk/library/special-collections/british-cartoon-archive.
5   The case is known as Chorlton v. Lings.

Object 4. An advertisement in the *Orkney Herald,* 4 October 1871

1   Scottish women ratepayers only achieved the municipal vote under an Act passed in 1881.
2   *Perthshire Advertiser*, 17 March 1870, 1.
3   *Paisley Herald*, 26 February 1870, 4.
4   *Orkney Herald*, 4 October 1871, 2.
5   *Orkney Herald,* 11 October 1871, 2.
6   *Orkney Herald,* 11 October 1871, 3.

Object 5. An engraving of a suffrage meeting, 1872

1   *The Graphic* was founded in 1869 to rival the well-established *Illustrated London News*.

2   https://victorianfictionresearchguides.org/the-illustrated-london-news-and-the-graphic/ and
     Hubbards Newspaper and Bank Directory of the World, 1882, 1089.
3   For Rhoda Garrett, see Elizabeth Crawford, *Enterprising Women: The Garretts and Their Circle*
     (London: Francis Boutle, 2002).
4   *The Graphic*, 25 May 1872, 3.
5   https://www.npg.org.uk/collections/search/portrait/mw166412/Dame-Millicent-Fawcett?LinkID=mp
     01548&search=sas&sText=millicent+fawcett&role=sit&rNo=1.
6   *The Examiner,* 3 August 1872, 21.
7   https://www.hibbitt.org.uk/biographies/bio-dando-william-elbert-1843-1918.html.

Object 6. Statue of John Stuart Mill, erected 1878

1   The total cost of the statue was £1,600; see *The Echo*, 26 January 1878, 3.
2   *Dundee Courier,* 28 January 1878, 2.
3   *Daily Mirror*, 21 May 1908, 4 and *Nottingham and Midland Catholic News*, 3.
4   *The Vote,* 27 May 1911, 56.
5   They were on sale at an exhibition of Woolner's sculpture. See *Common Cause*, 7 March 1913, 822.

Object 7. Annual reports of nineteenth-century suffrage societies

1   For the Women's Library Annual Reports collection, see https://digital.library.lse.ac.uk.

Object 8. The Haslam memorial seat, St Stephen's Green, Dublin

1   Carmel Quinlan, *Genteel Revolutionaries: Anna and Thomas Haslam and the Irish Women's
     Movement* (Cork: Cork University Press, 2002).
2   Jennifer Redmond, 'The "Success of Every Great Movement Had Been Largely due to
     the Free and Continuous Exercise of the Right to Petition": Irish Suffrage Petitioners and
     Parliamentarians in the Nineteenth Century', in Alexandra Hughes-Johnson and Lyndsey
     Jenkins (eds), *The Politics of Women's Suffrage* (London: UCL Press, 2021), 25–58. https://doi.
     org/10.14296/2111.9781912702985 (open access).
3   For the Minute Book of the DWSA, see https://www.nationalarchives.ie/article/minute-book-dublin-
     womens-suffrage-association-irish-womens-suffrage-local-government-association-1876-1913/.
4   James and Margaret Cousins, *We Two Together* (Madras: Ganesh, 1950), 164.
5   https://onlinecollection.hughlane.ie/objects/720/thomas-and-anna-m-haslam?ctx=7350eebbf7b5697
     1dd1984f220519fb16731a4ab&idx=0.

Object 9. *The Women's Suffrage Journal*

1   Helen Blackburn, *Women's Suffrage: A Record of the Women's Suffrage Movement in the British
     Isles* (London: Williams & Norgate, 1902), 101.
2   For the *WSJ*, see Williams, *The Great Miss Becker*, Chapter 5.

3 Under the 1870 Education Act women had become eligible both to vote for and to become members of School Boards. In 1870 the first to be elected were Elizabeth Garrett and Emily Davies in London and Becker in Manchester.

4 Pankhurst was a little careless of detail, remembering the *WSJ* as arriving weekly, rather than monthly. See Emmeline Pankhurst, *Suffragette: My Own Story* (Poole, Dorset: Solis Press, 2015), 7.

5 For instance, during final discussions on the 1884 Reform Bill when the 1 May issue of thirty-six pages was deemed a 'Double Number', priced at 2d.

6 For *WSJ*, see https://digital.library.lse.ac.uk/collections/list/collections/10.

Object 10. Invitation card to 'A National Demonstration of Women', 6 May 1880

1 From 1879 Gladstone conducted mass meetings in Midlothian, his prospective constituency, creating a new style of political campaigning.

2 *Women's Suffrage Journal*, 1 May 1880, 83.

3 Blackburn, *Women's Suffrage*, 153.

4 The '10' in the postmark was the code for South Kensington. Caroline Williams, heiress to a Welsh colliery, was a generous supporter of women's causes.

5 Family history suggests she may have given birth to as many as sixteen children; see https://www.levantineheritage.com/uvedale-barrington-tristram-family-in-turkey.html.

6 *Times*, 7 May 1880, 9.

7 *Christian World*, 13 May 1880, 317.

8 *Graphic*, 22 May 1880, 8.

9 *Women's Suffrage Journal*, 1 June 1880, 108.

Object 11. Oil painting by Richard Staunton Cahill, 1888, 'Mary Smith Lecturing on Woman's Rights'

1 Lydia Becker Letter Book (M50/1/3, Manchester Libraries, Information and Archives).

2 *West Cumberland Times*, 23 February 1884, 5.

3 Mary Smith, *Autobiography of Mary Smith: Schoolmistress and Nonconformist* (London: Bemrose, 1892), 94, 274.

4 *Autobiography*, 306.

Object 12. *Carte de visite* photograph, Sheffield 1882, annotated

1 Vero was writing after the vote was won; no other husband of the women pictured was then still alive. Vero's key is a little difficult to follow, but, from known images, the sitting women can be identified as Carbutt and Scatcherd, leaving the names of the standing four to be read from right to left as he sets out.

2 In 2022 Scatcherd was commemorated by a blue plaque at her former Morley home.

3 For mentions of Vero, Ellis and McCormick, see numerous references in Elizabeth Crawford, *The Women's Suffrage Movement: A Regional Survey* (London: Routledge, 2006).

4 For Vero's inscription, see Find a Grave via Ancestry.co.uk.

Object 13. Election handbill for Helen Taylor's candidature at the North Camberwell parliamentary election, 1885

1   Leach was a member of the Yarmouth School Board and an Irish Land League activist.
2   Janet Smith, 'Crossing the Border of Citizenship: Helen Taylor, the Independent Radical Democrat Candidate for Camberwell North, 1885', *Open Library of Humanities*, vol. 6 (no.2), 2020, 19. doi: https://doi.org/10.16995/olh.540.
3   Sandra Holton, *Suffrage Days* (London: Routledge, 1996), 49–69.
4   The leaflet was printed by Mayo, Dean Street, Fetter Lane, who also printed pro-home rule items, perhaps explaining Craigen's choice of printer. Both this and Object 13 were collected by Helen Taylor.

Object 14. An engraving of a meeting of the Women's Franchise League, 1891

1   This paralleled the split in the Liberal party. Followers of Gladstone backed home rule for Ireland; those against, Liberal Unionists, sided with the Conservatives.
2   Sandra Stanley Holton, 'Now You See It, Now You Don't: The Women's Franchise League and Its Place in Contending Narratives of the Women's Suffrage Movement', in Maroula Joannou and June Purvis (eds), *The Women's Suffrage Movement: New Feminist Perspectives* (Manchester: Manchester University Press, 1998), 15–36.
3   At this time Mrs Pankhurst ran an 'inexpensive art furnishers' shop, Emerson & Co.
4   *Graphic*, 12 December 1891, text 5, illustration, 6.
5   Alan Bott and Irene Clephane, *Our Mothers: A Cavalcade in Pictures, Quotation and Description of Late Victorian Women 1870–1900* (London: Gollancz, 1932), 165.
6   Estelle Sylvia Pankhurst, *The Suffragette Movement* (London: Longmans, 1931).

Object 15. Photograph of Elizabeth Wolstenholme Elmy

1   In 1907 Schmidt photographed Annie Kenney in mill-girl attire (London Museum, 50.82/1290.)
2   Maureen Wright, *Elizabeth Wolstenholme Elmy and the Victorian Feminist Movement* (Manchester: Manchester University Press, 2011). Wright suggests Elmy may have interacted with 7,000 correspondents. Most of Elmy's surviving papers are held in the British Library. (Add MSS 47449-55.)
3   For a detailed discussion of the work of the WEU, see Wright, Chapter 6.
4   *Personal Rights Journal*, November 1892, 213.

Object 16. Portrait of Mary Wollstonecraft

1   Unwin's wife, Jane, a daughter of Richard Cobden, was a leading Liberal suffragist. *Vindication of the Rights of Woman* was first published by Joseph Johnson, 1792. For Fawcett's Introduction, see Melissa Terras and Elizabeth Crawford (eds), *Millicent Garrett Fawcett: Selected Writings* (London: UCL Press, 2022), Section 11.
2   *Newcastle Daily Chronicle*, 22 November 1886, 4.

3 First published, 1884, in the United States, by Roberts in their 'Famous Women' series; in UK by W.H. Allen in 1885 in 'Eminent Women' series.

4 See, e.g., *Woman's Signal*, 12 August 1897.

5 Now held by the Tate Gallery, London. For a history of the portrait, see Eileen M. Hunt (ed.), *Portraits of Wollstonecraft* (London: Bloomsbury Academic, 2020), 21–4.

6 *Women's Franchise*, 19 December 1907, 283. Margaret Clayton, *Mary Wollstonecraft and the Women's Movement of Today* (London: Frank Palmer, *c.* 1910).

7 Banner and programme, both designed by Mary Lowndes, are held by the Women's Library collection, LSE. For Mary Lowndes' Album containing the programme, see https://www.flickr.com/photos/lselibrary/albums/72157692028437514/. For the banner, see https://artsandculture.google.com/asset/mary-wollstonecraft4-suffrage-banner/sQHU1ZbSmQlZbg?hl=en.

Object 17. Helen Blackburn's bookcase, 1897

1 Lady Frances Balfour, *Ne Obliviscaris: Dinna Forget,* vol. 2 (London: Hodder & Stoughton, no date) 129.

2 Balfour, *Ne Obliviscaris*, vol. 2, 129.

3 Blackburn, *Women's Suffrage*, 7, refers to the 4th edition of Astell, published in 1701, suggesting this was the edition Blackburn owned, now held in the Blackburn Collection.

4 Blackburn, *Women's Suffrage*, v.

5 For Guinness, see Elizabeth Crawford, *Art and Suffrage* (London: Francis Boutle, 2018).

6 Hallett to M. Pickton, 3 April 1903 (GCAC 4/6/3/3, Girton College Archive).

Object 18. Scenes at the National Convention for the Civic Rights of Women, magazine illustration, 1903

1 The Holborn Town Hall was then on the corner of Gray's Inn Road and Theobald's Road.

2 *Black and White* was a weekly illustrated magazine, carrying news and fiction, founded in 1891 and incorporated in *The Sphere*, 1912.

3 *Daily News*, 17 October 1903, 5.

Object 19. The Pankhurst home, 62 Nelson Street, Chorlton-on-Medlock, Manchester

1 Emmeline Pankhurst, *My Own Story* (London: Eveleigh Nash, 1914), 38.

2 *Manchester Courier*, 21 February 1885, 8.

3 *Woman's Herald,* 7 February 1891, 241–2.

4 Pankhurst, *The Suffragette Movement*, 167.

5 See, e.g. advertisement in *Clarion*, 22 April 1904, 4.

6 June Purvis, *Christabel Pankhurst: A Biography* (London: Routledge, 2018).

7 The Manchester Society was renamed the NESWS, 1897.

8 Lyndsey Jenkins, *Sisters and Sisterhood: The Kenney Family, Class, and Suffrage, 1890–1965* (Oxford: Oxford University Press, 2021), 3–4.

9 *Scotsman*, 6 June 1977, 8.

10 https://pankhurstmuseum.com and https://www.manchesterwomensaid.org.

Object 20. Photographic postcard of the 'Lancashire and Cheshire Delegates on the Women's Franchise Deputation to the Prime Minister', May 1906

1　*Daily Mirror*, 19 May, 3.
2　*Leeds and Yorkshire Mercury*, 19 May 1906, 5.
3　Jill Liddington and Jill Norris, *One Hand Tied behind Us: The Rise of the Women's Suffrage Movement* (London: Rivers Oram, 2nd ed, 2000).
4　For the Patent Cap Winders banner, see *Southport Guardian,* 23 May 1906, 10; for the Manchester and Salford banner, see *Sheffield Evening Telegraph*, 19 May 1906, 6.
5　*Sheffield Evening Telegraph*, 19 May 1906, 6.
6　For a discussion of Kenney's image, see Jenkins, *Sisters*, 112–21.

Object 21. A German photographic postcard, 23 October 1906

1　The phrase, with 'rouse' in quotes, is used by Sylvia Pankhurst in *The Suffragette Movement*, 197.
2　Pankhurst, *Unshackled*, 65.
3　*Daily Mirror*, 24 October 1906, 3.

Object 22. Illustration of 'The Mud March', February 1907

1　*Times*, 12 December 1906, 12.
2　Marianne Tidcombe (ed.), *E28: The Prison Diary of Annie Cobden-Sanderson* (Marlborough: Libanus Press, 2017).
3　*Brisbane Courier*, 27 May 1898, 6.
4　Elizabeth Crawford (ed.), *Campaigning for the Vote: Kate Frye's Suffrage Diary* (London: Francis Boutle, 2013), 29.
5　*Labour Leader*, 15 February 1907, 10.
6　*Nottingham Journal*, 14 February 1907, 5.

Object 23. Press photograph taken on 31 October 1906

1　In *The Suffragette Movement*, 216, Sylvia Pankhurst writes that, when she resigned as WSPU secretary in summer 1906, Despard was appointed joint honorary secretary with How-Martyn, but this is likely a misremembrance as it is contradicted by contemporary newspaper reports, see the *Morning Leader* 29 October 1906, 1. There are no reports of Despard being joint secretary before mid-October. See the *Daily News*, 8 October 1906, 8, for a letter from the WSPU signed by Edith How-Martyn as sole honorary secretary.
2　Held in the London Museum https://www.londonmuseum.org.uk/collections/v/object-292377/a-committee-meeting-of-the-suffragette-leaders-1907/.
3　*Leeds Mercury*, 16 September 1907, 5.

Object 24. Women's Freedom League Minute Book 1907–8

1   For the main WFL archive, see https://archives.lse.ac.uk/records/2WFL. For a podcast about the WFL by Dr Claire Eustance, see https://www.suffrageresources.org.uk/resource/3229/the-womens-freedom-league.

Object 25. A suffrage poster

1   For studies of suffrage art and artists, see Lisa Tickner, *Spectacle of Women* (London: Chatto & Windus, 1987) and, for Joan Harvey Drew, Crawford, *Art and Suffrage*, 77–82.
2   *Women's Franchise*, 17 October 1907, 4.
3   For discussion of the iconography of the suffrage movement, see Tickner, *The Spectacle of Women,* c Chapter 4.
4   For a social realist poster, see Object 34. See Alice Sheppard, 'The Relation of Suffrage Art to Culture', in R. Dotterer and S. Bowers (eds), *Politics, Gender, and the Arts* (Selinsgrove, PA: Susquhehanna University Press, 1992), 33.
5   Walter Crane, *Cartoons for the Cause* (London: Twentieth Century Press, 1897).
6   Jane Marcus, 'Women, War and Madness', in Alice Parker and Elizabeth Meese (eds), *The Difference within; Feminism and Critical Theory* (Amsterdam: J. Benjamins Publishing, 1989), 56.

Object 26. Suffrage scrapbook compiled by Mrs Spencer Graves

1   Maud Arncliffe Sennett, 'A Collection of Press Cuttings, Pamphlets, Leaflets and Ephemera', 37 vols (London, British Library, C.121.g.1).
2   Isabel Seymour's Scrapbook is held by the National Gallery of Victoria, Australia. https://www.ngv.vic.gov.au/exhibition/womens-suffrage-research-collection/ and Kitty Marion's by the London Museum. https://artsandculture.google.com/asset/scrapbook-compiled-by-the-suffragette-kitty-marion-marion-kitty/AQEjIoxG7PwDrg.
3   Cherish Watton, 'Suffrage Scrapbooks and Emotional Histories of Women's Activism', *Women's History Review*, vol. 31 (no.6), 2022, 1028–46. https://doi.org/10.1080/09612025.2021.2012343 (open access).

Object 27. Suffrage newspapers

1   Maria Dicenzo (with Lucy Delap and Leila Ryan), *Feminist Media History: Suffrage, Periodicals and the Public Sphere* (Basingstoke: Palgrave Macmillan, 2011).
2   For Wilson, see Crawford, *Art and Suffrage*, 226–7.
3   For Pearse, see Crawford, *Art and Suffrage*, 180–3.

Object 28. Women's Social and Political Union 'Haunted House' buckle and belt

1   *Daily News*, quoted in *Votes for Women*, 25 June 1908, 5.
2   The buckle was last advertised in *Votes for Women*, 11 June 1909, 29, alongside all these other items.
3   Christabel Pankhurst, 'The Political Importance of the Colours', *Votes for Women*, 7 May 1909, 632.
4   *Common Cause*, 26 May 1910, 99.

Object 29. Women's Freedom League 'Dorothy bag'

1   For a pattern for a Dorothy bag, see *The Lady's World Fancy Work Book* (London: Lady's World Publishing, October 1908).
2   *Sunderland Daily Echo*, 14 March 1912, 1.
3   *Votes for Women*, 30 July 1908, 12.
4   *Votes for Women*, 26 March 1909, 483.
5   *Nevinson Diaries*, 17 November 1911.
6   *The Vote*, 30 December 1909, 115.
7   Katherine Roberts, *Pages from the Diary of a Militant Suffragette* (Letchworth: Garden City Press, 1911), 108.
8   *Votes for Women*, 4 February 1909, 319. For the 'suffragette look', see K. Rolley, 'Fashion, Femininity and the Fight for the Vote', *Art History*, vol. 13 (no.1), March 1990, 47–71.

Object 30. 'Susan B. Anthony' suffrage banner, 1908

1   See, e.g., suffrage banners from the Women's Library collection at LSE. https://www.flickr.com/photos/lselibrary/albums/72157660179759073/with/44671987821 and those held in the London Museum. See also Tickner, *The Spectacle of Women*.
2   For Lowndes' Album, see https://www.flickr.com/photos/lselibrary/albums/72157692028437514/with/39963686741. For the Susan B. Anthony and Lucy Stone banners, see https://www.flickr.com/photos/lselibrary/albums/72157660179759073/.
3   https://images.hollis.harvard.edu/primo-explore/fulldisplay?docid=HVD_VIAolvwork20003298&context=L&vid=HVD_IMAGES&search_scope=default_scope&tab=default_tab&lang=en_US.
4   See https://www.flickr.com/photos/lselibrary/26091519498/in/album-72157692028437514. Christiana Herringham represented the ASL on the NUWSS committee organizing the 1908 procession.
5   *Morning Leader*, 15 June 1908, 4.
6   See https://phm.org.uk/collections-display/?irn=44103.
7   For details of these artists, see Crawford, *Art and Suffrage*.
8   *Votes for Women*, 25 June 1908, 14.
9   *Women's Franchise*, 9 July 1908, 4.
10   See https://www.digitaldrama.org/project/100-banners/.

Object 31. The train and the suffrage movement

1   *Votes for* Women, 25 June 1908, 258.
2   *Votes for Women*, 17 June 1910, 620.
3   For a map of the British railway network by the end of 1870 and 1879, see https://www.campop.geog.cam.ac.uk/research/projects/transport/onlineatlas/railways.pdf.
4   In 2025 only Galashiels has a station.
5   Blackburn, *Women's Suffrage*, 109.
6   Crawford (ed.), *Campaigning for the Vote*, 157.
7   *Grantham Journal*, 18 July 1914, 7.
8   *Suffragette*, 21 November 1913, 132.

Object 32. The bicycle and the suffrage movement

1   *Vote*, 6 June 1930, 182.
2   Pankhurst, *The Suffragette Movement*, 139, gives the date she and Christabel acquired bicycles as 1906, but from the context it was more likely to have been 1896.
3   *Votes for Women*, 4 October 1907, 11; *Women's Franchise*, 23 April 1908, 505.
4   The design was Sylvia Pankhurst's 'Angel of Freedom', *Votes for Women*, 14 May 1909, 675.
5   *Votes for Women*, 9 August 1912, 736.
6   NUWSS *Annual Report* 1914.
7   *Suffragette*, 28 March 1913, 385; *Reading Mercury*, 18 July 1914, 9.

Object 33. The car and the suffrage movement

1   *Northern Daily Telegraph*, 26 June 1906, 2.
2   *Votes for Women*, 14 May 1909, 667.
3   Listen to the 1962 interview. https://www.bbc.co.uk/sounds/play/p01ngy65.
4   Crawford (ed.), *Campaigning for the Vote*, 62.

Object 34. The caravan and the suffrage movement

1   *Women's Franchise*, 23 July 1908, 40.
2   2 July 1908, 7BSH/5/2/04, Women's Library collection, LSE.
3   *Newnham College Club Roll*, 1908.
4   *Suffragette*, 8 August 1913, 739.
5   *Suffragette*, 15 August 1913, 771.
6   *Suffragette,* 7 August 1914, 298.

Object 35. Suffrage offices

1   For a wider view and other, similar, photographs, see *Votes for Women,* 14 July 1911, 678.
2   Frederick Pethick-Lawrence, *Votes for Women*, 14 July 1911, 678.
3   Yoshio Markino, *My Idealed John Bullesses* (London: Constable, 1912), 151.
4   H.G. Wells, *Ann Veronica*, ed. S. Schutt (London: Penguin, 2005), 184.

Object 36. Women's Freedom League 'Proclamation' banner, 1908

1   *Daily Mirror*, 13 October 1908, 3.
2   *Ashbourne Telegraph*, 16 October 1908, 4.
3   *Aberdeen People's Journal*, 31 October 1908, 6.
4   *Yorkshire Evening Post*, 29 October 1908, 3.
5   *Hampshire Post*, 30 October 1908, 7.
6   *Wicklow News-Letter*, 31 October 1908, 5.
7   https://ukvote100.org/2017/08/23/the-ladies-gallery-grilles/.
8   https://unesco.org.uk/portfolio/memory-of-the-world/.

Object 37. Bow Street Police Court, 1908

1   Arthur Barrett is not to be confused with Alfred Barratt, another press photographer (see Object 23).
2   *Westminster Gazette,* 14 October 1908, 6.
3   https://www.londonmuseum.org.uk/collections/v/object-490352/photograph/.
4   Mrs Pankhurst was photographed in the Bow Street dock with Evelina Haverfield during their trial in July 1909.
5   https://bowstreetpolicemuseum.org.uk/.

Object 38. Photograph of women wearing replica prison dress, 1908

1   Diane Atkinson, *Rise Up, Women* (London: Bloomsbury, 2018), 123.
2   *The Essex Newsman*, 21 November 1908, 3.
3   *Votes for Women*, 19 November 1908, 127.
4   *Weekly Dispatch*, 22 November 1908, 2.
5   Although all women are named on the photograph caption, not all can now be identified with certainty.
6   *Votes for Women,* 3 December 1908, 164.
7   *Standard*, 30 November 1908, quoted in *Votes for Women*, 3 December 1908, 165.
8   https://www.londonmuseum.org.uk/collections/v/object-292484/the-suffragette-elsie-howey-in-a-replica-prison-cell/.

Object 39. Record of a speech made by Christabel Pankhurst, 1908

1   *Woman's Leader*, 28 August 1925, 242. The paper was the successor to *The Common Cause*.
2   *Daily Mirror*, 6 July 1959, 2.
3   Mentioned in cutting in Object 26.
4   *Coventry Evening Telegraph*, 28 May 1929, 1.
5   For the Pethick-Lawrence recording, see SC/24/6, Women's Library collection, LSE. For an excerpt, featuring Emmeline Pethick-Lawrence, see https://www.youtube.com/watch?v=7wWU73uFJUo.

For the Harrison tapes, see 'Oral Evidence on the Suffragette and Suffragist Movements: the Brian Harrison interviews, 1974–1988' (8 SUF, https://www.lse.ac.uk/library/collection-highlights/the-suffrage-interviews, The Women's Library collection, LSE).

6   Search YouTube to find a site playing the 1908 record.

Object 40. Tea rooms and the suffrage movement

1   Lynne Walker, 'Vistas of Pleasure: Women Consumers of Urban Space in the West End of London 1850–1900', in Clarissa Campbell Orr (ed.), *Women in the Victorian Art World* (Manchester: Manchester University Press, 1995), 70–88.
2   *Gentlewoman* 29 February 1908, 287.
3   The first advertisement appears in *Votes for Women*, 31 December 1908.

Object 41. Suffrage medals

1   *Halifax Daily Guardian*, 6 March 1908, 2.
2   *Common Cause*, 6 May 1909, 59.
3   *Votes for Women*, 6 August 1909, 1043.
4   Theresa Garnett's medal is held by the London Museum, Ada Wright's was sold at Bonhams, London, 21 June 2023.
5   *Votes for Women*, 5 November 1909, 84.
6   One was auctioned with the hunger-strike medal of WSPU member Gladys Roberts, Christie's 1981.

Object 42. Postcard advertising the NUWSS 'Pageant of Women's Trades and Professions', April 1909

1   For Mary Lowndes' Album, see https://www.flickr.com/photos/lselibrary/albums/72157692028437514/.
2   Diary of Kate Frye (KPF, Royal Holloway College University of London Archive).
3   For a description of the Pageant, see *Common Cause*, 6 May 1909, 59–61.

Object 43. China and the suffrage movement

1   *Votes for Women,* 19 May 1911, 547.
2   See https://www.flickr.com/photos/lselibrary/26462903619.
3   *Votes for Women*, 13 May 1910, 538.
4   *Votes for Women*, 30 May 1913, 644.
5   A 'portcullis' teapot, bowl and milk jug are among the collection of Hall's china now held by Birmingham Museum and Art Gallery.
6   The surviving pieces are a tea service held in the Women's Library collection (Archive Ceramic Box 10–11) and a single plate sold as Lot 22, Bonham's Auction 22 September–3 October 2023.

Object 44. Women's Freedom League petition badge, 1909

1   For a study of the part petitioning played in the suffrage movement, see Henry Miller, 'The British Women's Suffrage Movement and the Practice of Petitioning, 1890–1914', *The Historical Journal*, vol. 64 (no. 2), 2021, 332–56.
2   *Women's Franchise*, 19 August 1909, 736.
3   Margaret Wynne Nevinson, *Life's Fitful Fever* (London: A. & C. Black, 1926), 202–5 for an excellent description of the 'Great Watch'.
4   Mrs Lilian Hicks, quoted in *Daily News*, 29 October 1909, 7.
5   An abridged version of *At the Gates* was published in *The Vote*, 16 December 1909, 94.
6   *Daily News*, 24 September 1909, 4.

Object 45. Suffrage society badges

1   See Kenneth Florey, 'English Suffrage Badges and the Marketing of the Campaign', in Miranda Garrett and Zoe Thomas (eds), *Suffrage and the Arts: Visual Culture, Politics and Enterprise* (London: Bloomsbury, 2019), 137–55.
2   For the census boycott, see Jill Liddington, *Vanishing for the Vote* (Manchester: Manchester University Press, 2014).
3   For more about the CWSS and other religious suffrage societies, see Carmen Mangion, 'Religious Suffrage Societies', in Krista Cowman (ed), *The Routledge Companion to British Women's Suffrage* (London: Routledge, 2024), 306–21.
4   *Common Cause*, 28 November 1913, 626.
5   See Ryland Wallace, *The Women's Suffrage Movement in Wales, 1866–1928* (Cardiff: University of Wales Press, 2018).
6   Diary of Kate Frye, 18 November 1910 (KPF, Royal Holloway College University of London Archives).

Object 46. Designs for emblems of the federations of the National Union of Women's Suffrage Societies

1   *Common Cause,* 17 March 1910, 687.
2   Designs for all the federations were printed, in black and white, on the front page of *Common Cause*, 7 March 1912 and a description given on p. 820.
3   Ireland was outside the purlieu of the NUWSS.

Object 47. Photograph of Millicent Fawcett planting a tree in Annie's Arboretum, Batheaston, 1910

1   Cynthia Hammond, *Architects, Angels, Activists and the City of Bath* (Farnham: Ashgate, 2012), 163–236; Beatrice Dobbie, *A Nest of Suffragettes in Somerset* (Batheaston: Batheaston Society, 1979) and June Hannam, 'Suffragettes Are Splendid for Any Work', in Clare Eustance et al. (eds), *A Suffrage Reader* (London: Leicester University Press, 2000), 53–68.
2   Blathwayt diaries, Gloucestershire Record Office (D2659/21 and /24 and /27).

3   Quoted in https://catalogue.gloucestershire.gov.uk/records/D2659/5/12.
4   *Reynold's Newspaper*, 4 September 1938, 5.
5   *Bristol Evening Post*, 3 April 1964, 33.
6   *Bristol Evening Post*, 30 March 1962, 24.
7   Col. Blathwayt's glass plates are held by Bath Record Office. For the images, see 'Bath in Time' Bath in Time. The surviving tree plaques are held in the Roman Baths Museum, Bath.

Object 48. Photographic postcard of the Prisoners' Pageant, 23 July 1910

1   Tickner, *Spectacle of Women*, 111–15.
2   https://player.bfi.org.uk/free/collection/suffragettes-on-film.
3   For plans of the demonstration, see *Votes for Women*, 15 July 1910, 686.
4   *Votes for Women*, 15 July 1910, 686.
5   Quoted in *Votes for Women*, 29 July 1910, 726.
6   Diane Atkinson, '"A Riot of Colour": Mrs Broom's Suffragette Photographs', in Anna Sparham, *Soldiers and Suffragettes: The Photography of Christina Broom* (London: Museum of London, 2015), 41–86.
7   *Votes for Women*, 29 July 1910, 728.

Object 49. Suffrage shops

1   John Mercer, 'Shopping for Suffrage: The Campaign Shops of the Women's Social and Political Union', *Women's History Review*, vol. 18 (no.2), 2009, 293–309.
2   The building still stands (2025).
3   Blue for Conservative, yellow for Liberal and red for Labour. *Common Cause*, 9 November 1911, 536. But CC was muddled: Robinson was Labour and Stanley Liberal.
4   The photograph was published in *Common Cause*, 9 November 1911, 534. Another copy of the photograph is held by Oldham Council Heritage Collections.
5   *Women's Franchise*, 26 September 1907, 144.
6   *Women's Franchise*, 18 June 1908, 603.
7   *Votes for Women*, 4 June 1908, 212.
8   Rachel Ferguson, *We Were Amused* (London: Jonathan Cape, 1950), 170.
9   *Votes for Women*, 1 July 1910, 651.

Object 50. Suffrage postcards

1   Although US focused, Kenneth Florey's *American Woman Suffrage Postcards: A Study and a Catalogue* (Jefferson, NC: McFarland, 2015), which reproduces examples of a wide range of cards, many types of which were published on both sides of the Atlantic, is essential reading for anyone studying UK suffrage postcards. See also Ian McDonald, *Vindication!: A Postcard History of the Women's Movement* (London: Bellew Publishing, 1989); Norman Watson, *Suffragettes and the Post* (Forfar, Angus: Robertson Printers, 2010); 'Postcards' in Crawford, *Women's Suffrage Movement*, 562–4 and https://thesuffragepostcardproject.omeka.net/ (a site that contains details of both British and US suffrage postcards). For a study of one type of UK suffrage postcard, see https://

womenslibrary.org.uk/2024/06/27/suffrage-postcards-in-the-grip-of-the-law/. Search the GWL catalogue for others in their collection.

2   Lauren Alex O'Hagan, 'Contesting Women's Right to Vote: Anti-Suffrage Postcards in Edwardian Britain', *Visual Culture in Britain*, vol. 21 (no.3), 2020–09, 330–62, a study of the 'comic' commercial postcard, usefully identifies five key themes that link their depictions of women activists. However, knowing how such women as Lydia Becker were depicted in ephemeral publications in the nineteenth century, it is difficult to accept that twentieth-century postcard publishers were engaged in consciously anti-suffrage campaigning rather than merely reflecting the mores of the day. While the author suggests the National League for Opposing Women's Suffrage was involved with commercial publishers in launching an anti-suffrage postcard campaign, only one illustrated postcard (and one poster) was published by the NLOWS. Moreover, it is doubtful that, except for the most obvious allusions to a Pankhurst, the depictions of 'comic' suffragettes were based on real personalities. For instance, the author gives no evidence to support a claim that Mrs Fawcett was caricatured in this way.

3   Details from 1911 census.

Object 51. Suffrage games

1   *Votes for Women,* 29 October 1909, 76.
2   First advertised in *Votes for Women*, 8 October 1909, 80.
3   *Chiswick Times,* 17 December 1909, 4.
4   *Votes for Women*, November 1907, 28.
5   *Votes for Women* 3 December 1909, 157.
6   The only known example is held by the Women's Library collection, LSE.
7   The only known example is held by the Bodleian Library, Oxford.
8   *Votes for Women*, 17 December 1908, 194.
9   Florey, *Women's Suffrage Memorabilia*, 189, illustration B1.

Object 52. Suffrage jewellery

1   Object 52 is in the Women's Library collection, LSE; the other two Mills' brooches are in the London Museum.
2   For an overview of suffragette jewellery, see Elizabeth S. Goring, 'Suffragette Jewellery in Britain', *Decorative Arts Society Journal*, vol. 26, 2002, 85–99, and watch Elizabeth Goring, 'Wearing the Colours: Jewellery and the Women's Suffrage Movement in Britain'. https://www.youtube.com/watch?v=mHV0mLvYJI8.
3   *Votes for Women*, 14 October 1910, 32.
4   *Votes for Women*, 21 January 1910, 263; 3 January 1913, 211.
5   *Common Cause*, 24 March 1910, 707.
6   The pendant is now in the London Museum collection.
7   *Votes for Women*, 7 January 1909, 242.

Object 53. Suffrage plays

1   *Vote,* 9 December 1909, 84.
2   For a review of the first production, see *The Era*, 17 April 1909, 21; see also *Kensington News*, 3 December 1909, 4.

3   Naomi Paxton, 'Suffrage on the Edwardian Stage', in Cowman (ed.), *The Routledge Companion to British Women's Suffrage*. Some plays, monologues and duologues have been reissued, e.g. Naomi Paxton (ed.), *The Methuen Drama Book of Suffrage Plays* (London: Methuen Drama, 2018).
4   Naomi Paxton, *Stage Rights! The Actresses' Franchise League, Activism and Politics 1908–58* (Manchester: Manchester University Press, 2018).
5   Diary of Kate Frye (KPF, Royal Holloway College University of London Archives).

Object 54. Suffrage novels

1   Sowon S. Park, 'Suffrage Fiction: A Political Discourse in the Marketplace', *English Literature in Transition, 1880–1920*, vol. 39 (no.4), 1996, 450–61. https://muse.jhu.edu/article/367903 (open access).
2   Charlotte Despard and Mabel Collins, *Outlawed* (London: Henry Drane, 1908), Preface, November 1908.
3   *Outlawed*, viii.
4   *Outlawed*, 300.
5   Adrienne Mollwo, *A Fair Suffragette* (London: Henry Drane, 1909), 252.

Object 55. Suffrage songs

1   Ethel Smyth, *Female Pipings in Eden* (London: Peter Davies, 1933), 192.
2   Christopher St John, *Ethel Smyth* (London: Longmans, 1959), 151.
3   *Votes for Women*, 27 January 1911, 272.
4   See advertisements for various editions of 'The March' in e.g. *Votes for Women,* 24 February 1911, 339 and 3 March 1911, 356. Vocal cards cost 1d; the deluxe edition, 1s 6d.
5   For more information on suffrage songs and music, see Crawford, *The Women's Suffrage Movement*, 644–6; also, mainly relating to the US, but with UK material, Kenneth Florey, *Women's Suffrage Memorabilia*, 162–72.

Object 56. May Billinghurst's 'Velociman'

1   For Billinghurst's copy of 'March of the Women', see 7RMB/B/3/4, Women's Library, LSE.
2   So described by R.R. Billinghurst, April 2008 (7RMB/B/4, Women's Library, LSE).
3   *Daily Telegraph*, 6 April 1910, 15.
4   *Dublin Daily Express*, 24 November 1910, 8.
5   For Billinghurst's account of her treatment in Holloway, see *Suffragette*, 24 January 1913, 216.

Object 57. *A Votes for Women* poster highlighting male activism

1   Clare Eustance and Angela John (eds), *The Men's Share?: Masculinities, Male Support and Women's Suffrage in Britain, 1890–1920* (London: Routledge, 1997).
2   *Votes for Women*, 17 March 1911, 385.

Object 58. National Union of Women's Suffrage Societies flyer in support of the Second Conciliation Bill, 1911

1 *Common Cause*, 23 March 1911, 814.
2 Millicent Garrett Fawcett, *Women's Suffrage: A Short History of a Great Movement* (London: T.C and E.C. Jack, 1912), 75.
3 E.g., letter from A. Burgoyne Conservative MP for Kensington North, *Bayswater Chronicle*, 13 May 1911, 5. He voted for the bill.

Object 59. 'Votes for Women' novelties

1 https://davidskardon.wixsite.com/skardons-world/shops-hotels.
2 *Leeds Mercury*, 21 November 1907, 4.
3 See Lots 34 and 35 *Bonhams: Votes for Women: The Lesley Mees Collection.*
4 For 'Jack-in-the Box' and 'jig doll', see Lots 69 and 72 *Bonhams: Votes for Women: The Lesley Mees Collection.* For 'pneumatic' suffragette, see *Sphere,* 31 October 1908.
5 *Queen*, 21 December 1912, 1148.

Object 60. Diaries and suffrage

1 Fawcett, *Women's Suffrage*, 79.
2 Robins' Diaries are held in the Fales Library, New York.
3 Murray's Diary, 7EGM/1/2, Women's Library, LSE.
4 Crawford (ed.), *Campaigning for the Vote*. The many volumes of the original diary are held in Royal Holloway College Archive.
5 Tidcombe (ed.), *The Prison Diary of Annie Cobden Sanderson.*
6 7EWD/A/4/04, Women's Library, LSE.
7 7KGG/1, Women's Library, LSE.
8 7MAR, Women's Library, LSE.
9 7HFD, Women's Library, LSE.
10 For Lees, see 2OWS/1; for Ramsay, see 7ARA, Women's Library, LSE.

Object 61. 'The Pillar Box and the Suffragette' money box

1 Emily Wilding Davison, *Incendiarism* 7EWD/A/4/02, Women's Library, LSE.
2 *Morning Leader*, 15 December 1911, 3.
3 *Votes for Women*, 29 December 1911, 212.
4 *Suffragette*, 26 December 1912.

Object 62. Anti-suffrage flyer, 1912

1 Julia Bush, *Women against the Vote: Female Anti-suffragism in Britain* (Oxford: Oxford University Press, 2007).
2 *Evening Mail*, 1 March 1912, 6.

Object 63. German photographic postcard of a window smashed by suffragettes, March 1912

1   *Votes for Women*, 23 February 1912, 319.
2   Jennifer Godfrey, *Secret Missions of the Suffragettes* (Barnsley: Pen and Sword Books, 2024).
3   *Newcastle Daily Chronicle*, 4 March 1912, 3.
4   *Votes for Women*, 8 March 1912, 861.
5   MEPO3-1787 (6), The National Archives.

Object 64. 'Elusive Christabel', optic toy, 1912

1   *Kinematograph Weekly*, 10 August 1911, 1782.
2   *Daily Mirror*, 7 March 1912, 4.
3   For details of Christabel's escape, see June Purvis, *Christabel Pankhurst* (London: Routledge, 2018), 271–3.

Object 65. 'Topical Chessmen (Suffragettes v. The Law)'

1   *Western Echo*, 7 May 1910, 3.
2   *Votes for Women*, 25 October 1912, 58.
3   MEPO2/1566, The National Archives.

Object 66. A cloth embroidered with the signatures of suffragette prisoners, 1912

1   The 'Suffragette Handkerchief' is held by The Priest House, West Hoathly, West Sussex; Janie Terrero's embroidered panel by the London Museum.
2   Mrs Alec-Tweedie, *My Table Cloths* (London: Hutchinson, 1916).
3   For names of those arrested, see Index of 'Names of Persons Arrested 1906–14', HO45/24665, The National Archives.
4   For names of prisoners released by 17 April, see *Votes for Women*, 26 April 1912, 470.

Object 67. Forcible feeding: a 'comic' postcard

1   Research indicates that he was probably P.C. Wilfred Percival Armstrong, whose 21st birthday was on 5 August 1910.
2   *Votes for Women*, 1 October 1909, 2.
3   *Votes for Women*, 8 October 1909, 19.

Object 69. Report book kept by an organizer for the New Constitutional Society for Women's Suffrage

1 Krista Cowman, *Women of the Right Spirit: Paid Organisers of the WSPU* (Manchester: Manchester University Press, 2007), 12 and 79.
2 Although not a peripatetic organizer, the secretary of the Birmingham NUWSS kept a notebook labelled 'Town hall meetings: methods of organizing and procedure' (MS841/B/514, Birmingham Archives).
3 Kate Frye's diaries, 1887–1958 (KPF, Royal Holloway University of London Archives). See also Crawford (ed.), *Campaigning for the Vote* and Elizabeth Crawford, *Kate Parry Frye: The Long Life of an Edwardian Actress and Suffragette* (London: ITV Ventures, 2014, audiobook).

Object 70. A silver basket 'Sold for King's Taxes'

1 The banner is held by the London Museum. For the TRL, see Hilary Frances, 'Pay the Piper, Call the Tune', in Joannou and Purvis (eds), *The Women's Suffrage Movement,* 65–76.
2 *Norwood News*, 18 May 1912, 5.
3 *Norwood News*, 3 May 1913, 5.

Object 71. The pendant/brooch presented to Millicent Fawcett by the National Union of Women's Suffrage Societies, 1913

1 Edith Palliser, 10 February 1913 (2LSW/E/07/142, Women's Library Collection, LSE).
2 E.g. the 'Tudor Rose' badge designed by the Artists Suffrage League, *Common Cause*, 24 March 1910, 707, 716.
3 Stephen Pudney, 'Florence Rimmington and the Fawcett Jewel', *Decorative Arts Society Journal*, vol. 46, 2022, 75–87. For *Englishwoman* exhibition, see *Common Cause*, 14 November 1912, 554.
4 *Common Cause*, 17 January 1913, 700.
5 *Common Cause*, 31 January 1913, 735.
6 Letter from Philippa Strachey, 11 February 1913 (London Museum).

Object 72. Photographic postcard of 'Suffragette Fire, Nevill Cricket Ground, Tunbridge Wells'

1 *Illustrated Police News,* 27 February 1913, 7.
2 *Suffragette*, 18 April 1913, 452.
3 See Oral Evidence on the Suffragette and Suffragist Movements: the *Brian Harrison* interviews, 1974–88, especially interview with Maude Kate Smith (8SUF/B/030, Women's Library collection, LSE). For Lenton, see '1955: Suffragette Anniversary'. https://www.bbc.co.uk/videos/crgygjwz68yo. See also Simon Webb, *The Suffragette Bombers* (Barnsley: Pen and Sword, 2014).

Object 73. A lily carried at Emily Wilding Davison's funeral, 14 June 1913

1 Liz Stanley and Ann Morley, *The Life and Death of Emily Wilding Davison* (London: Women's Press, 1988).
2 Vivien Gardner and Diane Atkinson (eds), *Kitty Marion: Actor and Activist* (Manchester: Manchester University Press, 2019).
3 https://www.youtube.com/watch?v=um9GV6_AILM.
4 *Times*, 11 June 1913, 15.
5 *Coventry Times*, 11 June 1913, 8.
6 For a recorded interview with Roe, see 8SUF/B/007, Women's Library collection, LSE; for her description of organizing the procession. https://www.youtube.com/watch?v=K_TmP1svQEM; also *Suffragette*, 13 June 1913, 581.
7 For newsreel of the funeral, see https://www.youtube.com/watch?v=v8WF2CMJmD8.
8 *Suffragette*, 25 July 1913, 711.

Object 74. National Union of Women's Suffrage Societies Pilgrimage haversack, 1913

1 Jane Robinson, *Hearts and Minds: The Untold Story of the Great Pilgrimage* (London: Transworld, 2018).
2 *Common Cause,* 9 May 1913, 67.
3 *Common Cause,* 9 May 1913, 76.

Object 75. A still from the film *The Hunger Strike*, 1913

1 *Sketch*, 11 June 1913, 26.
2 https://player.bfi.org.uk/free/film/watch-milling-the-militants-a-comical-absurdity-1913-online.
3 *Bioscope*, 14 March 1912, 736.
4 Charles Urban, *The Cinematograph in Science, Education, and Matters of State* (London: Charles Urban Trading, 1907), 17.
5 Gardner and Atkinson (eds), *Kitty Marion: Actor and Activist*, 171.

Object 76. Group photograph of delegates to the Church League for Women's Suffrage General Council Meeting, 2 July 1913

1 The identification was made by Clare Wichbold.
2 *CLWS Monthly Paper*, 1 April 1914, 68.
3 For an overview, see Mangion, 'Religious Suffrage Societies', in Cowman (ed), *The Routledge Companion*, 306–21.
4 *CLWS Monthly Paper*, for meeting see, e.g., 1 July 1914, 119, for letter, see August 1913, 259.
5 *Free Church Suffrage Times*, 15 March 1917, 23.

Object 77. *The Suffrage Annual and Women's Who's Who, 1913*

1   *The Suffrage Annual and Woman's Who's Who* is available online https://archive.org/details/the-
     suffrage-annual-and-women-s-who-s-wh.
2   Jihang Park, 'The British Suffrage Activists of 1913: An Analysis', *Past and Present*, vol. 120 (no.1),
     1988, 147–62.
3   *Votes for Women*, 21 February 1913, 297.
4   *Standard,* 14 December 1912, 13.
5   A blank form, indicating information requested, is included in the correspondence (2LSW/E/20/8,
     Women's Library collection, LSE).
6   E.g. *Daily Mirror*, 5 June 1913, 4.
7   *Newcastle Daily Chronicle*, 1 May 1913, 7.

Object 78. Mrs Pankhurst's shoe

1   Crawford (ed.), *Campaigning for the Vote*, 188–9.
2   Pankhurst, *The Suffragette Movement*, 54, 56.
3   *Daily Mirror*, 5 April 1912, 5.

Object 79. *Irish Citizen* leaflet, 15 August 1914

1   Louise Ryan, 'The Irish Citizen, 1912–1920', *Saothar*, vol. 17, 1992, 105–11.
2   Senia Pašeta, *Irish Nationalist Women, 1900-1918* (Cambridge: Cambridge University Press, 2013).
3   *Irish Citizen*, 17 August 1914, 98; 22 August 1914, 105.

Object 80. A Flyer for 'The Right to Serve' March, 1915

1   HO 45/24665/253239 (National Archives).
2   Christabel Pankhurst, *The War* (London: WSPU, 1914), 16.
3   Alexandra Hughes-Johnson, 'Keep Your Eyes on Us Because There Is No More Napping', in
     Alexandra Hughes-Johnson and Lyndsey Jenkins (eds), *The Politics of Women's Suffrage* (London:
     University of London Press, 2021), 129–59.
4   June Purvis, *Emmeline Pankhurst* (London: Routledge, 2002), 276.
5   The Munitions of War Act was passed on 2 July 1915.
6   *Suffragette*, 9 July 1915, 195.
7   Crawford (ed.), *Campaigning for the Vote*, 209–10.

Object 81. East London Federation of the Suffragettes: First Annual Report

1   Estelle Sylvia Pankhurst Papers, International Institute of Social History, Amsterdam. https://
     access.iisg.amsterdam/universalviewer/#?manifest=https://access.iisg.amsterdam/iiif/presentation/
     ARCH01029.216/manifest.

Object 82. Photographs of ambulances of the Scottish Women's Hospitals for Foreign Service. 1915–17

1   Eva Shaw Maclaren, *A History of the Scottish Women's Hospitals* (London: Hodder and Stoughton, 1919), 7.
2   Wendy Moore, *Jack and Eve: Two Women in Love and at War* (London: Atlantic Books, 2024).
3   *Common Cause*, 4 September 1914, 418.
4   Ray Strachey, *Women's Suffrage and Women's Service* (London: London and National Society for Women's Suffrage, 1927).

Object 83. 'The Suffrage Oak', Kelvingrove Park, Glasgow

1   See Krista Cowman, "A Party between Revolution and Peaceful Persuasion": A Fresh Look at the United Suffragists', in Joannou and Purvis (eds), *The Women's Suffrage Movement*, 77–88.
2   Millicent Garrett Fawcett, *Women's Victory – And After, Personal Reminiscences 1911–1918* (London: Sidgwick and Jackson, 1920), 146.
3   Glasgow Society for Equal Citizenship Scrapbook (GWL-2016-140-2 Glasgow Women's Library).

Object 84. Mrs Despard's election card, 1918

1   *Britannia*, 20 December 1918, 236.

Object 85. Lady Astor's parliamentary outfit

1   *Daily Mirror*, 2 December 1919, 2.
2   Mari Takayanagi et al., *Voice and Vote: Celebrating 100 Years of Votes for Women* (London: Regal Press, 2018).
3   *Times*, 29 November 1919, 7.
4   The painting was donated in 1925 to Plymouth, now held in The Box collection.
5   Jacqui Turner, 'First Woman to Take Her Seat in the UK Parliament, 1919', in Rosemary Auchmuty et al. (eds), *Women's Legal Landmarks in the Interwar Years* (Oxford: Hart, 2024), 41–8.
6   See photographs of Astor in the National Portrait Gallery, London.
7   https://www.londonmuseum.org.uk/collections/v/object-495402/suit-womens-suit/.

Object 86. Helena Normanton's KC jabot

1   Judith Bourne, 'Great Expectations and Hard Times: The Advent of the Sex Disqualification (Removal) Act 1919 and Women's Entry to the Legal Profession', *Women's History Review*, vol. 32 (no. 6), 2022, 793–808. https://doi.org/10.1080/09612025.2022.2138017 (open access).
2   Normanton was one of nine women called that day. The first, Ivy Williams, had been called on 10 May 1922.

Object 87. A Minerva Club plate

1   Minutes of Proceedings of the Metropolitan Board of Works, 9 August 1861, 624.
2   *Vote*, 27 February 1920, 519.
3   *Truth*, 29 March 1957, 340.
4   For a description of the Club in the late 1930s listen to an interview recorded by Prof. Sir Brian Harrison of Mrs Marion Johnson, daughter of a former WFL member (8SUF/B/041, Women's Library collection, LSE).
5   For clubs associated with the suffrage campaign, see entry 'Clubs' in Crawford, *The Women's Suffrage Movement*, 117–30.

Object 88. Photograph of a garden party at Aubrey House, Kensington, 1925

1   *Woman's Leader*, 10 April 1925, 84.
2   *What the Vote Has Done* (London: NUSEC, 1926).
3   See Section 49, Terras and Crawford (eds), *Millicent Garrett Fawcett*, 376–90.

Object 89. A poster advertising *Time and Tide*

1   *Westminster Gazette*, 24 July 1925, 8.
2   Catherine Clay, *Time and Tide: The Feminist and Cultural Politics of a Modern Magazine* (Edinburgh: Edinburgh University Press, 2018).
3   *Time and Tide*, 6 August 1926.
4   *Time and Tide*, 19 November 1920.
5   Crawford (ed.), *Campaigning for the Vote*, 213.

Object 90. 'Pilgrimage of Peace' banner, 1926

1   *Wiltshire Times*, 1 May 1926, 2.
2   *Central Somerset Gazette*, 4 June 1926, 6.
3   The Women's Library Collection also holds the banner for the Street Women's Suffrage Society.

Object 91. Postcard of members of the National Union of Societies for Equal Citizenship photographed at Westminster, 2 July 1928

1   No recording of the broadcast survives. For the text, see Terras and Crawford (eds), *Millicent Garrett Fawcett*, 404.

Object 93. Mrs Pankhurst's grave

1   *Eastern Post*, 5 February 1927, 5.
2   *Vote*, 27 February 1927, 57.
3   *Western Morning News*, 5 February 1927, 7.
4   *Vote*, 3 June 1927, 173.
5   Purvis, *Emmeline Pankhurst*, 344.
6   Crawford (ed.), *Campaigning for the Vote*, 213–14.
7   *Daily Express*, 19 June 1928, 3.
8   *Northern Whig*, 19 June 1928, 8.

Object 94. A pamphlet, *Women and the General Election,* 1929

1   *Leicester Evening Mail*, 23 April 1929, 1.
2   *Vote*, 17 May 1929, 157.
3   Margaret Bondfield, *A Life's Work* (London: Hutchinson, 1948), 276.

Object 95. Library, Women's Service House, Westminster, London

1   Strachey, *Women's* Suffrage, 1927.
2   *Woman's Leader*, 16 May 1924, 126.
3   Fawcett was presented with a ceremonial trowel (7MGF/0/02, Women's Library collection, LSE).
4   *Woman's Leader,* 5 August 1927, 7.
5   Sir Almroth E. Wright, *The Unexpurgated Case against Women's Suffrage* (London: Constable, 1913), 1.
6   *Woman's Leader*, 24 March 1922, 6.

Object 96. Sign for the Suffragette Fellowship's 'Women's Record House', Westminster, London

1   Suffragette Fellowship Constitution, post-1940, Teresa Billington-Greig Papers (7TBG Box 401, The Women's Library collection, LSE).
2   *Reynolds Newspaper*, 17 January 1932, 3.
3   *Birmingham Weekly Mercury*, 8 November 1936, 3.
4   Object *96* is held in a collection of material donated to the Women's Library by the family of Rose Lamartine Yates.
5   Letter to the *Times*, 14 October 1947, 5.

Object 97. Sylvia Pankhurst's typewriter

1 Underwood Typewriter Serial Numbers. https://typewriterdatabase.com/underwood.4.typewriter-serial-number-database. With thanks to Hannah Priest of the Pankhurst Museum.
2 *Yorkshire Post*, 29 June 1931, 6.
3 For instance, Richardson places herself at the 1913 Epsom Derby, even though there was no contemporary evidence of her presence there.

Object 98. The Suffragette Fellowship Memorial, Christchurch Gardens, Westminster, London

1 Eileen Luscombe, *History and Legacy of the Suffragette Fellowship* (London: Routledge, 2024).
2 Communication from Lorne McKean to the author, January 2015.

Object 99. 'New Dawn', a contemporary light sculpture celebrating the campaign for women's suffrage, sited at the entrance to St Stephen's Hall in the Houses of Parliament, 2016

1 *New Dawn* by Mary Branson, commemorative booklet, Parliamentary Curator's Office, 2016.
2 *Dundee Courier*, 15 July 1993, 8.
3 For Bertha Newcombe, see Crawford, *Art and Suffrage*, 167–70.
4 The Fawcett Society, together with its invaluable collection of books and papers, was based at Wilfred Street between 1956 and 1977.

Object 100. The statue of Millicent Garrett Fawcett in Parliament Square, London, erected 2018

1 Mayor of London press release, 24 April 2018, https://www.london.gov.uk/press-releases/mayoral/historic-statue-of-suffragist-leader-unveiled.
2 From a letter by Ray Strachey quoted in Stanley and Morley, *The Life and Death of Emily Wilding Davison*, 172–3.
3 In April 2025 Object 100 was defaced during a transgender protest.
4 https://www.independent.co.uk/news/uk/home-news/domestic-abuse-bill-protest-migrant-women-parliament-a8957536.html.

RESOURCES

All URLs here and in the Notes were correct when checked on 26 January 2026.

Key Online Sites

London Museum Online Collection https://www.londonmuseum.org.uk/collections/
LSE Digital Library – for a wide range of suffrage material https://digital.library.lse.ac.uk.
LSE The Women's Library Archives Catalogue https://archives.lse.ac.uk/.
LSE The Women's Library Flickr https://www.flickr.com/photos/lselibrary/albums/72157660822880401/.

Other Useful Online Sites

Bonhams: Deeds Not Words: A Women's Suffrage Collection, 10–20 November 2025 https://www.
bonhams.com/auction/31671/deeds-not-words-a-womens-suffrage-collection/.
Bonhams: Votes for Women: The Lesley Mees Collection, 22 September–3 October 2023 https://www.
bonhams.com/auction/29249/votes-for-women-the-lesley-mees-collection/.
Glasgow Women's Library: The Museum Collection https://womenslibrary.org.uk/explore-our-
collections/the-museum-collection/.
Ken Florey: Women Suffrage Memorabilia http://womansuffragememorabilia.com/.
National Museum of Scotland, Edinburgh https://www.nms.ac.uk/national-museum-of-scotland.
National Museum of Wales, Cardiff https://museum.wales/cardiff/.
People's History Museum, Manchester https://phm.org.uk/collection/.
V. & A. London https://www.vam.ac.uk/collections.
My website, https://womanandhersphere.com, contains numerous articles discussing suffrage objects.
In addition, do consult the websites of your local history museum and archives to discover if they hold
any suffrage material.

Newspapers and Journals

The ability to search a wide range of national and provincial newspapers, as well as the papers published
by the suffrage societies, has proved invaluable. Apart from *The Times*, which I accessed via the
London Library, all papers referenced in the Notes are included in either the 'British Newspaper
Archive', which I accessed via www.findmypast.co.uk, or in the LSE Digital Library.

Select Bibliography

Where appropriate, online links appear in the Notes.

Key Texts: Suffrage

Atkinson, Diane, *Suffragettes in the Purple, White and Green*. London 1906–14. London: Museum of London, 1992.

Atkinson, Diane, *The Suffragettes in Pictures*. Stroud: Sutton for the Museum of London, 1996.

Atkinson, Diane, *Rise Up Women!: The Remarkable Lives of the Suffragettes*. London: Bloomsbury, 2018.

Cowman, Krista (ed.), *The Routledge Companion to British Women's Suffrage*. London: Routledge, 2024.

Crawford, Elizabeth, *The Women's Suffrage Movement: A Reference Guide 1866–1928*. London: UCL Press, 1999.

Crawford, Elizabeth, *Art and Suffrage: A Biographical Dictionary of Suffrage Artists*. London: Francis Boutle, 2018.

Florey, Kenneth, *Women's Suffrage Memorabilia: An Illustrated Historical Study*. Jefferson, NC: McFarland, 2013.

Garrett, Miranda and Thomas, Zoe (eds), *Suffrage and the Arts: Visual Culture, Politics and Enterprise*. London: Bloomsbury, 2018.

Hughes-Johnson, Alexandra and Jenkins, Lyndsey (eds), *The Politics of Women's Suffrage: Local, National and International Dimensions*. London: University of London Press, 2021. https://doi.org/10.14296/2111.9781912702985 (open access).

Robinson, Jane, *Hearts and Minds: The Untold Story of the Great Pilgrimage*. London: Transworld, 2018.

Tickner, Lisa, *Spectacle of Women*. London: Chatto & Windus, 1987.

Key Texts: Material Culture

Dyer, Serena, 'State of the Field: Material Culture', *History*, vol. 106, no. 370 (2021), 282–92. https://doi.org/10.1111/1468-229X.13104 (open access).

Gerritsen, Anne and Riello, Giorgio (eds), *Writing Material Culture History*. 2nd ed. London: Bloomsbury Academic, 2021.

Hannan, Leonie, *History through Material Culture*. Manchester: Manchester University Press, 2017.

Prown, Jules David, 'Mind in Matter: An Introduction to Material Culture Theory and Method', *Winterthur Portfolio*, vol. 17, no. 1 (1982), 1–19.

Other Works Cited

Atkinson, Diane, *Mrs Broom's Suffragette Photographs*. London: Nishen Photography, 1989.

Auchmuty, Rosemary, Rackley, Erika and Takayanagi, Mari (eds), *Women's Legal Landmarks in the Interwar Years*. Oxford: Hart, 2024.

Beckett, Jane and Cherry, Deborah (eds), *The Edwardian Era*. London: Phaidon Press and Barbican Art Gallery, 1987.

Blackburn, Helen, *Women's Suffrage: A Record of the Women's Suffrage Movement in the British Isles*. London: Williams & Norgate, 1902.

Bourne, Judith, 'Great Expectations and Hard Times:-The Advent of the Sex Disqualification (Removal) Act 1919 and Women's Entry to the Legal Profession', *Women's History Review*, vol. 32, no. 6 (2022), 793–808.

Branson, Mary, *New Dawn*. London: Parliamentary Curator's Office, 2018.

Bush, Julia, *Women against the Vote: Female Anti-suffragism in Britain*. Oxford: Oxford University Press, 2007.

Clay, Catherine, *Time and Tide: The Feminist and Cultural Politics of a Modern Magazine*. Edinburgh: Edinburgh University Press, 2018.

Cowman, Krista, *Women of the Right Spirit: Paid Organisers of the WSPU*. Manchester: Manchester University Press, 2007.

Crawford, Elizabeth, *Enterprising Women: The Garretts and Their Circle*. London: Francis Boutle, 2002.

Crawford, Elizabeth, *The Women's Suffrage Movement: A Regional Survey*. London: Routledge, 2006.

Crawford, Elizabeth (ed.), *Campaigning for the Vote: Kate Parry Frye's Suffrage Diary*. London: Francis Boutle, 2013.

Crawford, Elizabeth, *Kate Parry Frye: The Long Life of an Edwardian Actress and Suffragette*. London: ITV Ventures, 2014 (audiobook).

Dobbie, Beatrice, *A Nest of Suffragettes in Somerset*. Batheaston: Batheaston Society, 1979.

Doughan, David and Sanchez, Denise, *Feminist Periodicals 1855–1984: An Annotated Critical Bibliography of British, Irish, Commonwealth and International Titles*. Brighton: Harvester Press, 1987.

Eustance, Clare and John, Angela (eds), *The Men's Share?: Masculinities, Male Support and Women's Suffrage in Britain, 1890–1920*. London: Routledge, 1997.

Eustance, Clare, Ryan, Joan and Ugolini, Laura (eds), *A Suffrage Reader*. London: Leicester University Press, 2000.

Fawcett, Millicent Garrett, *Women's Suffrage: A Short History of a Great Movement*. London: T.C and E.C. Jack, 1912.

Fawcett, Millicent Garrett, *Women's Victory and After, Personal Reminiscences 1911–1918*. London: Sidgwick and Jackson, 1920.

Florey, Kenneth, *American Woman Suffrage Postcards: A Study and a Catalogue*. Jefferson, NC: McFarland, 2015.

Gardner, Vivien and Atkinson, Diane (eds), *Kitty Marion: Actor and Activist*. Manchester: Manchester University Press, 2019.

Gaskell, Ivan and Carter, Sarah Anne (eds), *The Oxford Handbook of History and Material Culture*. New York: Oxford University Press, 2020.

Goring, Elizabeth S., 'Suffragette Jewellery in Britain', *Decorative Arts Society Journal*, vol. 26 (2002), 85–99.

Grant, Jane, *In the Steps of Exceptional Women: The Story of the Fawcett Society 1866–2016*. London: Francis Boutle, 2016.

Grant, Jane, *The Other Emmeline: The Story of Emmeline Pethick-Lawrence*. London: Francis Boutle, 2023.

Hammond, Cynthia, *Architects, Angels, Activists and the City of Bath*. Farnham: Ashgate, 2012.

Holton, Sandra Stanley, *Suffrage Days*. London: Routledge, 1996.

Jenkins, Lyndsey, *Sisters and Sisterhood: The Kenney Family, Class, and Suffrage, 1890–1965*. Oxford: Oxford University Press, 2021.

Joannou, Maroula and Purvis, June (eds), *The Women's Suffrage Movement: New Feminist Perspectives*. Manchester: Manchester University Press, 1998.

Leneman, Leah, *A Guid Cause: The Women's Suffrage Movement in Scotland*. Revised ed. Edinburgh: Mercat Press, 1995.

Liddington, Jill, *The Life and Times of a Respectable Rebel: Selina Cooper 1864–1946*. London: Virago, 1984.

Liddington, Jill, *Vanishing for the Vote*. Manchester: Manchester University Press, 2014.

Liddington, Jill and Norris, Jill, *One Hand Tied behind Us: The Rise of the Women's Suffrage Movement*. 2nd ed. London: Rivers Oram, 2000.

Linklater, Andro, *An Unhusbanded Life: Charlotte Despard, Suffragette, Socialist and Sinn Feiner*. London: Hutchinson, 1980.

Luscombe, Eileen, *History and Legacy of the Suffragette Fellowship*. London: Routledge, 2024.

Mayhall, Laura E. Nym, *The Militant Suffrage Movement: Citizenship and Resistance in Britain, 1860–1930*. Oxford: Oxford University Press, 2003.

McDonald, Ian, *Vindication!: A Postcard History of the Women's Movement*. London: Bellew Publishing, 1989.

Mercer, John, 'Shopping for Suffrage: The Campaign Shops of the Women's Social and Political Union', *Women's History Review*, vol. 18, no. 2 (2009), 293–309.

Miller, Henry, 'The British Women's Suffrage Movement and the Practice of Petitioning, 1890–1914', *The Historical Journal*, vol. 64, no. 2 (2021), 332–56.

Moore, Wendy, *Jack and Eve: Two Women in Love and at War*. London: Atlantic Books, 2024.

Mukherjee, Sumita, *Indian Suffragettes: Female Identities and Transnational Networks*. Oxford: Oxford University Press, 2018.

Pankhurst, Christabel, *Unshackled*. London: Cresset Press, 1987.

Pankhurst, Emmeline, *My Own Story*. London: Eveleigh Nash, 1914.

Pankhurst, E. Sylvia, *The Suffragette Movement: An Intimate Account of Persons and Ideals*. London: Virago, 1977.

Pankhurst, Richard, *Sylvia Pankhurst: Artist and Crusader*. London: Paddington Press, 1979.

Park, Jihang, 'The British Suffrage Activists of 1913: An Analysis', *Past and Present*, vol. 120, no. 1 (1988), 147–62.

Park, Sowon S., 'Suffrage Fiction: A Political Discourse in the Marketplace', *English Literature in Transition, 1880–1920*, vol. 39, no. 4 (1996), 450–61.

Pašeta, Senia, *Irish Nationalist Women, 1900–1918*. Cambridge: Cambridge University Press, 2013.

Pudney, Stephen, 'Florence Rimmington and the Fawcett Jewel', *Decorative Arts Society Journal*, vol. 46 (2022), 75–87.

Purvis, June, *Emmeline Pankhurst: A Biography*. London: Routledge, 2002.

Purvis, June, *Christabel Pankhurst: A Biography*. London: Routledge, 2018.

Quinlan, Carmel, *Genteel Revolutionaries: Anna and Thomas Haslam and the Irish Women's Movement*. Cork: Cork University Press, 2002.

R., A.J. (ed.), *The Suffrage Annual and Women's Who's Who*. London: Stanley Paul, 1913.

Raeburn, Antonia, *The Militant Suffragettes*. London: Michael Joseph, 1972.

Raeburn, Antonia, *The Suffragette View*. Newton Abbot: David and Charles, 1976.

Rubinstein, David, *A Different World for Women: The Life of Millicent Garrett Fawcett*. Brighton: Harvester, 1991.

Ryan, Louise, 'The Irish Citizen, 1912–1920', *Saothar*, vol. 17 (1992), 105–11.

Ryder, Kirsty, 'Purple, White and Green: The Material Construction of Women's Suffrage', Ph.D. thesis, University of York, 2024.

Sheppard, Alice, *Cartooning for Suffrage*. Albuquerque: New Mexico Press, 1994.

Smith, Janet, 'Crossing the Border of Citizenship: Helen Taylor, the Independent Radical Democrat Candidate for Camberwell North, 1885', *Open Library of Humanities*, vol. 6, no. 2 (2020), 19. https://doi.org/10.16995/olh.540 (open access).

Stanley, Liz and Morley, Ann, *The Life and Death of Emily Wilding Davison*. London: Women's Press, 1988.

St John, Christopher, *Ethel Smyth*. London: Longmans, 1959.

Strachey, Ray, *Women's Suffrage and Women's Service*. London: LNSWS, 1927.

Strachey, Ray, *The Cause: A Short History of the Women's Movement in Great Britain*. London: Virago, 1978.

Takayanagi, Mari, Unwin, Melanie and Seaward, Paul, *Voice and Vote: Celebrating 100 Years of Votes for Women*. London: Regal Press, 2018.

Terras, Melissa and Crawford, Elizabeth (eds), *Millicent Garrett Fawcett: Selected Writings*. London: UCL Press, 2022. https://doi.org/10.14324/111.9781787358638 (open access).

Urban, Charles, *The Cinematograph in Science, Education, and Matters of State*. London: Charles Urban Trading, 1907.

Walker, Lynne, 'Vistas of Pleasure: Women Consumers of Urban Space in the West End of London 1850–1900' in Clarissa Campbell Orr (ed.), *Women in the Victorian Art World*. Manchester: Manchester University Press, 1995.

Wallace, Ryland, *The Women's Suffrage Movement in Wales, 1866–1928*. Cardiff: University of Wales Press, 2018.

Watson, Norman, *Suffragettes and the Post*. Forfar, Angus: Robertson Printers, 2010.

Wiley, Christopher and Rose, Lucy Ella (eds), *Women's Suffrage in Word, Image, Music, Stage and Screen: The Making of a Movement*. London: Routledge, 2021.

Williams, Joanna M. *The Great Miss Becker*. Barnsley: Pen & Sword, 2022.

Wright, Maureen, *Elizabeth Wolstenholme Elmy and the Victorian Feminist Movement*. Manchester: Manchester University Press, 2011.

INDEX